C000178114

HYPNOSIS FOR RUNNING:

Training Your Mind To Maximise Your Running Performance

Adam Eason

Awake Media Productions Ltd
28 Winston Avenue
Poole
Dorset
BH12 1PE

Published by Awake Media Productions Ltd
First Published — January 2013

ISBN 978-0-9575667-0-5

© Adam Eason, 2013

All rights reserved. No part of this publication may be
reproduced, stored in a retrieval system, or transmitted, in any
form or by any means, electronic, mechanical, photocopying,
recording or otherwise, without the prior permission of the
publishers

Dedication

I dedicate this book to my wife.

She swears blind that no matter how many times my running kit
is washed, it smells the same washed as when it is dirty, post-run.
Katie waves me off on my training runs, she supports my efforts
and cheers me on from the sidelines during races. Without her,
I would not be able to run with anything like the commitment
that I do. She enthuses about my running when it is not really her
thing. She watches me peel off nip-guards after long runs and put
them in the bin. She puts up with me rolling my legs out on the
foam roller in front of the telly in the evenings.
I think about her when I run. Katie, I love you.

Sincere and hearty thanks:

Thanks go to Gary Turner, someone I feel privileged to call
a friend and someone who I am honoured to know. Not just
because he is a 13 time world champion in a variety of fighting
disciplines. Not just because of his passion for being a sportsman
and ability as a runner is so inspiring. Not just because he
contributes so generously to the world of hypnotherapy that I
belong to. It is because of all these things that he does, he does
them in such a kind, well-meaning fashion and with a smile on
his face. Thank you for writing the foreword to this book Gary.

My thanks also to you, for investing the time and money in this
book. I hope to reward you and your running greatly as a result
of that investment.

> "I always loved running… it was something you could
> do by yourself, and under your own power. You could go
> in any direction, fast or slow as you wanted, fighting the

wind if you felt like it, seeking out new sights just on the strength of your feet and the courage of your lungs."

Jesse Owens

Contents

323

Foreword, by Gary 'Smiler' Turner

*"The smiles and excited chatter ceased. Around 150 ul-
tra-marathon racers sparked into life and surged forward
over the start line. I bumbled forward, the line went
taught, and I was away — my two huskies pulled forward
ahead of me, we turned sharply right, and started to
scramble up the first craggy climb. The Brecon Beacons
Ultra-Marathon had started. Ahead of us lay 42 miles of
mud, ice, bog, shale, rock, water crossings and some of the
biggest mountains in Wales.*

*I wasn't worried about going up the mountains — I was
concerned about the downhill sections. On my own I can
run downhill very well, almost detaching my legs at the
hips and just letting them turn. However, I was running
canicross (canine cross country, running with trained
dogs in harness) with my two young huskies. They pull
steadily going uphill, yet, they also pull hard going
downhill. This meant that on every downhill I would be
leaning back and braking against 58kg of husky powering
forward — on very difficult conditions underfoot, for
miles at a time. I would not gain anything here running
with huskies, in fact, I would be hindered. This was not
going to be an easy race. It was also my first ultra-marathon. It was also a week after I received an early copy of
this book."*

Let me introduce myself. I'm Gary 'Smiler' Turner, and I have had
a successful sporting career. I have been fortunate enough to win
thirteen World Titles across three different fighting sports. I've
competed in over twenty-five countries and been an international
since 1983. I've been in three different British Teams. I've had a
satisfying career.

I retired from competition a couple of years ago and needed a new focus in my life to keep me fit. So I started running for fun. I once read a sign that said "age doesn't make you inactive — inactivity makes you age". I wasn't going to let myself age. I was going to keep active. I did some research, lots of thinking, and welcomed two young huskies into my home. They now ensure I get up and out every single day.

I run canicross. My huskies and I all have appropriate harnesses on and are linked by a bungee cord. My huskies 'line out' in front of me, and we're away. Every day we go out running anywhere from two to a maximum recently of thirty miles. It keeps me fit, healthy, and satisfies the huskies' genetic need to run. I run for my life and health — I also run to give the huskies a good life. A happy husky is a tired husky.

I am also a hypnotherapist (clinical hypnotist) and through hypnosis is how I met Adam Eason. We were both booked to give talks at the prestigious School of Medicine at Kings College London on particular uses of hypnosis. I was presenting on the use of hypnosis for sports performance, and Adam was presenting on self-hypnosis.

I had networked with Adam for a couple of years before we met. I already knew that he is very well respected amongst all of my leading peers, is arguably the best hypnotherapy trainer in the UK, a world renowned expert when it comes to self-hypnosis, a published author, an exceptional speaker, and has a brilliant depth of knowledge in respect to hypnosis — both the science and the application. To be honest, he and I are both geeks. Always learning, testing, developing and thinking. This will be to your advantage as you read this book.

When we finally met in person I also discovered he was indeed a thoroughly nice man too, amiable, and very giving in time, attention and knowledge.

Adam is also a marathon runner and a fast one. Combine this with being possibly the world's leading expert on self-hypnosis, and there is no better person available to present you with the knowledge in this book.

> *"My legs were wobbling and cramping at the same time*
> *— in fact, it was the cramping that was probably stopping*
> *me from falling over, providing some stability. I had*
> *braced against the huskies, holding them back with leg*
> *strength as we dropped 300m in elevation before driving*
> *upwards once more for another 400m. Now my legs were*
> *telling me they'd had enough. And I'd only done 13 miles*
> *at this stage.*
>
> *As I wobbled onto the ridge of the mountains the sleet*
> *drove horizontally in my face. The wonderful view*
> *had disappeared with the arrival of the weather-front,*
> *bringing with it cloud that covered the mountainside. I*
> *stumbled as my foot broke through ice into a knee deep*
> *bog. The huskies drove forward. I put one foot in front of*
> *the other. I smiled. 'Just one more step, just one more step,'*
> *I repeated in my mind, focusing on just what I needed to*
> *do. I kept my legs turning. My body started to relax, my*
> *form improved, the cramping and wobbling eased, and*
> *my pace picked up. And my smile grew larger."*

I have been a very successful sportsman. I've also completed events such as the Red Bull 24hr Mountain Bike Race and the London Marathon. I know what is needed to be the best. As a successful sportsman I state that performance relies 100% on the mind. Sure, your body conditioning and your technical ability are necessary — yet if your mind is not in the right place these will never be developed.

This book is aimed at runners and is unique in approach. It focuses on all the mental skills you need to be a great runner and helps you achieve them. I consider it the fast-track to running success and enjoyment. As you read this book you will learn how to run faster, easier, more efficiently, run for longer distances, achieve your running goals, increase and maintain motivation — it will help you improve every area of your running. At the same time, and perhaps most importantly, you'll learn to enjoy every step too.

> "As I approached Checkpoint 6, the 30 mile point, I was in a great deal of pain. Pen Y Fan had nearly broken me physically. The 350m of near vertical ascent across slippery icy granite had been incredibly hard on already tired legs, yet was nothing compared to holding back the huskies on the descent the other side. Bracing against the huskies with tired legs conspired with a slippery slurry of mud on the slope to produce a good ten or so tumbles coming down the mountain.
>
> I gave my number at the checkpoint and I understood that the race was about to get even harder. The difficult terrain, the surfaces under foot, finding my way was all about to be complicated by darkness. I put my head torch on and shuffled onwards. 'Only 12 miles to go,' I thought. 'Excellent!'"

When the draft of Adam's book dropped through my door the timing couldn't have been better. One week before my first ultra-marathon. I eagerly turned the pages and found it a compelling read. It completely captured my attention, as I'm sure it will yours. The information and knowledge, and the application of it, is first class. Being a fast reader I read it three times in as many days. I checked the contents, studied the steps, researched the reference material, and became a vastly better runner — just through the knowledge from the book alone.

Then the real magic happened. I started to put into practice the steps in the book. I practiced dropping myself in and out of self-hypnosis using Adam's methods. It was easy to achieve. I just followed his clear steps. From here I started to work through the book, one step at a time, carrying out all the self-hypnosis applications he lists. My final loosening run, two days before my race, was one of my best runs ever. It just 'happened' that way. I didn't need to consciously think, I was just in a perfect state of 'flow'.

The night before my Ultra-marathon I slept in my truck in a small village nestled amongst the Brecon Beacons. The huskies snuggled in against my sleeping bag to keep me warm and I dropped into self-hypnosis one last time. I mentally rehearsed every part of the run. I went through the pre-race preparation, the terrain, and how I would easily get through every worst case situation I could think of. I mentally planned for every eventuality. I rehearsed my physical state throughout the race. I rehearsed my mental state, ensuring that I always maintained a smile especially for the tougher sections. I was not stepping into the unknown. I had made it known.

> "The final approach to the race HQ was heart-warm-
> ing. A huge grin appeared on my face. 'Hike on!' I
> commanded the huskies and they gave a final surge
> forward. My legs drove onwards to keep up. The only
> word I can use to describe the final sprint is 'awesome'!
> All the runners and support crew who had completed the
> race to this point were out on the finish line, out in the
> cold, clapping, cheering and giving support, having left
> their warm meals and hot drinks inside, all to bring me
> home.
>
> 'Easy!' I commanded and we slowed as we crossed the
> line, laughing, the other runners instantly making a fuss
> of the huskies. They didn't even appear tired. Yet, at that
> moment, I didn't appear to be either. I was elated. I had
> finished the Brecon Beacons Ultra-Marathon — 42 miles
> of the toughest terrain and the greatest distance I had
> ever run. I am now an 'Ultra-Runner'."

I am an Ultra-Runner. I love the sound of that. I feel even better about it when I consider the terrain that I had covered. The Brecon Beacons are used for UK 22 Regiment SAS training for a good reason — the environment is tough! I ran 42 miles across these mountains. This is the type of event where if your mind is not right you would not finish. Luckily, thanks to carefully preparing and using the guidance of this book, I not only finished,

I enjoyed every single step along the way — as could you by applying the knowledge in this amazing book.

Gary Turner

World Champion Sportsman, Hypnotherapist, and now Ultra-runner too.

Author of the book, *'No Worries'*

www.garyturner.co.uk

Chapter One:
Introducing Hypnosis For Running

"The miracle isn't that I finished. The miracle is that I had the courage to start."

John Bingham

Welcome to Hypnosis for Running. My name is Adam Eason and I am addicted to running... And to all things hypnosis...

I am combining two of my greatest loves here: I ran my first marathon back in 2000 and have been a full-time hypnosis professional since 1996. And I'm not just combining things for the sake of it, this is not purely some flight of indulgence (though there is some of that here, I must confess) though I think I could merrily research, read around and mine both subjects for the remainder of my days and be quite satisfied.

Although I wish it were larger, there is an impressive body of evidence to support the way the mind influences and affects sporting performance and the physiology in general. My own running has benefited enormously as a result of the processes and techniques that I use from the fields of cognitive behavioural hypnotherapy, neuro linguistic programming, rational emotive therapy and a wide array of other influences ranging from self-hypnosis, mindfulness and meditation processes, to trans-actional analysis, gestalt therapy and the vast field of sports psychology. Facets of all these fields have affected the way I run and how I approach my running and training. All are used and applied within the pages of this book.

It is a great joy for me to run along the sea front where I live in Bournemouth and, although the bay itself is only 7 and a bit miles (14 miles there and back) of which I am well acquainted with every square inch personally and in great detail;. getting there from home is a few miles longer/further. This means even my 20–22 mile training runs when preparing for a marathon can be accommodated and include plenty of sea air without too much time dodging traffic on roads.

I regularly do battle with the strong sea winds that make it feel like I am running on the spot one way and then being pushed strongly along in the other direction at certain times of the year. Then there is the incline of the promenade, slanting as it does, ensuring that one leg is worked more than the other at times, and I make sure I come back on myself so that I do not have one leg bigger than the other (like tennis players whose racket arm is muscular and the other resembles that of a T-Rex). There is, as well, the uneven and unpredictable surfaces of the neighbouring forest and woodland areas which I tell myself aids proprioceptive muscle development of the core, and we have the steep hills and demanding zig-zags going down to the beach areas of my run (and of course having to face running back up them on the way back). I think the conditions give me a good workout that gives me speed on flat road race courses.

My legs and feet get a lot of respect from me these days. Having experienced several bouts of shin splints, plantar fasciitis and every toenail having gone at some point in my training schedules — poor legs and feet. Where I once had soft baby feet, blisters upon blisters have turned them into tough hard leathery things that give me an unfair advantage at the firewalk events I organise to raise money for the charities I run for. My thick set build is of a very different design to the world's fastest marathon runners who are very slight and nimble, but I get motivated seeing James Cracknell completing sub-3 hour marathons regularly.

This all gives you a taste of my ongoing running experience, filled with challenges, laughs and the odd pain in the arse. I prefer training in the cold: us red-heads were not designed for the warmer climes and I find training in the summer months tougher and more physically demanding. I ran the 2007 London marathon, the hottest on record, and they ran out of water for many of the people in the latter stages of the race because selfish people like me kept pouring it on our heads.

The races I run are what continue to motivate and inspire me and I have done a fair few of them over the years. I love being around runners who train with discipline and create such a supportive environment at races. I plan in great detail for my races — I stick to my schedules and though I do enjoy the journey, my schedules tend to be on track throughout. I am such an airhead that if I were not to adopt such an attitude with my running and life in general (my business too) things would get messy. I need a regimen and sticking to it gives me as much of a sense of achievement as getting a marathon PB or crossing the line at a demanding race.

Anyhow, throughout the years of running and having a successful hypnotherapy practice and hypnosis training school, in addition to my other audio programmes and books that sell globally, I quietly and slowly compiled a body of work to help runners get better at running and enjoy running more — using their minds.

In April and May 2012, I ran the Brighton marathon, then London marathon, then Milton Keynes marathon one after the other in successive weeks and then ran Edinburgh 2 weeks later. I charted my training, my toils, my trials, my use of my mind to help assist my progress, my needless consumerism of running gadgetry, kit and gear, my influences, my ways of keeping motivated and keeping myself sane while also maintaining my marriage on my blog, **hypnosisforrunning.com**. Today, the blog still thrives, and gives me the opportunity to vent my spleen and vocalise my ongoing relationship with running and hypnosis. As I move into ultramarathon running with some of the world's toughest events in my diary for upcoming years, I'll be needing my mental skills more than ever.

This book has a number of aims that I hope to get across to you, the reader, within this introduction. One aim is to provide inspiration for runners of all levels, as well as instruction and ideas for improving your mental approach. I have aimed to make it as evidence-based as possible, though there are facets of this book and techniques offered that are without randomised controlled trials supporting them and are just recommended due to my experience of running and working with runners and clients within my consulting rooms.

I did also want to quickly add, when I refer to runners, I often use 'him' or 'himself' as a term. This is simply because I often write from my own personal perspective and simply was not inclined to keep writing 'him or her' and 'himself or herself' at the end of every single reference just to make it seem more agreeable. I hope you female readers understand and empathise.

Evidence For The Use Of Hypnosis For Runners:

We use our legs to run, don't we? As a result, surely we just need to run and keep on running, as Forrest Gump would say. Isn't this the case?

Though these days marathon running is my sport, I have played football to a fairly high standard and various sports throughout my life and I think just about everyone who has ever participated in any kind of sport can remember when our state of mind interfered with a good performance.

I am going to add here that when I refer to the 'mind' I am speaking of mind and body as one. The literature and evidence from the fields of psychology, neuroscience and psychosomatic medicine dispute the concept of dualism, that of the mind being distinct to the brain. Throughout this book, the mind of the runner is therefore considered and thought of as part of the mind-body being one.

Of course, it is not just about running and endurance performance either, many men encounter anxiety with sexual situations which affects their ability; for others similar anxiety may have affected performance in an exam or test of some kind.

In sports, this might occur in an important competition. We all saw how Rory McIlroy lost his healthy lead in the US masters in Augusta in 2011, before recovering mentally and showing some amazing resilience to go on and win the 2011 US Open golf major in tremendous style a few months later.

Those of us in the UK, in particular, may be familiar with the 1985 World Snooker championship final (watched by 19 million viewers past midnight) whereby the seemingly undefeatable reigning world champion Steve Davis missed a chance to cut in the final black ball in the final frame before Dennis Taylor potted it. The pressure on both players in that final frame was massive and clearly affected their ability.

My own sporting hero, the former Nottingham Forest and England left back, Stuart Pearce, was usually a man of steel and nerve, but then missed a crucial penalty when stepping up in the football World Cup semi-final in 1990. He usually scored penalties and free kicks for fun.

We have seen how tennis players struggle with those important points in big championships and how our football teams get affected by the crowd when they play away from home.

For runners, this might affect our performance in races as well as in our important preparation. So of course, us runners use more than just our legs.

There is a great deal of research evidence that supports the view that psychological factors affect and influence the performance of an endurance runner *(Morgan and Pollock,1977; Morgan and Costill, 1972; Morgan, 2001; O'Connor, 1992).*

I think everyone knows, these days, that our state of mind affects how we perform, yet it seems quite common for individuals to lack understanding of how to get in control of their own mentality, especially when it comes to sports performance.

In this book, I have written a lot about how to use your mind, and how to use hypnosis, hypnotherapy and cognitive behavioural principles for enhancing running ability, and ensuring the mind of a runner is as equipped and trained for the endurance running event as the body is with all those miles under the belt.

Within the research that I have been conducting as I have compiled the chapters of this book, it is amazing to read accounts of athletes and sports people giving the reasons behind the wide variation in their sporting performance and results. Very, very few (top elite athletes included) actually perform with major consistency. I know within my own running circles, there are many, many anecdotal observations that people offer up regarding their endurance and running performance.

Injuries and health issues aside, the vast majority of the accounts that I have encountered in my consulting rooms, or on a personal level at races and events, suggest that most runners believe their own differences in performance are due to parallel variations in their state of mind. Many runners I encounter tend to suggest that it is 50/50 physical and mental when it comes to their sporting performance and, though this is only subjective evidence based on my limited encountering of runners, I would say that it is a very low percentage (3–10% max) of training time that is spent on the psychological skills and mental abilities required for peak performance.

It is a rare occurrence to encounter an athlete or sports person who spends a great deal of time and effort on their psychological skills and the mental side of training. Let's make this clear — the presupposition of this book is that the psychological side of training is just as important as anything else when it comes to endurance performance. The athletes at the very top of their game are the ones who know this more than the rest and that is often why they are there.

Let's take a look at the very famous Roger Bannister, cited here, there and everywhere due to his achievement of being the first man to run the four-minute mile: on the 6th May 1954 he ran the mile in 3 minutes and fifty-nine seconds. Many runners had got close to that time, but many questioned whether it was actually possible.

Swedish runner Gunder Hågg had run 4:01.4 and his fellow runner Arne Anderson had run 4:01.6. Their countryman and sports psychologist of the time (when Hågg had held world records at one mile, two mile, three mile, 1500m, 3000m and 5000m), Dr Lars-Eric Unestahl, had openly stated that perhaps Hågg and other runners were convinced that the four minute mile was impossible and therefore there was a mental barrier stopping runners achieving it.

Bannister was confident it could be done and even later wrote:

> *"Though physiology may indicate respiratory and circulatory limits to muscular effort, psychological and other factors beyond the ken of physiology set the razor's edge of defeat or victory and determine how close an athlete approaches the absolute limits of performance."*
>
> *(Bannister, 1956)*

Once Bannister had run the sub-four minute mile, many others followed in rapid succession and it made sure that runners and other athletes started to look at their psychology as an important way of becoming a better runner or athlete.

Of the research and studies available to us today, we can learn a great deal about the importance of psychological factors when it comes to running.

Morgan and Costill *(1972)* and Morgan and Pollock *(1977)* looked at the psychological characteristics of runners and while they did show that runners tended to have notably lower anxiety levels than other people, it was unclear as to whether that was due to being a runner (there is evidence to suggest running is good for mental health) or to other conditions. Elite marathon runners have been shown in these studies to have what is termed the "iceberg" profile of a mood state, and earlier studies suggested that these runners tended to lean more towards the introvert than extrovert, despite some exceptions and evidence to suggest extroverts can actually perceive high intensity exertion as less effortful.

The studies did show that elite runners all tend to experience lower than average levels of depression, anxiety, anger and confusion, and so I think it is safe to say that if you look after your general levels of mental health, you'll be equipped to run

There are differing types of goals that runners can have. Real elite athletes may well have outcome goals that comprise of where they wish to finish in the race: *"I want to be first,"* or, *"As long as I finish in front of Haile Gebrsalassie I'll be happy."* (I'm kidding with that one.)

Some runners will look at process goals, which focus on how you perform: *"My goal is to run this training run and pump my arms throughout,"* or, *"I make sure I run by lifting my legs with my hamstrings instead of my quads,"* for those that are getting technical or looking at their running technique.

However, most runners are more likely to be using performance goals, which are goals that you set relating to your own level of ability such as, *"I want to run a personal best time at this race,"* or, *"I want to run this marathon in under 3 hours."* The different types of goals can be useful for us in different ways and can influence and affect us by directing our thoughts in different ways.

There has been a good amount of study and research conducted on setting goals in sports and exercise. Rising up out of the academic work of Ryan *(1970)* and Taylor *(1967)*, in more recent times the major contributor to the study of goals in athletic performance is Locke *(1966, 1968, 1978 and with colleagues in 1981 and 1990)*. Since then, hundreds of studies have been conducted in a wide variety of settings in business and industry and have shown impressive results. However, it was really only in the mid 1980s that goal setting in sport was examined.

Locke and Latham *(1985)* suggested that goal setting could work much better in sports due to the fact that sportspeople are more objective about their performance. More recently, studies have shown a mix of support for goal-setting effectiveness in sport. A number of studies have not supported the notion of it being so effective *(Burton 1992; Weinberg, 1992, 1994)*.

If we look at a number of more recent studies *(Burton, Weinberg, Yukelson, & Weigand, 1998; Filby, Maynard, & Graydon, 1999; Weinberg, Burke, & Jackson, 1997)* as well as the impressive meta-analysis of Kyllo and Landers *(1995)* we can see that there are some consistent notions within the literature regarding goal-setting in sport:

1. The vast majority of athletes do use some form of goal setting as a means of enhancing their performance and find it to be fairly effective.

2. Athletes that engage with a variety of goal setting strategies get the best results in measured performance.

3. The main reason for setting goals is that it focuses and directs the individual.

4. The main barriers preventing individuals from using goal-setting systems are lack of time, stress, tiredness and other pressures.

5. Goals are more effective if they are moderately difficult, challenging, but kept realistic.

6. Athletes benefit more when they have short-term goals and long term goals.

7. Having an action plan to accompany a goal makes it more effective.

So how is it that goals actually help sporting performance?

Locke et al. *(1981)* suggested that goals are effective on performance for four main reasons:

1. Having goals directs attention.

This is about us runners keeping focused and being aware of the cues we are presented with when training or preparing for an event of some kind.

For example, if we want to run a sub 4 hour marathon, we need to be aware of what pace we can maintain in our long runs, we need to know that we are doing enough miles each week to have built up our endurance. We may find that we can easily run for 3 hours, but it may be slower than we wish and therefore we may decide that in order to achieve our goal, we need to look at our pace and speed work — this could lead to other, smaller goals to be set for achieving speed or simply hitting speed work targets.

Also, if we had no goal at all, we may simply be running without a sense of purpose; it may not be compelling to be without an aim of any kind and thus may result in us lacking motivation.

2. Having goals mobilises effort.

By having feedback as we progress towards the goal, we have a means of keeping on with our effort.

3. Having goals enhances persistence.

Many people in my therapy rooms tend to find the real long-term goals are not all that compelling. Even a marathon that is 16 weeks away can seem like a distant thing to be aiming for. So looking at short-term goals is often a great contributor to those longer term ones.

I know that with the 16 week training schedules I used to download at **Runners World** website when training for marathons, they would offer up a monthly goal too, such as, *"Your goal this month is to run a 1 hour 45 minute half marathon,"* or, *"Your goal this month is to taper ready for your marathon,"* and so on.

Likewise, if someone wants to reduce their weight by 6 stone, that may not happen immediately and it would not be safe for it to happen too quickly. So you may decide to have shorter term goals that lead up towards that bigger goal such as, *"I aim to reduce my weight by two pounds this week,"* as a compelling shorter term achievement.

Shorter goals also indicate success is being achieved and when we feel like we are achieving, it becomes a lot easier to persist with our training and endeavours.

4. Having goals develops new learning strategies.

What is meant here is that when we set goals, often strategies are put in place by those advising us, such as coaches at running clubs or other runners that help us move towards our goals.

I know that the advice I have had via resources at Runners World, books, magazines, coaches, trainers, seasoned runners at running clubs, fellow competitors at events and friends have often resulted in me applying new skills and strategies to my training schedule to help meet my next goal.

Since I started running on the front of my feet more than I used to, my times have got quicker as I have got older. Since I pumped my arms better during sprints, I generate more speed. Please note, these things are not considered generally good for all runners, but helped me personally to improve. There are other examples too, examples that have all contributed to me wanting to develop to achieve those goals I had set.

However, in more recent times, there has been some caution with regards to goal setting. Burton (1989) suggested that goals can increase anxiety and even knock confidence if they are based on factors outside an individual's control. For example, if you have a goal to finish in the top 100 competitors at London marathon, you cannot account for the other runners and how they run on the day. If that person got a personal best time but came 200th, they may feel disappointed, despite what many would consider to be a fabulous performance.

Therefore, setting personal performance goals is recommended based upon our own considered level of ability and measuring up against ourselves — it requires us to be realistic and it also suggests that goal setting is a skill to be developed and practiced in order to derive the most benefit.

Goal orientation theory has been written about by many authors *(Duda, 1992; Roberts, 1992; Dweck, 1986, for example)* and suggests that the goals we set ourselves affect the way we evaluate our own ability and performance and the way we attribute success or failure. These thoughts, ideas and other cognitions in turn then influence the strategies we take forward in training, how we behave during training and when competing, and influence our motivation and persistence.

I write about this attribution of success and failure in a later chapter in this book when I discuss Martin Seligman's Learned Optimism and Albert Ellis's REBT approach.

The studies suggest that each individual's perception of their own ability is affected by how they interpret success and failure, which then affects and influences goal-directed behaviour in relation to running performance, training and racing.

There is a great deal of research to support the use of goal-setting, but also a great deal of research to suggest that they must be carefully and diligently constructed with realism and set in relation to our own performance and that, when done properly and carefully, can aid our performance.

Now let's look at and explore the key principles to engage in when goal setting and also how to actually go about setting goals when running.

The Principles Of Goal Setting For Runners:

Let us now explore and examine some of the most important evidence-based underlying principles for goal setting. Then I'll finish this chapter off with suggestions on how to actually devise a system to set goals to enhance your running performance and enjoyment.

Facets of this are going to remind you of the classic SMART goals strategy which is very well known, highly regarded by many and well worth researching and investigating if you do not already know about it.

I hope it came across in the early part of this chapter, that the evidence and research on goal setting suggests it can enhance performance and our general development as a runner when used diligently, regularly and properly.

I also hope that it came across, that goal setting is not universally effective in every way for every runner. Different types of goals for different types of activities will vary depending on the runner.

Some goals will enhance motivation, some will help a runner persist in the face of adversity, and some will let the runner feel more in control of some goals than others.

Throughout the literature and research though, some key points stand out and are consistent considerations when setting goals, if you wish them to help you advance.

Principle 1:

Firstly, goals produce higher levels of performance enhancement when they are specific than if someone is simply attempting a goal of *"doing their best" (Weinberg & Weigand, 1993)*. Those club coaches, fellow runners or family members who tell the runner to go out there and *"do their best"* might help the runner to feel motivated, but it is not as effective (for helping the runner stay motivated and perform better) as it is to encourage them to go out and achieve a particular and specific goal.

Additionally, as an evidence-based hypnotherapist who employs a lot of cognitive behavioural processes within my therapy rooms, it is a tendency of mine to prefer to use therapeutic interventions that can be measured. We set therapeutic goals along the way and measure our progress towards them each session — likewise, specific goals when it comes to running are goals that can be measured.

As runners, we may well want to become faster or fitter or slimmer, but these are all vague, generic goals. Taking 5 minutes off your personal best 10k time within the next 8 weeks, or being able to run 10% further in the same time within 16 weeks are more specific and measurable goals that are more useful for the runner.

Principle 2:

The next principle is one that requires some thought and consideration — that goals ought to be challenging, with a good level of difficulty, but ultimately attainable (Locke and Latham, 1990). If a goal is too easy, it may not present a challenge and not result in the full effort being invested by the runner. This can also therefore lead to average performances instead of pushing ourselves in training, subsequent races or events.

Of course, the flip side of that is that if the goals set are too difficult or just unrealistic, they can result in failure and subsequent feelings of defeat, lack of motivation and lowered belief in oneself.

So when setting running goals, the runner will benefit from striking a balance of aiming to improve and achieve the desired successful outcomes, whilst avoiding pressure and potential failure by keeping the goal realistic and suitably challenging.

From my own point view, I have found the balance hard to strike sometimes. After a couple of years off running in the early 2000s, I subsequently got back into running and ran the London marathon in 4hrs 30mins that season. The next year I ran the London marathon in just under 4 hours, then the subsequent year I ran it in 3 hours 15 minutes as I trained harder and better, I also found making gains tougher. When you are a 14 stone man, then thinking of taking another 15 minutes off your marathon time to get that golden fleece of a sub 3 hour marathon is a tough goal to set. It would be some feat and require a lot of consideration — I was not getting any younger either! It is a tough balance that requires healthy, intelligent consideration (I did achieve it though).

Principle 3:

Previously, I mentioned how long term goals can seem less compelling. A runner may be running just because he wants to reduce his weight by 4 stone in the next year. That year can seem like a long way away. Likewise, I used to set myself targets for each marathon season, culminating in the time I wanted to run the marathon in that year. I think a lot of people set these kinds of longer-term goals when they start.

The research suggests that having short-term goals as well as those longer-term goals will enhance motivation and performance more effectively *(Weinberg et al., 1993, 2000)*.

Short term goals can give us good indicators of the progress we are making, they give us success along the way, they give us measurable evidence that we are progressing toward that longer term goal and can be more compelling. With running, having a weekly and monthly objective and goal that is specific, can really help us notice our improvement and let us get on with those training schedules where the end seems a long way off, especially if you are training in poor weather conditions in winter, for example.

With my own goal setting for running a sub 3 hour marathon, I would set weekly mileage goals, as well as having particular pace goals and time goals for each and every run, which I think is pretty much the way most people train for marathons. With the emergence of GPS running watches (how I love my Garmin 610), it is made so much easier. However, prior to each run, I get focused, really tune in to my objective for that run and make it a specific, short-term goal. I knew that if I simply kept on achieving these short term goals with this much regularity, then my longer term goal would be made easier, more attainable and more realistic.

Gould *(1988)* stated that many athletes find it easier to get motivated and ready for a game, competition or event, than it is to get motivated for training. I know runners who are well pumped prior to races, but struggle to train with consistency. Therefore, as well as long and short term goals, make sure you have goals for training, as well as for your race performance and specific longer term outcomes.

Goals set for training can help apply some healthy pressure similar to that experienced with races — I know runners at clubs I have attended that are goal oriented during training, who really have some (self-induced) pressure on them for the final speed interval or that final mile to make sure they hit that training goal. Filby et al. *(1999)* showed that goals set for training are just as important as those set for races and competitions.

Both long-term and short-term goals are equally important, getting them both set up is going to serve you really well. Which then brings me on to the next principle very nicely...

Principle 4:

Get your goals written down. This is not just supported by sport psychologists *(Gould, 1998; Weinberg et al., 2000)* but also other published psychologists and therapists. The research tends to suggest that if the goals are written and then displayed where they can be seen, goals set will be more effective in enhancing performance.

Remember in the boxing films, the boxer had his opponent's photograph pinned to his mirror? I keep my long-term goals on paper pinned to a mirror despite my wife's protestations and I keep another pinned to the noticeboard beside my work desk in my office.

The idea is to keep the goal visible and to keep it in mind. Sometimes goals get swept away in the midst of training or end up stuffed in the bottom of a kit bag or at the bottom of a drawer; we want to keep them fresh in our minds.

Principle 5:

Earlier in this chapter, I mentioned that Locke (1968) wrote that one of the key benefits to goal setting in sports was that it helped develop learning strategies.

With runners therefore, we need to look at what we can be doing to advance our skills, technique, mindset, endurance and anything else required to help us achieve our goal.

A runner might read about technique, or get a coach to look at their technique, or see a physiotherapist. A runner might look at ways to recover more effectively after training runs. A runner might look at understanding nutrition to best fuel the new levels of exertion. A runner might look at other means of training, perhaps using hills, or a track for speed sessions, or working on the arm swing to generate pace in speed sessions. You can see the wide variety of ways we could look at learning how to improve our chances of achieving our goal.

Rather than letting it become a by-product of our goal setting, it is recommended that the runner actively pursue ways and means of developing new strategies to enhance performance.

Principle 6:

The research, studies and literature do show that goals are helped greatly by social support when it comes to us keeping driven, motivated and overcoming obstacles to success *(Albrecht and*

Adelman, 1984; Cohen, 1988; Hardy, Richman & Rosenfeld, 1991). One study in particular demonstrated that having the support of your spouse, having told them of the goal and advising of ways the spouse can help support, is a great way to get the goals achieved.

Therefore, tell close friends and family, perhaps even colleagues (ones who might hold you accountable) of your aims for your races or ongoing training. What time do you plan to finish that 10k, that half-marathon, that marathon, that ultra marathon? How many miles do you plan to run in total this month? Let them know and then also suggest how they can support you. I'll be writing in more detail in a later chapter about the benefits of using encouragement to run better.

As well as helping to encourage you and hold you accountable for the goal, you also then have an outlet for discussion if you wish to discuss any struggles you encounter working towards the goal.

Principle 7:

Finally then, we look at goal evaluation. This is having a way of assessing what you did with your previous goals. Locke *(1981)* found that getting accurate feedback was important in sports, but those of us without coaches or people to derive feedback from in any detailed fashion, can look at being reflective and applying some sort of critique to how it went, what you did, and what you can do different next time. This is going to help you with setting your next set of goals too.

In my consulting rooms, we (my clients and I) often look at Problem Solving Therapy (PST) as a means of assessing a problem and putting a plan in place to overcome it. The same strategy of reflecting intelligently and considering what to do differently next time (if you plan on doing anything different at all) is an important part of making the most out of goal setting.

I have not written in any detail about having specific outcome goals as this book is not really aimed at elite runners — but aiming to win races, or beat other runners in races is a proven way of enhancing performance *(Kingston & Hardy, 1997; Orlick and Partington, 1988)*. However, for the rest of the running community, having well formed specific goals aimed at your own performance is going to be what helps enhance your running results and enjoyment.

I really hope this is getting your juices flowing and getting you thinking about how you'll develop your own running goals. Now let's explore how to actually set up your own goal setting system so that you run faster, better and further.

Creating Your Own Goal Setting System To Advance Your Running:

This is the final phase with regards to goal-setting. Having had a look at the evidence supporting goal setting and then also exploring the principles of goal setting as we have done in the previous parts of this chapter, you should have a good starting place for setting your running goals. Let's be sure to do it right though and look at how to systemise your goal setting to derive the greatest running gains.

When any runner takes on the marathon, for example, they plan it. At least, those savvy runners do. They put a schedule together, they plan and prepare well. Not just the training, but the organisation of the event itself requires preparation and planning. Your goal setting is the same, and requires the runner to plan accordingly too.

Runners that have a coach or experts at their running club can enlist the assessment skills of that person or people. However, in the absence of such, most runners will need to conduct some sort of objective assessment. For runners, this is usually best done prior to your training schedule getting underway, or in the months where you are running less, or out of the main running season. Ideally, you assess your needs and abilities before you begin your training programme.

Having examined your own speed, endurance, and considered how you felt last time you were out running, thinking about your current fitness level, and looked at previous performances (heck, you might consider looking at your current weight and other elements of physical condition too) then you are better informed about the realism of the goals you will subsequently set yourself.

It is important for me to stress the afore-mentioned word "objectively." That is, make sure that you assess yourself with honesty and candour and don't go convincing yourself that you are fitter, faster or healthier than you actually are. Be objective in your assessment of yourself.

With that assessment completed, the runner sets goals based upon any needs identified and current levels of fitness, speed, endurance, etc. Set long-term goals, or have one single main goal, and then set some short-term goals that will provide evidence that you are successfully making your way towards the longer-term goals. Think about making sure the goal is based on your own performance and is therefore within your own control, and apply the principles to your goals that I wrote about previously.

Be sure you set the goals when you are capable of being objective and measured too. If you set goals when you are emotional or behaving emotively, then you might not be setting them with the most amount of intelligence, and this may consign the goal to failure before it has begun.

Consider also the kinds of needs you have, psychologically. Consider your psychological needs, consider technique and set goals for those areas too. Remember we want to think about more than just the miles we run and the speed we run them. Do you need motivation? Do you need inspiration or encouragement? Do you need to learn more about nutrition, or ways to enhance recovery times, or how to build your resilience in the face of adversity?

With each goal in place and initially written up, the runner then intelligently considers and plans it. That is, you now plan a strategy. Build an action plan that details what you are going to do in order to attain that goal. This is more than simply typing up your daily mileage output. Do you need to research and get resources or information? Do you need to develop new strategies, new running techniques? Be as diligent as possible at this stage and you will reap the rewards, I assure you.

A couple of words of warning here, though. Runners and athletes of other kinds tend to get excited and pumped up when first setting goals. Be aware of setting too many at the early stages. You don't want to drown in goals! You also do not want to set so many goals that it becomes unmanageable to adhere to them. One of the pitfalls of goal setting is getting blown over by the crest of our own wave. Make sure you are not setting too many goals at the beginning.

With this planning and preparation done, you then need to put in place some way of evaluating your goals so that they do not wither. I see it happen all the time; runners get fired up, get their goals beautifully crafted, intelligently planned and prepared for, then a few weeks down the line, the goals are almost forgotten about and the runner loses sight of them and the goals are not serving their intended purpose of advancing our performance.

The runner benefits from staying focused on the goals. Having short term goals to tend to helps, and if we can add some way of evaluating and staying on track, then that is going to help keep the runner focused and on track.

One way to do so is to re-evaluate the goals at regular intervals. At the end of each month, you might like to check in and see if you are on track, maybe even assess your capabilities and fitness compared to when you set the goal, see if you can measure your progress. Have you completed all the planned training runs? Have you explored all the new learning strategies? Have you addressed your psychological needs? Are you remaining motivated?

Be objectively reflective and examine your progress at regular intervals that you diarise. Any good coach or trainer will assess progress and even have regular review meetings to assess where you are at, so you can look at this and do this. Heck, if you have a supportive colleague or spouse, then you may even want to enlist their help with looking at your ongoing progress and seeing if you need to tweak your goals or amend them in any way as a result of your re-evaluation.

When you assess your progress, you might be off target, you may be flying and exceeding expectations, or you may be perfectly on track. Wherever you find your progress, you may need to make the longer-term goal slightly less demanding, or more of a challenge, or leave it as it is. Goals are not immovable objects that remain the same throughout. You can adjust them and tweak them as you move forwards in order that you keep on track and on target and derive the most benefit from the focus you put on them.

One of the ways that goals often get left to fizzle out in the distance is failing to evaluate, monitor and subsequently tweak the goals. Make absolutely sure that you set some time aside to assess where you are at and to be reflective, objective and consider any changes that need to be made.

In early 2012, when I was training for the five consecutive marathons I was going to be running that spring, I got a really bad flu bug. It set my training schedule back quite a bit as I had 10 days off running and then felt groggy when I did get back on the road. My goals and training targets required me to adjust them and reassess my progress.

Sadly, it is a fact of life for runners that we get injuries or experience illness, so readjusting goals is one of the things that is going to be required to keep our goals helping us enhance performance.

I want to repeat here something that I covered earlier too. That is that goals are likely to be far less useful and beneficial if they are not specific and measurable. When setting your goals, refer to that principle mentioned previously and ensure that your goals are not just, *"I want to run further," "I want to run faster," "I want to reduce my weight,"* because these are vague and very difficult to measure. Get specific with times, distances, and make them measurable so that you can gauge your progress.

As part of the ongoing process, you want to keep encouraging yourself and driving yourself with your goals. There are a number of ways of doing that and these are shared in later chapters. As runners, we want to be encouraged with our goals. If you can't or won't rely on yourself to keep providing that encouragement, then seek it from running partners, colleagues or your loved ones, or join a running club where your fellow runners can help give you that.

With the goals then set and in place, do check them against the principles written in this chapter and make any final tweaks that you deem necessary. Then you are going to have a finely tuned set of goals with an accompanying goal orientation mindset within your running that can fuel your training and have you enhancing your running performance.

Memories of the Future:

To gain the maximum effect from setting your self goals, runners should get themselves acquainted with all those fabulous good feelings they are going to experience when they achieve that goal.

Whenever we complete a marathon in a specific time, complete an interval session without having to stop to catch our breath, or hit a different goal of some kind, it makes everything worthwhile, and it feels really good. So how about getting familiar with that feeling before it has happened in reality?

We'll be looking at specific mental imagery techniques later on in this book, but for now, you can use your imagination to advance your goal setting skills.

These good feelings (of achieving the goal) can generate passion for the goal. Thus, an effective part of our goal setting process can include you imagining that you have achieved your particular goal set for some moment in the future: You imagine the satisfaction of success, the glow of accomplishment. This satisfaction serves as a real motivation, a passion for achievement that will last through practices.

So when setting your goals and writing them up, also consider creating "memories of the future" that is, you are going to imagine achieving that goal and be aware of how it feels, how it looks, how it sounds when you achieve it.

When you establish your challenging running goals and image the powerful, enjoyable, positive, satisfying feelings that you get when you achieve those goals, then your goals become more motivating, more empowering, more inspirational, and will drive you onwards with more impetus.

Joe Montana *(Montana & Weiner, 1997)* encourages storing future memories in this way:

> *"If you are in a slump, focus on your mental approach before you mess around with what you are doing physically. Visualizing specifically and realistically what you will be doing will help you move from stressed-out to confident and relaxed... This isn't fantasizing, it's rehearsal."*

Joe Montana

Effect on Confidence:

Imagining successful achievement of our goals helps us runners to perceive achieving a potentially difficult goal as a real possibility that we are very much capable of. Building this kind of confidence motivates you, the runner, to expend the energy necessary to achieve the goal. After imaging success, one runner recently said to me that he knew he could finally crack a one and a half hour half-marathon because he felt he had already done it with the goal-achieving imagery.

Lots of people view their future through their past. They think because they have always done certain things a certain way, then they will continue to happen that way. Whereas creating your own future memories is going to enable you to have a vision of the future — which can be a much more powerful force in determining the future than is often given credit for.

When I first was introduced to the world of personal development in my late teenage years and early twenties, I recall reading a classic self-help book by James Allen, entitled, *'As A Man Thinketh'*. In it, he suggests that we all imagine that the mind is like a fertile garden and the thoughts that you have in your mind are seeds. All that your thoughts need to grow, is your attention. Your attention is like the rain and sunshine that the seed needs to grow. So, if you allow old, limiting thoughts and beliefs to continue to grow and then keep focusing on them, you are going to have a mind filled with fruit of the belief that you do not know how to overcome obstacles or worse still, a mind filled with failure or lack.

In upcoming chapters, we'll be looking at ways of using our internal dialogue effectively and how to use mental imagery in a wide variety of ways to enhance and advance our running performance.

Before we get into that in more detail, while you are setting goals and desired outcomes, follow these basic steps to create future memories to aid with your goal setting:

Step One:

In a quiet and comfortable place, create a picture in your mind of your desired outcome; this might be successfully completing a race, training well for an event, crossing the finish line or just achieving any other running goal. Place that picture in your mind as if you were looking at it on a big screen.

These do not have to be perfect cinema screen pictures by the way, just imagine it as best as you can. Just imagine and have the right intention behind actively imagining as best as you can and that is going to be just fine.

Step Two:

As you look at the image of that desired outcome, make it as vivid as you can. Add your favourite motivating sounds, maybe a favourite piece of inspiring music, or even imagine someone with a wonderful voice, motivating you or giving you inspiring messages, or even the voice of a loved one congratulating you or telling you how proud they are of you.

Then add some wonderful feelings to that version of yourself as you look at it. As you look at the version that has achieved that goal, how does that make you feel? Where in the body are those feelings of achievement? Make the picture as sensory rich as you can. Use colours and details as much as possible.

Step Three:

As you look at this image of yourself in your imagination, think to yourself, *"I just know that is going to happen,"* the same way that you know a brick will fall to the floor if you let go of it. Convince yourself of it and really believe in it as you look at it.

Then, think to yourself, *"I deserve that."* Really know that you deserve it. Finally, think that this is enjoyable, fun, fulfilling; perceive it as an enjoyable thing to do that is rewarding and fun. When we take our goals too seriously, we often make them too rigid and they are not very compelling. Think to yourself that the journey to your desired outcome is going to be enjoyable and fun!

Step Four:

Next, step into that image of you in your mind. Wear it, act like it. When you pretend to be a certain way, you are learning how to be that way at the deeper behavioural level. Really, truly associate with it, feel the feelings of it and get it lodged into your mind. How does that version of you think, how does that version of you hold their body? Then do those things and BE that version of yourself. Mentally rehearse that future scenario in your mind.

Here you are acquainting your mind with that outcome, you are teaching it how to be that way. You are creating your future successful running memory. Spend some time on this step and really associate with that outcome. See what you would be seeing, hear the sounds of your success, feel the feelings that you would feel. Experience it as if it is happening right now.

Use this basic technique and start getting yourself associated with those future memories of achieving the running goals you have set for yourself in line with the principles laid out earlier in this chapter.

Chapter Three:
The Runner's
Understanding of Hypnosis

This chapter title is probably misleading as it is not really offering up an in-depth understanding of hypnosis. It is showing you how to do hypnosis. Self-hypnosis is an active process and this chapter is going to show you how to "open the door" and access hypnosis for you to use in conjunction with all the other instructional chapters coming up.

There are a number of models of hypnosis for people to understand — but they are not really relevant to the aim of this book, which is to help you use your mind and hypnosis to enhance your running performance. If you want to truly understand hypnosis, there are monumentally massive volumes of work by academics that you can wade through.

It is going to help to have some level of understanding and I aim to ensure there are no myths or misconceptions about hypnosis, but I do not want us to study in any great depth what hypnosis is. I simply want you to be able to use it and then apply the rest of the material in this book to yourself in order to advance your running.

Are Runners Using Self-Hypnosis During Their Runs Without Realising?

When getting close to finalising this book, my continued research led me to stumble across an article published in a 1983 volume of the *American Journal of Clinical Hypnosis* and it is entitled 'Auto-Hypnosis in Long Distance Runners' by Kenneth Callen. Needless to say, my eyes lit up, and I began reading in some depth. What could be more wonderful? An academic journal attempting to correlate hypnosis and running! For me, it was a golden few moments when I read it for the first time.

Before I start to explain how to hypnotise yourself, I could not resist sharing with you some of the findings of this study, because they are fascinating. First up, here is the abstract for the study, which as every good abstract aims to do, explains the study and its findings:

> *Four hundred and twenty-four runners completed a questionnaire concerning their running habits and the mental processes which occur while running. Over half of the respondents experience a trance-like state with wide variation in depth, along with increased receptivity to internal events, absorption, and vivid imagery, all hallmarks of auto-hypnosis.*
>
> *The techniques used to get into a trance are the same as those commonly employed in hetero-hypnosis; rhythmical deep breathing, eye fixation, and repetition of a sound or phrase. Many of the runners become more creative during these trance-like states, and some feel their athletic performance is enhanced.*

Well, this is exciting stuff for us here, on many levels. The study does really conclude by asking more questions and suggesting more research is needed. However, I thought I'd share with you some of the key findings in this particular study, which make for fascinating reading, even if the study does not offer up any particular tool or methodology for our own gain, which is usually what piques my interest.

Prior to this study, the vast majority of research had looked at the end result of exercise and running performance. The authors noted that very little research examined the mental processes which occurred *during* running.

With my own running experiences and having worked with so many runners and met so many over the years at races, clubs, events and so on, I found myself agreeing with some of the opening statements framing this study —

> *Running is a natural process which under ordinary circumstances requires very little concentration or attention, thereby, freeing the mind to wander in pleasant fantasy. Most runners tend to run alone and many seek out isolated areas with few distractions, such as parks and country roads.*

Some might even add, this is a perfect environment for self-hypnosis being described here?

Many runners describe the 'runner's high' which I mention later on in this book and show you how to develop. There is also a great deal of literature where people refer subjectively to their running experience as delving into other worlds and realms of altered consciousness, etc. Which is all very good, but how is this related to or pertaining to hypnosis?

The authors of this study suggested that there were some parallels to be drawn between some formal definitions of major authors in the field of self-hypnosis, and the psychological experience of runners detailed in the study.

For example, Fromm et al *(1981)* refer to self-hypnosis as trance-like states with wide variation in depth, increased receptivity to interval events, absorption, and vivid visual imagery — which is very similar to a number of accounts given by runners when describing their own mental experience during running. Likewise, the very same authors Fromm et al *(1981)* who have conducted a great deal of research on the phenomena of self-hypnosis also call for more research on the subject of 'alert self-hypnosis' such as that experienced by runners.

So I wanted to share some of the results of this study:

1. 267 (54%) of the sample indicated that they sometimes feel they are in a 'trance' or altered state of consciousness while running.

36 (16%) of this group have been hypnotised before and 26 (11%) have been exposed to other techniques such as transcendental meditation, yoga, and autogenic training.

Interestingly, comparing the 165 respondents with no previous experience with the 62 who had used hypnosis (or other techniques) before reveals no significant difference on any of the items asked within the questionnaire.

Of those who stated they experienced 'trance-like' states when running, 70 (31%) described the methods they used to get into those states:

- 24 (35%) used their own breathing as a technique. They described rhythmical breathing, counting and stride patterns.

- 18 (26%) use imagery which is frequently described as 'out of the body' whereby the runner watches himself from a dissociated perspective.

- 9 (13%) of those using imagery had a grandiose quality to the imagery used — such as winning a big marathon event or Olympic gold.

- 6 (9%) used music to induce a trance. Often using some of the lyrics over and over in the mind.

- The remainder focused attention on a particular point or would allow their mind to wander.

2. 196 (46%) of the runners stated that they repeated words or phrases in their heads when running. 43% of them used music lyrics or music to repeat. 15% stated that they used encouraging words to themselves such as "you can do it," etc. 12% employ counting such as counting steps, breaths or passing cars.

The runners were also asked what mental processes they used to run faster and better. 108 (25%) described techniques fitting into a variety of categories:

- 18% use imagery relating to body parts working well or their body functioning smoothly.

- 16% use distractions such as talking to someone else or focusing elsewhere, getting absorbed in the scenery or used sexual thoughts.

- 14% used goal setting and rewarding themselves for hitting targets.

- 14% focused on their form throughout in an attempt to keep efficient and effective.

3. 245 (58%) of those runners in the survey engaged in mental imagery of some kind when running.

- 34% try to form images.

- 66% say that the images happen spontaneously without effort.

- 35% use imagery that involves watching one's self running and often crossing the line at the end of a run. Many see themselves as fit and healthy.

- 18% engage in grandiose imagery, such as winning races.

- 18% imagine pleasant scenes such as beaches or forests.

4. 251 (59%) of runners in this study felt that they become more creative when running. They found themselves able to find solutions to problems, generate ideas better and with less effort.

It would be an interesting study that examined whether running somehow does help us create new ideas or if it is lowering anxiety in order to enable a free flow of thoughts.

It is a fascinating study for sure. Even though runners may seem blank and withdrawn and quiet inside, this study suggests that the opposite is true and that the majority are engaged in some mental activity. The study even suggests that what many runners experience is similar, if not the same, as self-hypnosis. Which is very useful for you to know as a runner who is about to read the rest of this chapter which is designed to instruct you how to use structured self-hypnosis.

Fromm et al *(1981)* describe self-hypnosis as being characterised by *"an expansion of attentional range, increased receptivity to internal events and an increase in the quantity and quality of imagery."* The mental processes occurring during running tend to meet all these criteria for self-hypnosis. Though heck, no-one single definition of self-hypnosis is as of yet agreed upon and tends to be open to plenty of debate.

Typically, runners being dissociated or absorbed in something else or engaged in other types of reality are also considered characteristics of both hetero- and self-hypnosis.

This study (especially with my level of biased interpretation) might suggest that running naturally enhances hypnosis skills of the individual.

Spanos et al *(1986)* and Fromm et al *(1981)* demonstrated that those who practiced their self-hypnosis skills became more responsive and more hypnotisable. Most runners train 3–5 times a week and so get to practice their own mental strategies that many times too. Runners really do therefore (surely!) have the capacity to become exceptional self-hypnotists — especially if trained how to use it effectively instead of just using spontaneous forms as noted and reported on within this study. That is the direction we go in now with the rest of this chapter.

For me, it gives me even more encouragement about the usefulness, relevance and benefits of runners learning to use self-hypnosis skills to advance their running performance.

What is Self-Hypnosis?

In this book, you are going to be learning how to use self-hypnosis. Your application of self-hypnosis is then taken for granted in subsequent chapters where you learn how to employ mental imagery, cognitive strategies and other methodologies within self-hypnosis sessions. This chapter gives you instructions on how to access hypnosis for yourself.

A decade after the first definition of hypnosis was crafted, the executive committee of the APA Division 30 Society of Psychological Hypnosis *(Green, Barabasz, Barrett, and Montgomery, 2005)* revised their definition to encompass the widely used clinical technique of self-hypnosis, described as, *"the act of administering hypnotic procedures on one's own."*

The idea that hypnosis involves two people, a hypnotist and a subject, would seem immediately contradicted by the phenomenon of self-hypnosis, in which there does not seem to be any hypnotist at all. At one level, we can say that there is no contradiction, because in a very real sense all hypnosis is self-hypnosis. The hypnotist can recite an induction procedure and make suggestions for various experiences, but it is the subject (the person being hypnotised) who must actively participate in the process; without that active participation, nothing happens.

You are essentially going to be engaging in the hypnotic process by yourself, without the hypnotist doing the induction or leading the session.

Comparisons of self-hypnosis with more traditional 'hetero-hypnosis' show that they are highly correlated *(Shor and Easton, 1973; Orne and McConkey, 1981; L.S Johnson et al 1983)*. However, the two are also different and it is likely to be misleading to suggest here that your experience of self-hypnosis is going to be the same as the experience you'd have with a professional hypnotist.

It may be more difficult to give yourself certain types of suggestion that a hypnotist could give you. However, it is clear that the overlap between the two forms of hypnosis is considerable.

At the same time, it must be said, that much of what passes for 'self-hypnosis', especially in a clinical setting, more closely resembles a relaxed state of reverie and imagery, in which subjects are allowed to construct their own experience without any particular direction from the hypnotist *(Fromm et al., 1981; Olness, 1981)*. The relationship of this form of hypnosis to the more traditional 'hetero' form is open to question *(Khan et al., 1989)* — as is the question of whether this form of 'self-hypnosis' should really be called hypnosis at all.

The important thing for you to consider and be aware of, is that as you are guiding yourself into and through the hypnosis sessions, you need to engage, have a good level of focus and awareness and it'll be nothing like being unconscious: quite the contrary, you'll have a heightened level of awareness and that is quite different from popular media portrayals of what hypnosis is.

Is All Hypnosis Self-Hypnosis?

Several people in the field of hypnosis and hypnotherapy, whose work I truly love, have offered up the notion that all hypnosis is self-hypnosis. They believe that the power is with the client: the person who is guided into hypnosis.

In fact, in 2006, the National Guild of Hypnotists (NGH) stated in print that the hypnotist will "induct a client into a self-hypnotic state." Several other hypnosis associations have followed in a similar vein.

In the 1985 book by Lynn and Garske, entitled **Contemporary Psychotherapies,** in a chapter titled "Hypnosuggestive procedures as catalysts for psychotherapies", Theodor Barber contended that most hypnosuggestive procedures can be truthfully defined as self-hypnosis. Additionally, work by Orne and McConkey in 1981 *(Toward convergent inquiry into self-hypnosis, International Journal of Clinical and Experimental Hypnosis)* and Sanders in 1991 *(Clinical Self-Hypnosis: The Power of Words and Images)* state the same. Parts therapy and regression proponent Roy Hunter and his mentor, Charles Tebbetts, stated the same — that hypnosis is self-hypnosis. In fact, in Roy Hunters book **The Art Of Hypnotherapy,** he states that Tebbetts, whilst still alive, began every hypnosis session with the statement, *"All hypnosis is self-hypnosis."*

The founder of the American Board of Hypnotherapy held that same opinion as stated in *The Wizard Within* by Krasner in 1990 *(published by ABH Press).*

In 1995, in *Essentials of Hypnosis*, Michael Yapko suggested that whatever power the hypnotherapist has, is acquired from the client and of course, can be terminated by the client.

As far back as 1965, in *Hypnosis Induction Technics,* Tietelbaum stated that if a hypnotist attempts to be too powerful, then the client might lose rapport and reject suggestions given.

Really, it is the guys in the 19th century, born out of Mesmerism and the dark ages, that created the notions of hypnosis **'being done to'** another individual.

Ultimately, the person being hypnotised is responsible for generating the suggestion inside their own mind, the relevant imagery to go with it, and combining with it all their own experience and behaviours in response.

One of the benefits of such a theory and approach to hypnosis, is that it does lend itself wonderfully well to the runner using hypnosis techniques at home and can therefore be taught in a number of techniques to advance running performance. This is made difficult if the person being hypnotised believes that they can only enter hypnosis if the all-powerful hypnotist needs to be around to induce it.

This way of explaining hypnosis to my hypnotherapy clients is also very useful because it helps to bypass resistance and fear associated with the notion of being under the control of another person.

Practicing self-hypnosis, the runner becomes an active agent in the process of advancing their own performance. You become your own hypnotist. Let's learn how to do that.

Using Self-Hypnosis:

Before we start with the variety of techniques, themes, strategies and various other facets of this book, you'll need to be able to hypnotise yourself.

The self-hypnosis sessions you engage in will require you to loosely follow a five step structure, with a model that takes you through Steps A to E:

Step A — You Access hypnosis.
There are a wide number of means and ways that you'll be given here to help you do this.

Step B — Being in control.
This helps you to focus and keep on track.

Step C — Continually deepening.
You deepen your perception of your experience of self-hypnosis in a variety of ways that you'll be shown.

Step D — Deliver your suggestions.
This is where you'll engage in the change-work, or apply the cognitive strategies or simply affirm suggestions to yourself.

Step E — Exit hypnosis.
You bring that self-hypnosis session to a conclusion.

We are now going to go through the steps (A–E) one at a time in more detail, offering up options and variety for each step. Many academics tend to believe that it is much easier to access hypnosis once you have been hypnotised by a professional. If you have been hypnotised formally by a hypnotist before now, it is likely to advance your skills as a self-hypnotist.

If you have not, there is no need to worry, everything you need is explained here, however, if you wish to experiment and advance your skills you can download a full safe controlled relaxation hypnosis session from my website for you to practice entering hypnosis: **www.adam-eason.com**.

There are a number of options and instructions given here for doing the various steps. It is not by any means fully exhaustive; that would require another full book, not just a single chapter. Do therefore consider visiting the blog of my website for other ways of inducing and deepening hypnosis.

Step A: Access Hypnosis:

Our first step gets a lot of attention in literature on hypnosis: what hypnotists refer to as the induction, whereby hypnosis is induced. This is where us self-hypnotists access hypnosis and induce hypnosis for ourselves. Please read the techniques in this chapter before you start practicing them. Get a general under-standing and then practice them before you proceed with the applications going forward.

On my self-hypnosis seminars, I hypnotise the delegates and set up an easy way for them to do Step A, the access. I install a trigger that they use to access hypnosis readily from there onwards. They then test it, practice on the seminar and learn how to make it even better. As I said previously, you can download the audio session for free from my website to do the same if you wish.

Here are a number of different ways of accessing hypnosis, inducing hypnosis, or more simply, opening the door of hypnosis.

1. Using Eye-Fixation For Self-Hypnosis

On my hypnotherapy training diploma, the eye-fixation induction is kind of the "hypnosis 101" induction that all students learn before any other inductions and, here, I want to show you how to apply it to yourself rather than do it with another person.

This method of inducing hypnosis was originally developed by James Braid, believed by many of us in this field to be the founder of hypnotherapy as we know it today. As well as being a medical man of the day, James Braid specialised in eye treatment and as a result, having coined the term 'hypnosis' and moved the understanding of hypnosis away from the field of Mesmerism, it was natural that his initial methods of inducing hypnosis would involve the eyes and fixing their attention. What's more, there is a great deal more research that has been conducted on this induction than the majority of the hypnosis field.

The basic premise is to attempt to produce a level of strain on the eye muscles by having an individual look upwards with the eyes and without moving the head.

After trial and error with a variety of ways of doing this, Braid used an object, such as his lancet case and elevated it in front of the individual to the point where it would be a strain to continue looking at it. If such an object was not used, an individual could be asked to look at a point on the wall or ceiling, without moving

69

their head, which caused them to slightly strain their eyes if the gaze was fixed for a while.

Here, for the purpose of using this technique for inducing self-hypnosis, we tend to suggest that the individual look up at their own forehead, though again, picking a spot on the wall or ceiling to create more strain can be done if necessary.

The reason that the gaze is pointed upwards in this way is of course to advance and enhance the tiredness felt in and around the eyes in a fairly speedy timescale. Importantly, you do not tilt the head backwards at all, otherwise you assist the eyes and just end up staring upwards with a bent neck. You move the eyes only with the head in its usual, balanced position upon your neck.

With the eyes fixed in this way, creating some minor strain, the individual induces a slight sensation of the eyes being sleepy as they close in this slow manner. Importantly though, this process gets the individual to concentrate in an intense fashion by staring at that point.

Braid actually attempted to call hypnosis 'monoideism' at one stage because of the importance he placed upon getting some focus and attention to achieve it.

When doing this with an individual, taking them in to hypnosis, they tend to close their eyes after around 30 seconds or so. When using this to induce hypnosis in yourself, you should consider aiming for a similar timescale to close your own eyes.

Once you have adopted a comfortable, seated position, with your head facing forward, without moving your head you move your eyes to the elevated position whereby it is a slight strain to hold them there, you then need to employ your imagination to make your eyes feel like closing. This is incredibly important. You must help the process along with your thoughts — imagine that your eyelids are getting heavier, tell yourself that they want to close and that it will be so nice and comfortable when they do so.

All the time that you are communicating with yourself in your mind in this way, ensure that you keep your gaze fixed in that same position without wavering or moving or allowing your eyes to relax by compensating in some other way. Keep your head and eye position in the position that ensures the eyes become tired.

Then, once they are ready to close, you let them close and that is the initiation of your hypnosis. You then proceed with the subsequent Steps B through to E.

Some theorists of hypnosis also offer up some ways of advancing the success you have with this process, which I thought I'd add here too. For example, you could adopt the behaviours of someone who is in hypnosis. That is, act as if you are hypnotised to enhance the fact that you are and enhance your openness to it. Take on the posture of someone who is initially concentrating very hard, who then falls asleep as the eyes close.

You've seen what happens when someone is fighting falling asleep. Like when I am sat in front of the fire with the TV on after my dinner in the evenings. I get that sensation in my eyelids where they start to close and I keep snapping them open to regain my focus! Adopt that same behaviour; let your eyes close slowly and adopt the posture of someone drifting on in this way.

To further complement this, you can let your body relax deeper when you close your eyes as you proceed on to whatever deepening strategies you are going to use.

As you purposely take on these behaviours, the idea is that you'll start to take on some of the things you are acting — the same way

71

a method actor takes on characteristics of their character when acting — you then notice how you do actually start to feel slightly drowsy as your eyes flitter, and slowly close.

As I alluded to earlier, it is also important how you communicate your thoughts throughout the process. Use your imagination to advance the process and make it more effective.

You can simply tell yourself you are feeling more relaxed and that your eyelids are feeling heavier, for example, using your internal dialogue. You could imagine them closing and getting heavier during the straining process. You can imagine them closing and imagine how much more relaxed they are when closed.

You might remember times when you have been drowsy or sleepy and your eyelids felt heavy and wanted to close. As you remember that sensation, tell yourself that this is the same.

You might imagine a light shining in your eyes or a gentle breeze blowing toward them, exaggerating the desire to close them and let go. Use a gentle, relaxing tone when you communicate with yourself, encourage yourself by telling yourself how well you are doing this and use your imagination and cognitions in whatever way helps advance the overall process.

As with any self-hypnosis process, repetition makes it better. So practice this over and over to get really good at it. Use your thoughts and posture in line with the structure and really get good at using this method.

2. Heavy Arm Self-Hypnosis Induction Method:

Here is our second way of doing Step A and accessing hypnosis.

This is a self-hypnosis induction technique that engages the imagination and makes use of nature's law, in a way that many hypnosis professionals refer to as a 'biological' induction.
It includes inherently within it a convincer, too — that is, it convinces you that self-hypnosis is occurring by the way it is carried out.

Important note: The people who benefit the most from these types of self-hypnosis inductions are the ones who really engage their imagination, focus on the instructions and absorb themselves in the process. What would you rather do: nothing, or engage your imagination, focus and absorb yourself to benefit the most?

Throughout this book, I use a step-by-step method of explaining many of the processes, which is going to start from here onwards. Follow these simple steps to induce hypnosis using the heavy arm method.

Step One:

Just get yourself comfortable and be in a place where you will be undisturbed for the duration of this session, ideally sat up in a chair with your feet flat on the floor and your arms uncrossed and ready to begin.

Just allow yourself to get settled and comfortably seated, with your feet flat on the floor and your arms and legs uncrossed and not touching each other.

Adjust yourself so that your head is nicely balanced and comfortable upon your shoulders and your body is at a most comfortable posture.

Throughout this hypnosis induction process, you may notice certain changes happening immediately whereas others might take a few moments, trust that you are doing this in the way that is right for you, you are unique and respond in your own unique way.

Then take a nice deep breath and as you exhale, allow your eyes to comfortably close and begin.

As I say in many of my audio programmes, you don't have to sit perfectly still throughout these self-hypnosis induction processes, but the more still you are, the less spatial awareness you'll start to have of your physical body as the session progresses and so, the deeper your experience may well be, so experiment with stillness as much as you find it comfortable to do so. Stillness means you tend to get less distractions and so do consider benefiting from incorporating stillness into your sessions.

Then move on to the next step.

Step Two:

You are in this nice seated posture, with the crown of your head pointing to the ceiling and your shoulders relaxed.

It is an attentive posture you want to have, with your feet flat on the floor and your hands by your sides or on your lap and not touching each other. I prefer to be attentive than too slouched and relaxed which tends to encourage people to wander off, lack focus and even fall asleep, which is not all that useful — unless you want and need more sleep.

With your eyes closed, take your right hand and arm and hold it straight out in front of you, palm facing down. Simply hold your right arm and hand straight out in front of you, palm facing down and with it there in that position, be aware of the feelings that you are having in your right arm and hand right now at this time while it is being held aloft and in front of you like that.

Imagine that there is a bucket resting on your hand, and every relaxed breath you breathe from here onwards and for the duration of this induction process, fills the bucket with more water, making it feel as if it is getting heavier and heavier.

Get really mindful of the sensation that exists within the arm, become aware of as much as you possibly can about the arm. Scan along it and within it with your mind.

Start to notice what you notice. Is there tension anywhere? Are any (even tiny and subtle) movements occurring? What else are you noticing? Tell yourself and feedback to yourself what you notice as you hold your arm out. Become as aware of the entire arm as possible in these moments.

Imagine the bucket continuing to fill with water with each breath you breathe, getting heavier and heavier and harder to keep in that position and then move on to the next step.

Step Three:

Now continue to pay attention to that arm because this is the stage all the fun and hypnosis is going to start happening.

Imagine it (your arm) is beginning to feel heavier and heavier, imagine it is getting heavier and let it feel heavier and heavier. This is made easier by the fact it is being held and gravity is naturally pulling on it, but start to let it take over a little bit by advancing that sensation of heaviness using your imagination.

As you imagine the arm getting heavier, notice that thinking about the heaviness creates a tendency for your arm to become heavier, feeling as if it is getting heavier and heavier. Affirm this by saying to yourself those words "heavier and heavier" repeatedly as you continue to let your imagination make the arm feel heavy.

As it feels as if it is getting heavier and heavier, also imagine the arm starts to, very slowly but surely, move downwards.

Tell yourself what that feels like, tell yourself using your internal dialogue in your own head, feeding back as you did earlier. State to yourself that your arm is moving downwards.

The heaviness in your arm grows with your continued imagination of such and as it grows and feels heavier, so you want to also become more relaxed, more comfortable and at ease. So imagine that each movement of your arm going downwards starts to make every other muscle in your body more relaxed and comfortable.

Continue paying attention to your arm all the time as it feels as if it is getting heavier, you imagine it getting heavier, as it moves downwards, so you relax and now start to tell yourself you are going deeper into hypnosis.

Tell yourself this with volition, do not allow other thoughts in to distract, repeat that sentiment, relax with the sentiment (too much effort or stress can impede the progress you make) and repeatedly tell yourself to go into hypnosis as you focus on the arm moving downwards and the body relaxing everywhere else.

You might notice your breathing changing as you relax more, if so, enjoy that and tell yourself that it is happening.

You are creating a chain of progressive things occurring here:

Imagine your arm is moving lower and feeling heavier in order to show you how deeply hypnotised you are becoming and how much more relaxed you are right now.

Just as you think your hand is going to reach the chair or your lap or anything else, move on to the next step.

Step Four:

When your hand reaches your lap, it rests, it relaxes and flops into a comfortable position where the relaxation continues to spread through your body. Imagine the newly experienced relaxation in the resting arm spreading to everywhere else. Maybe even let out an audible 'sigh' as the arm reaches the lap or chair and then enjoy the relaxation developing from it.

Use words like "relaxing" and "comforting" to describe your ongoing experience and enjoy the arm no longer being heavy, just relaxed and feeling so good. Continue to affirm that you are drifting deeper into hypnosis, and you can commence with the latter stages of the self-hypnosis session.

You then follow the other steps from B through to E.

3. Using Magnetic Palms To Induce Hypnosis:

This is our third way of inducing hypnosis, still on Step A of our A–E steps for our self-hypnosis sessions.

Many street hypnotists and stage hypnotists use this process in inducing hypnosis and preparing people for hypnosis induction and I have seen many professionals use this kind of process when hypnotising others. Here, I'm explaining how to use the same process to induce self-hypnosis.

This is all about 'magnetic palms'.

Before hypnosis was officially even called hypnosis, before it existed in the way we know it today, Mesmerists used to believe that there was an invisible magnetic energy that flowed through each and every one of us. Out of that era came a number of tests that are used today within the field of hypnosis and though they really have nothing to do with actual magnetism, they are really useful in developing hypnotic responsiveness, and tuning up self-hypnosis skills.

This process of 'magnetic hands' is very simple to do, you just hold your hands out in front of you with your palms facing each other, just 10–20 centimetres or so apart. The aim for you is to then use your imagination and self-hypnosis suggestions to get the hands to move together without actually closing them in a usual deliberate manner.

It won't happen magically and there is not actually a Mesmeric 'magnetic force' pulling your hands in towards each other. Your muscles still do that for you. It is just that instead of you moving them in a voluntary, deliberate fashion as you usually would, you are now using your imagination and a number of different sensations instead of conscious control.

As with the vast majority of self-hypnosis skills, this requires some practice to help develop fluency and overall betterment of your self-hypnosis.

Firstly, on a physical level, if you position the hands 10–20 centimetres apart and have your arms relaxed and at ease, with your eyes fixed on the space in between them, gravity will help them to feel as if they are drawing in that direction.

If you rub the hands together immediately prior to doing this, really rub them together fast and generate some heat in the palms, then the heat in the hands and the 'energy' created from that movement will enhance the physical tendency for them to feel as if they are drawing closer together anyway.

To really advance this in order to subsequently advance your self-hypnosis skills though, you need to engage your thoughts and imagination.

This can be done in a wide variety of ways, but I recommend you start by imagining that there is a magnetic force pulling your hands together. Imagine that you can feel it happening, as if it is a distinct sensation all of its own that is drawing the hands in. You might also say to yourself the words "my hands draw closer together with each breath I breathe" to advance the flavour of the action happening in response to your imagination. When you say it to yourself, absolutely convince yourself of the hands being drawn together, say it to yourself in such a fashion that makes you believe in it 100%.

For those that prefer something more visual, you might like to imagine the 'magnetic force' as a light or a colour that aids the process of drawing the hands in together. Or you may wish to imagine that string is tied around the hands and is being pulled tighter as the hands draw closer. You could imagine someone pressing the backs of the hands and they are getting closer. Basically, anything that you can imagine that would force the hands closer together, make it as vivid as you can and let the process happen.

Keep the remainder of your body relaxed and be fascinated in the process, enjoy it and it'll be much more effective as you will not be clouded with any unwanted feelings or thoughts.

Expectation is incredibly (powerful?) with hypnosis. If you expect certain outcomes, they are more likely to occur. The same is true here. If you expect the hands to move closer together, then they will. Be positive about it, really expect it to happen and engage your imagination as best as you can and you'll start to develop your self-hypnosis skills for use in a wide variety of other ways.

When the hands touch together, then let them drop into your lap and you proceed with Steps B through to E.

4. Hand To Face Induction:

Over the years, I have offered up a number of ways, methods and means to commence with self-hypnosis sessions, through the format of a structured induction. Many authors might suggest that this is not always necessary, but structured inductions have been something that has worked incredibly well for me, with my own subjective experience and as a result of teaching self-hypnosis since 1996.

This induction process for self-hypnosis is actually a great one and is a bit more advanced than the previous three, it is also more demanding. The reason is that often we use nature to advance our imagination. For example, imagining your arm getting heavier when you hold it outwards is easy to do as it would perhaps feel heavy anyway as a result of gravity and the slight strain of doing so; the same goes for imagining your eyelids getting heavier when you use an eye-fixation process. This technique here today involves some fixation, it eventually utilises nature but importantly requires some real purposeful use of the imagination.

Within this process, you are required to engage your imagination and to elicit some 'hypnotic phenomena' within yourself. If your internal dialogue or belief starts to defy your imagination, then quiet it by imagining a volume control of your internal dialogue, or wrapping duct tape around the voice of your internal dialogue or doing whatever you need to do to keep it quiet while you engage your imagination. Follow these simple seven steps for the hand to face induction method:

Step One:

Of course you want to be in a place where you are going to be undisturbed for the remainder of this session.

Be sat in a comfortable, upright position, ideally with your feet flat on the floor and your arms uncrossed. Be in a receptive posture, and not slouched, your posture will help you to engage with the process and be attentive to it.

Have your hands resting in your lap, upon your legs with the palms facing upwards. Once you have got yourself into this physical position, then you keep your eyes open and proceed to Step Two.

Step Two:

Keep your head in the same, still position while you look at your hands. Focus all your attention, all your awareness and gaze attentively at the palms of your hands resting in your lap, whilst keeping your head completely still, just moving your eyes to look at them.

As you look at them, start to be mindful of your hands. That is, notice any sensations within them, which there are likely to be more of when you really focus and heighten your awareness.

Notice the temperature of them, are they hot or cold or somewhere in between? Are they perfectly still or is there the tiniest fraction of movement within them? Notice the details of the lines in the hands.

When you have really engaged with your hands, move on to the next step.

Step Three:

As you continue to look at your hands, work out which of them feels the heaviest. Even if it is just a tiny bit more than the other, which one feels more settled in its position.

When you have worked that out, turn your attention to the one that feels the lightest. Stare at a fixed point on that palm, the palm of the hand that feels lighter than the other.

Enjoy the fact that it feels lighter than the other for a couple of moments.

Now start to imagine it is feeling lighter with each breath that you breathe. Almost as if each inhalation is making the hand and arm feel as if it is getting lighter and lighter. You have to really engage your imagination and believe that this is absolutely the case.

Use your internal dialogue and cognitions to dominate your thoughts while you imagine this and say to yourself with real purpose and volition "my hand is feeling as if it is lighter and lighter" and keep repeating it as you imagine your hand moving up off your lap.

Keep repeating the phrase with real meaning, keep engaging the imagination and as soon as you get a tiny movement of any kind upwards with the hand, then move on to the next step.

Step Four:

Now engage your imagination further by imagining that in the palm of this lighter, slowly moving hand is an incredibly powerful magnet. A really incredibly powerful magnet. Imagine a second magnet is on one of your cheekbones and that it is attracting the palm of your hand closer and closer.

Watch as the magnet pulls the hand toward your face. Stare at the palm of the hand, imagine it is moving more purposefully towards your face as the magnet pulls the hand to your cheekbone.

Some people like to imagine that they can see some sort of magnetic force that is present and is drawing the hand closer to the face. You can do this if you want to.

Now start to engage your internal dialogue, again suggest to yourself using an affirmation; "the magnetic force is pulling my hand to my face" and repeat it with meaning, say it to yourself like you really believe in it 100%. Over and over in your mind as you imagine that magnet and the magnetic force pulling the hand to your face in easy movements at a pace that is right to you.

This is key: now make an important distinction, think carefully as the hand moves towards the face. Work out if the hand is being pulled more strongly by the magnet in the palm or the magnet on your cheekbone. Make sure you can tell where the magnetic force is stronger.

When you know that, move on to the next step.

Step Five:

Continue to engage really purposefully with all the above steps and watch the hand move closer to the cheekbone, and as you watch it arrive beneath your eye line, let your eyes continue to look downwards and then just close as any part of your hand gently touches your face.

As your eyes close, take a deep breath and imagine the magnetic force is cut. Imagine that as your eyes closed, the magnets were switched off in some way.

With them switched off, notice how your hand and arm feel heavier and heavier and you tell yourself that the arm feels heavier and heaver and imagine it floating slowly back to its original position on your lap. Imagine it drifting back down and as you imagine that, let it relax, feel heavier and tell yourself "as my arm drops, so I go deeper and deeper into hypnosis" and keep repeating the words "deeper and deeper" as the arm floats all the way back down to the lap.

Let each exhalation increase the heavy sensation as the arm drifts to your leg where it began this exercise.

Once it reaches the lap, as it touches, exhale deeply and let the relaxation in that arm spread throughout the body and then move through Steps B to E.

There are four fairly simple methods to practice Step A and access hypnosis. Remember, we open the door with Step A, we get focused and begin our self-hypnosis sessions with the induction. Do not expect lightning bolts to fire from the sky and give you some definitive sign that you are hypnotised. As you practice and get persistent with it, you'll start to notice the qualities of self-hypnosis and the signs will demonstrate to you that you are getting better and more adept at inducing hypnosis. Now once you have done Step A and have induced hypnosis, you move on to Step B.

Step B: Being in Control.

With this step, you signal your intentions to yourself, you develop focus and you set up the session. This is done very simply and quickly by using your internal dialogue and acknowledging that you are in control of the session.

This is not essential and there is no evidence to suggest that this enhances self-hypnosis, but my own experience over the years has suggested that it gets the mind receptive and also has you taking charge in a progressive, determined way.

Simply affirm to yourself, something along the lines of the following:

>*"I am hypnotised."*
>
>*"I am in full control."*
>
>*"I respond to my intended suggestions."*
>
>*"I am protected from random thoughts, sounds and images."*

You acknowledge and impress upon yourself that you are indeed in hypnosis. You remind yourself that you are in control of the session. You give authority to your intended suggestions (or change-work, as per the array of techniques and strategies following in this book) and you are protected from random thoughts, sounds and images that may occur while you are engaged in this self-hypnosis session.

Now that you have induced hypnosis with Step A, and taken control with Step B, you move on to Step C.

Step C: Continually deepening:

There are a very wide range of deepening methods. The idea here is to deepen your perception of your hypnotic experience. Please note, you are not actually going deeper, it is a concept, a metaphor or a level of perception. Traditionally, it was suggested that the deeper you were, the better you would respond to suggestions or change-work. However, it is very difficult to measure actual depth of hypnosis beyond individual responsiveness to suggestions.

Some of the techniques that you are going to be using to advance your running performance will enable you to dismiss using a deepener as suggested here. That is because the technique itself has a structure that can substitute a deepener; you'll be advised if that is the case.

This step is referred to as 'continually deepening' not just because the letter C fits in with my model, but because at times, when you are engaged and focused within a session, it might feel as if your hypnosis got lighter, or was less profound. If so, you can administer a deepener at your own discretion to deepen accordingly. Thus, you continually manage your depth, by deepening as you see fit. You'll learn to recognize when you might need to do that.

Here are a number of ways that you can deepen your experience of hypnosis.

1. Progressive relaxation:

Progressive relaxation can be used as an induction too. You might simply start a session using progressive relaxation to enter hypnosis. You can engage in progressive relaxation in a number of ways:

1. You can simply breathe and say the word 'soften' to yourself as you think of the muscles of your body. Work your way through your body, using your awareness, starting at one end of your body and moving all the way through to the other end. This is a process I learned from Richard Bandler, one of the co-creators of the field of NLP (neuro linguistic programming) when attending a seminar of his.

2. You can imagine a relaxing colour, and then spread that colour through your body, one muscle at a time. Tell yourself that as the colour spreads, it relaxes the muscles.

3. Imagine light and/or heat spreading through you, relaxing you deeply.

4. Imagine that you are a rag doll and that your muscles are loose, limp and dormant.

5. Imagine being close to a heat source that spreads throughout you.

There are many, many other ways to use progressive relaxation. Just use whatever process you know of to deeply relax and allow your body to be more and more relaxed. In a later chapter in this book, we focus on relaxation and you'll be shown how to use a very particular method of relaxation for de-sensitisation purposes that can also be used as a deepener.

2. Imagining Going Deeper:

The most obvious way to deepen hypnosis is to use the classic types of means and use mental imagery that involves going deeper; skiing or trekking down a mountain, going down stairs, drifting into outer space, diving deeper into the sea, walking deeper into a landscape of your own design.

You could simply spend time imagining being in a favourite place, or you might also imagine watching the numbers in your mind as you count downwards and backwards from 100 down to 0, telling yourself that each number takes you deeper.

3. Quiet The Mind— Bubble Time Deepener:

Bubbles can sometimes be the sort of material that is a bit fluffy, a bit too alternative and the sort of thing that does not necessarily suit me. So I was naturally delighted a few years back when I re-read the Charles Tebbetts self-hypnosis book, which incidentally is a bit fluffy, alternative and esoteric, but is an important contribution to the library of anyone exploring the field of self-hypnosis. Anyhow, it used a rather lovely process that involved bubbles that I have adapted and use a great deal still today.

Many people learning self-hypnosis or practicing their own skills often talk to me or ask me about getting distracted or explain that their mind wanders and that they feel they get easily distracted. This in turn serves to fuel their opinion that they are not progressing.

We get distracted. We all do. There are monks out there who dedicate their entire lifetimes to getting stillness and deep peace of mind and even they rarely attain absolute perfection in that regard. My message is to persist and with practice things get easier, and to accept distractions and continue regardless of them... *"Oh no, I left the cutlery drawer open at home when I left for work... I think... Did I?"* Can be simply followed with, *"... And back to my self-hypnosis practice..."* for example. No big deal.

However, the reason I mention the bubble related theme at the beginning is because you can use a deepening process that I am about to give (involving bubbles) that can be used to enhance the peace of mind and quiet and that actually utilises distractions or unwanted thoughts and allows them to form part of your self-hypnosis session.

Step One:

Induce hypnosis and take control as we did in Steps A and B.

Step Two:

Now imagine a large body of water of some kind. This can be an ocean, a sea, a lake, a river or even a large pool of some sort. A lake would be ideal for the first few times you use this process as it is more still and has less movement occurring within it that lends itself well to the very nature of this type of session.

As you imagine that large body of water, imagine being sat on the bed of it, the floor of it and use your imagination to let you breathe easily and comfortably.

Just be mindful at this stage. Observe yourself, your breathing and don't try to change anything and don't try to stop anything from changing. Sometimes things change just by being observed. Enjoy some quiet. Just be comfortable imagining this rather unusual idea that you are breathing comfortably and easily whilst sat at the bottom of a large body of water.

When you have got comfortable with that notion and are imagining it as clearly and vividly as possible, move on to Step Three.

Step Three:

After any period of mindfulness and quiet reflection occurs, eventually a thought is likely to cross your mind. As soon as any thought enters your mind, watch and imagine a bubble rising out of the ground, rising up to the surface of the water.

So if and when any image, sound, dialogue or thought comes into your mind, you watch and see a bubble rise up out of the water bed, it then floats up and up and you watch it go out of view as it reaches the surface of the water.

Imagine that the bubble is the thought and that you simply let go of the thought as the bubble drifts and floats far away. The thought then leaves your mind quiet and peaceful again.

Continue doing this for a few moments. As you continue to do this, tell yourself that with each bubble that floats up, with each thought that dissipates, and with each breath you breathe comfortably at the foot of this body of water, you go deeper and deeper into hypnosis.

You might simply say the words "*deeper and deeper*" (for example) to yourself as a deepening mantra and a means of keeping the mind still while letting go of any other thoughts as bubbles that float up and away.

Once you have got comfortable doing this, move on to Step Four.

Step Four:

Let the bubbles rising and floating away be mirrored with your breathing rate. That is, create the bubble and get it rising as you inhale. Then as you exhale push it all the way out of the water and into the air to dissipate. Some thoughts may persist and continue, in which case, be patient and accept the repetition and keep repeating the process gently and easily as you breathe gently and deeply.

Do not judge or try to interfere with the thoughts you have. Just notice them, watch them happening, accept them and then let them go by imagining the bubble. Allow each facet of this mindful bubble process to take you deeper into hypnosis.

As you go deeper, and once you have done this for a comfortable period of time, move on to the next step.

Step Five:

Once you feel that your hypnosis is of a sufficient depth, then you continue with your change-work or self-suggestion as you would do usually, before moving on to the final step. This entire process can also be done simply to derive the benefits of mindfulness and enjoy a quiet, relaxed and peaceful mind for the duration of the session. (We discuss mindfulness in more depth later on in this book too).

You then follow Steps D through to E and open your eyes to bring this session to an end.

As with all of the techniques and processes I have shared here, practice and repetition will advance the effectiveness and your own responsiveness. You might want to experiment with the amount of time you can keep going with the process and build up your time doing this as a stand-alone technique.

4. Mind's Eye Deepener:

One of my favourite deepening processes in hypnosis is one championed, and often referred to, by Michael Yapko, and is called the mind's eye closure.

I like it because it is fairly quick, really does the job of deepening well and helps in a variety of ways with the session. The technique involves offering suggestions about imagining the presence of a "mind's eye" as the (albeit metaphorical) part of our mind which thinks and imagines stuff even when our body is relaxed, comfortable and still.

This process offers up a notion of using your imaginary mind's eye and the eyelids of that mind's eye (like an imaginary version of the eye fixation we learned about earlier in this chapter). You guide yourself and imagine the mind's eyelid getting heavier, for example, and you then extend the metaphor so that this (imaginary) eyelid closing also helps the mind to quieten and be less distracted.

It is great to use if you are about to engage in hypnosis following some time in a busy environment, or if you are a little fidgety at the beginning of a session, for example.

This is the way Michael Yapko suggests it is done and can be found in his book **Trancework** in the chapter on **"Strategies of Hypnotic Induction"**. He suggests you word it something like this, having ideally completed an initial induction of some kind:

> *"...just as you have eyes that see the world around you, you have an inner eye that many people refer to as the "mind's eye"... and it can see images and process thoughts even as you relax deeply... and you can think of your mind's eye as having an eyelid... and like your physical eyes your mind's eyelid can gradually grow more tired and heavy, and it can begin to drop... and as it begins to close it slowly closes out more of those stray thoughts and stray images and leave your mind clearer and clearer, more quiet and open and free to experience whatever you would choose... and it's closing more and more... and your mind grows quieter, more restful... and now your mind's eye can close... and close out any stray thoughts or images that you don't want to interfere with how relaxed you are..."*

I like the way this technique can help people 'switch off' and get focused on the hypnosis. I tend to prefer that you suggest the mind is more and more clear rather than it is perfectly clear, because if you have some minor internal dialogue, you may feel that what you are suggesting is not working and as such develop some resistance to the procedure.

There are a number of deepening methods and that concludes Step C.

Step D: Deliver Suggestion or do change-work.

You are going to be given a wide array of techniques, methods, strategies and processes to do at this stage throughout the book. Once you have induced hypnosis, taken control and deepened (if you needed to) you then get to the important part of the process, which is the change-work, the process that is going to advance and contribute to your running performance in some way.

These are coming up within the remainder of the book.

Step E: Exit from Hypnosis:

You conclude the hypnosis session by simply counting from 1 to 5. You can count aloud or in your mind. Whichever way you do so, when you count 5 and open your eyes, you signal the end of that self-hypnosis session.

Each of the numbers can represent a number of different things, so you might like to consider that the first few times you exit hypnosis, you even tell yourself the following:

> "When I count 1, I have full control, flexibility and coordination throughout my entire body, from the tips of my toes to the top of my head, from the tips of my fingers and thumbs to my shoulders. Any feelings of lightness or heaviness return to their true and correct perspective."

Here we have put all our bodily sensations back as they should be. Sometimes, prolonged stillness in hypnosis can, for example, alter our sensations of lightness and heaviness in our limbs, and some of the inductions we use may have altered sensations and perspective that we want to return to usual.

"When I count 2, I position myself back in the place where I entered hypnosis, remembering and recalling what was to my left and right, above and below, remembering and recalling some features of the place."

This is important if you spent some time in a favourite place or used your imagination vividly to be somewhere else. Some of the mental imagery techniques we use later in this book require you to imagine rehearsing skills when running or being somewhere else in your mind, for example. You are ensuring that you reconnect with the place that you are actually in once again.

"When I count 3, all sounds return to their true levels of importance and have the correct perspective."

Some people find that, while in hypnosis, their hearing can become altered slightly. For example, a lady I once hypnotised commented that my voice seemed like it was background noise even though I was sitting right next to her and that the traffic outside seemed louder. Our focus can sometimes make sounds seem different. Likewise, a strong imagined experience can have our hearing tuned differently potentially, so we like to make sure that is all back in place too.

"When I count 4, I am keeping and bringing with me all the wonderful benefits of this hypnosis session."

All the good stuff that you have worked on in the self-hypnosis session can now be brought back with you into your real-life. Make sure it is integrated and is not left in the domain of hypnosis.

"When I count 5, I open my eyes to be fully emerged and out of hypnosis."

You then count from 1 to 5 and open your eyes. That particular session is completed. I strongly suggest that you revisit this chapter now and run through the A to E protocol, practice the various inductions and deepening skills, then you are ready to start using it all for the upcoming ways of advancing your running performance.

Your Internal Dialogue — The Language of Self-Hypnosis

We are going to discuss self-talk in more detail later on in this book. For now though, when engaging in some of the earlier self-hypnosis sessions, be aware of how you use your language when talking to yourself in hypnosis.

I encourage you to use language in a progressive (positive?) way to ensure your internal dialogue can be as useful as possible within your self-hypnosis sessions. You do not have to be sickly sweet or incongruent, just be as progressive as you can be.

Think about an occasion in your life that was a wonderful occasion; maybe a happy birthday, the birth of a child, a wedding or a celebration, maybe a time when you achieved something, when you succeeded or maybe a time when you felt the full force of joy or love. Really think about that experience. Remember what you saw, remember and think about the sounds that you heard and think about how you know now and how you knew you felt so good then. Whereabouts in your body were those good feelings? Now, as you really think about that memory and immerse yourself in it, think about the words that you would use to describe that experience.

These are the words that are going to elicit the most powerful response from within you when you use them in self-hypnosis sessions and when you communicate with yourself at any time.

Have a think about these questions; what words make you feel good? Which words give you good feelings? These words will serve you well when used appropriately in self-hypnosis sessions.

Words in Self-Hypnosis:

Now, I am going to add a couple of words here for you to think about. Think about the words more and more and increasingly. These words are going to be important to create growth, power and fluidity in your mind. Let me explain how.

Consider the sentence, *"As a result of achieving my ideal weight, I am happy."* This is a nice way to remind yourself that achieving this particular goal (whatever it might be for you) you are happy. Great. However, we can make that more powerful by changing a rather static happy to *more and more happy*. I don't know about you, but I would never want to think that I ever reached the pinnacle of happiness and could not go any further.

Happy is static. In order to supercharge your self-hypnosis sessions and the way you utilise language in self-hypnosis, you can mobilise the words and get them moving onwards and upwards for you. You can change *happy* to *happier and happier*, or *more and more happy*, or *increasingly happy*, or *progressively more happy*, or *more and more appropriately happy*. Use whatever feels right for you, just use other words to develop and power it up. Make sure you do this appropriately and usefully of course. It may not always be right for you or your outcomes.

Words to avoid in Self-Hypnosis:

Some of these words may seem fine and feel fine to use for you. I am just giving you ideas and considerations when using these words in a self-hypnosis session.

When communicating with yourself , my recommendation is that you consider avoiding the following words and types of words;

Words that elicit bad feelings. Words that are ambiguous. Words that are limiting, restrictive or disempower you. Words that you are uncomfortable with.

Words that elicit bad feelings in Self-Hypnosis:

So, firstly, I want to point out some words that can elicit bad feelings: Try, can't, won't, don't, should, shouldn't, must, mustn't, jealousy, temper, no, lose, will, sad, difficult, but. I want to point out a couple of these words in particular.

The word **try** is limiting for some people. When you are trying to do something, you are not doing it. You may be building in failure by using the word try.

The word **will** is another one to avoid if you can. Will is not actually happening, it is something you will do rather than actually are doing. It never occurs. You know, you can put almost any sentence together with the word will in and simply remove that word to make it more progressive and positive for your self-hypnosis requirements.

Have a go at doing that. (I realise that there is likely to be at least one wise guy who now uses the word as in "last will and

testament", yes, very clever. I have not heard that one before.)
Here are a couple of examples;

As a result of stopping smoking **I will be healthier**. Now
becomes; As a result of stopping smoking **I am healthier. I will
successfully achieve my goals** is transformed into **I successfully
achieve my goals.** Here we have just removed "will" to make it
more progressive.

We are going to examine some thinking errors and distortions
later on in this book; we'll look at *musterbation* — using the
word "must" implies it is an obligation to do that thing rather
than actually wanting to do it. Likewise, the issue of *shouldism* is
whereby you feel you should do something rather than actually
wanting to, so be aware of some of those types of words for now.

This might not always be the case for you; just consider your own
language when using self-hypnosis.

Put Down the Put-Downs:

I recommend that you really do avoid using words that are
put-downs. They don't really have a place in self-hypnosis or your
mind at all. Avoid the following words and words like them:

Untidy, Dirty, Smelly, Ugly, Stupid, Lazy, Hopeless, Disliked,
Unkempt, Smelly, Idiot, Embarrass, Ridiculous. I know you know
lots more.

I don't really like even having to write these in this chapter. Your
internal dialogue and self-hypnosis sessions are better without
these words.

You can allow yourself to find the right solutions and methods for you. As you get more and more used to being in self-hypnosis or just communicating with yourself more progressively and discovering the kind of suggestions and words that have the most powerful effect for you, then you can fine-tune your use of them.

Revise this chapter, and then we are ready to start applying these skills to enhance running performance.

Chapter Four:
Loving Running, Banishing Excuses
And Getting Motivated

"Nothing is impossible; there are ways that lead to everything, and if we had sufficient will we should always have sufficient means. It is often merely for an excuse that we say things are impossible"

Francois de la Rochefoucauld.

If you are already absolutely driven, motivated and free of excuses and are head over heels in love with running, then you might feel inclined to skip this chapter and get onto the strategies for improving running performance, I understand that. However, the processes in this chapter are great ways to start applying your self-hypnosis skills. Spanos *(1986)* with his 'Carleton hypnotic skills training programme' showed that when you practice self-hypnosis, you become more hypnotisable and better at using hypnosis. You can move on to more sophisticated methods of applying it too.

If you start with some of these simpler strategies, then they'll serve you well as we move into the latter chapters for advancing your running performance.

When people consider running or training, they often go through that phase of rationalising it with themselves. You use that language at times, don't you?

"I **ought** to start my training schedule."

"I **should** do some physical exercise."

"I **must** get out on a run tonight. "

This sort of language shows that running is sometimes something we don't really want to do, but it is somehow necessary for us to get something else; it is a means to an end and not very compelling. We want to be slim, we want to fit into a different waist size of trousers or a smaller dress, we want to feel fitter when playing with the kids, we want to be able to see our toes when on the scales, we want to be perceived in a particular way — exercise is the means of doing it for many people.

There are very few people that first start out on the path to being a runner that actually think to themselves and tell the world around them:

"I **want** to run."

"I **enjoy** running."

"I **love feeling the sensation** of running."

It often takes us a while to develop this perspective on running. Whenever I say these kinds of things, many people look at me as if I am some sort of nut-job.

It tends to then feed my motivation to run further and keep on doing it. It is now an intrinsic and automatic part of my life and my day-to-day regimen.

"What? Is that it, Adam? That is your strategy for getting motivated? Just keep on doing it until you like it?!"

Nope. That kind of suggested process is likely to end up in as many January gym subscriptions that get used 20 times in January, 10 times in February and then never again.

Many people have an unusual psychological association with running when they first start and some of us go through dips in our motivation to get out running. Some runners think of running as some sort of a chore and think of doing it with some kind of begrudging mindset, like it is a punishment; often perpetuated by those that insist on "no pain, no gain", or other outdated 80s idiocy that only deserve to be repeated at select nostalgic moments when refusing to throw away your 'Frankie Says Relax' t-shirt.

If you consider running to be something you must/should/ought to be doing because you have to lose weight somehow, or because you promised to raise funds for a charity at a running event and you have to sacrifice some comfort and exchange pain, hassle and have various other misgivings, then of course you are not going to be motivated to run or train accordingly.

To get you underway with some processes to use straight away, this chapter offers up a couple of simple and basic ways to use self-hypnosis, mental imagery and a bunch of other stuff (excuse the technical jargon) to show you how to get motivated for running and end up wanting to do it, feel good doing it, and enjoy running. This then leads on to a process of falling in love with running and abandoning any excuses for not training. It is a great way to start to frame our running experience as we move forward to the more sophisticated processes and techniques that follow which advance your running performance.

Before we start with this first, motivating process, write up a list or have a mental note of all the reasons that you want to be a runner — all your motivations. Word them in a positive frame. By that I mean, state that you want to, *"Achieve your ideal size, shape and weight,"* and not, *"I don't wanna be fat."* Make sure your reasons are things that you strive to achieve rather than things you want to avoid — at least for this exercise, we are going to be positive.

I appreciate that many people are motivated by fear and avoiding things that they do not want, but this particular process lends itself better to being progressive.

With that in mind, also now think of some really marvellous statements that are inspiring and motivating to you, such as those I gave earlier: *"I love to run more and more,"* and, *"I increasingly enjoy being a runner,"* and, *"My body loves rigorous, healthy running,"* or word things however you choose, in your own preferred way.

So with that set of great reasons for running in mind, and with a set of positive affirmations to deliver to yourself later on, let the fun begin.

Seven Steps To Getting Motivated To Run:

Step One:

Induce hypnosis using any of the techniques from the previous chapter.

Once you have induced hypnosis, move on to Step Two.

Step Two:

You may choose to remember a time you enjoyed running, where you had a really good workout and you felt great for it. Alternatively, you can imagine and create such an experience...

Spend a few moments imagining that you have just completed a run of some kind. You decide what kind of run it was. Notice what you see all around you, notice the sounds of the environment you are in and, most importantly, start to feel the sensations of having enjoyed a spectacular uplifting exercise session.

Imagine the endorphins that your brain is pumping through your body that reach every cell of your body. Notice the warm tingle of heightened sensation in your muscles as they relax after the exertions, like it is a glowing, joyous sense of satisfaction. Imagine feel-good chemicals working through your system.

You might choose to imagine the good feelings as a colour working through your body and mind, or as a sound, or even just get a physical sense of it working through your body and concentrate on it.

Really spend plenty of time making sure you generate a very real and observable sensation in your mind and body that represents the sensation of having just exercised beautifully well. As you do it, tell yourself that you are going deeper inside your mind and use this step to deepen your own hypnosis at the same time.

When you are certain you have that, move on to the next step.

Step Three:

Now we benefit from one of the main abilities and characteristics of hypnosis. Magnify and increase that magnificent feeling. Maybe you imagine a dial in your mind, maybe you imagine the colours spreading or becoming brighter, maybe you sense the feelings expanding, maybe you just tell yourself they are amplifying, maybe you move the feelings (or your imagined feelings) faster and faster through your body and build them up to a feverishly delightful and delicious joyous feeling.

Take all the time you need and really practice expanding and developing this glorious feeling of post-run bliss and ecstasy.

When you are sure that you have grown it and amplified it to a memorable level, move on to the next step.

Step Four:

Holding those great feelings, recall all the reasons you have for running. All those great reasons and motivations you have. Remind yourself of all those wonderful reasons you have for running and start to imagine how good it is going to be when you achieve those desired outcomes — maybe it is reducing your size to fit into new clothes, maybe it is wanting to feel good, or prove to people that you can do this, maybe it is completing a marathon for a worthy cause you support; whatever the reasons, imagine you have achieved them and notice how good the feelings of achievement are. Bask in them and combine these feelings with those that you already have.

Build and develop and amplify, then move on to the next step.

Step Five:

Continue to build and amplify the good feeling and now state those affirmations to yourself, those positive statements. Start to say to yourself any one of the affirmations or positive statements that you decided upon prior to starting this session, for example:

> *"I love to run more and more."*

Or...

> *"I get increasingly more enjoyment from running."*

Repeat the chosen statement over and over in your mind and imagine that these words are getting combined with that good feeling, so that if you say these words to yourself outside of hypnosis, they install the feelings.

Imagine the words rolling around your mind and body and let these words become associated with that great, motivating feeling. When you are sure that these words have been repeated enough times in your mind to really have an effect in real-life, then move on to the next step.

Step Six:

To bring this together, now imagine being in a typical situation in your life when you are about to choose whether to go for a run or not. See the sights, hear the sounds, be in that place, that environment of your life.

Now mentally rehearse that in that situation, you state those words to yourself, you feel those feelings begin to grow and develop within you, you are inspired into action and you decisively choose to run.

Step Seven:

Tell yourself that every time you practice this process, it becomes easier to do in real-life. Tell yourself that each time you have to decide whether to run or not, you start to automatically feel really good at the prospect of it, knowing the great feelings you get and knowing the wonderful outcomes that await you. Think about a run that you can go and do within the next 48 hours and decide to do that.

Exit hypnosis by counting from 1 to 5, wiggling your fingers and toes, and then open your eyes.

Go and take some action, go and partake in that run that you planned and notice how much more enjoyment you get from it, notice how much more you can motivate yourself to engage in running and how much easier it becomes to instigate it more and more regularly.

Neat technique to start with, eh?

Fall In Love With Running:

With your new-found self-hypnosis skills then, here is your second technique to practice. It is a very simple process for you to practice and helps you to fall in love with running.

This is a lovely and rather novel process. It is based upon an NLP (neuro linguistic programming) technique that I have seen used and that has been published by a variety of authors in that field. It lacks the evidence base of many of the processes I share within this book, but stands upon some solid foundations used in the work of Pavlov and his stimulus response theory.

There are times when we all tend to fall in and out of love of running. I go through highs and lows and my motivation wanes from time to time and getting motoring is a lot easier when I am in love with running.

I tend to fall in love with running just before and after big events, when I have bought running gear, when the latest edition of Runners World magazine falls through the letterbox and when I talk to my brother about our running schedules each week. However, there are various other means to have a love for running that don't require the external stimulus that I mentioned in this paragraph.

Step One:

Before we start with the self-hypnosis process, create a list of the feelings you'd like to have about and towards running. You can write them down and have a written list (which I advise) or you can create a list in your mind as preparation for this exercise.

Your relationship with running may have wavered in a variety of ways over the years, or even if you are just starting out running, so being aware of how you wish to feel towards running is going to help you in the process of actually having that sort of regard towards it. Plus, having a vivid idea of the feelings you want to have beforehand is going to ensure that you enhance the relationship with running and help those feelings be ignited later on in this process.

Once you have a good comprehensive list drawn up, pick the 4 or 5 top things from it in order of preference and jot down an occasion when you felt that way before. Just briefly remind yourself of those occasions and have an idea of them in your mind. With the list of occasions, besides your top 4 or 5 ways that you wish to feel towards running (love, affection, inspiration, motivation, excitement, enjoyment, fun, healthiness, etc.), then proceed on to Step Two.

Step Two:

Induce hypnosis using any of the techniques shown in Chapter Three.

Once you have induced hypnosis, move on to Step Three.

Step Three:

With hypnosis induced, now run through your top 4 or 5 feelings in the following way whilst associating them with running:

Remind yourself of one of your listed feelings that you wish to have, then recall the occasion you felt it before; make sure you imagine seeing the sights, hearing the sounds and feeling that feeling as vividly as you possibly can.

Generate some of that feeling and then spend a couple of minutes growing it and magnifying it and enhancing it. You might imagine it as a colour that you spread in your body and mind, it might be a sensation that you develop further, or even a sound that resonates within you. Really develop and build that feeling within you, then move on to the next step when you can feel it vividly.

Step Four:

Once you can feel plenty of that feeling, think about going running whilst keeping that feeling. Imagine a future run you are going to go on whilst feeling that sensational state within you and associate that feeling with running. Get the great feeling intertwined unmistakably with the experience of running.

Once you feel that you have merged the feeling with running, then move on to the next step.

Step Five:

Repeat Steps Three and Four with the other feelings and occasions you previously listed until you have done this with all the feelings you wish to have towards running.

Make sure you take all the time necessary and do this thoroughly and diligently, you'll benefit greatly from doing so. Each time you do this; imagine developing a strong bond, a wonderful relationship with running. Remind yourself of how much good it is doing you and how much your love for running is building and get excited about running.

Really develop these states and enjoy feeling them and associating them with running and once you have gone through the list, move on to the next step.

Step Six:

Once you have developed these feelings you wish to have towards running, then imagine going out on a run (final time for this exercise) and combining all those wonderful feelings. Imagine them merging and associating wonderfully with your run. See the sights of the places you run in, hear the sounds and really imagine being on your run whilst feeling this way towards your run. As you do that, think the words "I love running" to yourself.

Say the words in a way that is undeniably convincing to you that you do love running. Say it with vigour and meaning and in a way that you feel like you truly believe it.

Then you can use those words to stimulate these feelings when you plan to go running and throughout your runs. Heck, at the end of a great run, say the words to yourself to anchor those great post-run feelings to the words so you can use them to get your relationship with running developed and built massively.

Step Seven:

Once you have done the previous steps, then exit as shown in Chapter Two by counting from 1 to 5.

You might like to take a couple of deep, energising breaths and open your eyes to bring this part of the session to an end.

Test and practice using the words in your mind and really fall in love with running. You see, when you love it, you'll be more inclined to do it.

There you have it: let's start the 'hypnosis for running experience' off by truly falling in love with running so that we have a wonderful foundation to build upon, and so that we are not in any way finding the running experiences that lie ahead of us to be any kind of a chore.

Let Go of Excuses to Not Train:

Many runners find themselves making excuses not to train and run, so in addition to getting motivated to run and falling in love with running, to round off this basic chapter nicely, let's also equip you with a self-hypnosis process to banish excuses.

You'd be amazed at the excuses that I am given from clients in therapy excusing their issues. Of course, some are very valid and not to be ignored. Yet in therapy and in life, so many people insist on excusing themselves for all manner of behaviours, thoughts, limitations and mistakes. Runners are no exception.

Whatever goals and outcomes you have for your own running, do you have a set of excuses that you offer up to yourself and others that makes it OK not to do those things?

This third self-hypnosis process is all about blasting away and getting rid of old excuses not to run and stopping procrastination about running.

Step One:

Just ensuring that you are in a comfortable position where you are going to be undisturbed for a while, induce hypnosis using any of the processes from Chapter Two. Once you have induced hypnosis, move on to the next step.

Step Two:

In this receptive state of mind, have a really good think about a running goal that you wish to achieve. Perhaps think about a desired running outcome you'd like to achieve but that you are perhaps procrastinating about, or making excuses for not doing.

Importantly at this stage, as you think about that outcome, that goal, or that running achievement, think about the actions you'd have to take, the actions that are required for you to accomplish this running goal.

When you think about those actions you'd have to take, notice and become really tuned in to yourself. What is it that you actually do instead? What feelings and thoughts come up before you get sidetracked? What are the excuses that you come up with to make it OK not to accomplish?

If the excuses do not directly make themselves obvious, perhaps notice how your thoughts redirect you, and what thoughts do actually redirect. We can refer to those thoughts as excuses for the rest of this exercise.

All the time, notice subtle thoughts, images in your mind, feelings that you feel and be very perceptive of this. Being in self-hypnosis is likely to amplify those and make them more obvious than usual.

You might find that if you attempted to put these feelings or thoughts into words, they possibly sound silly — that is the stuff we are after! They are deep-rooted rationalisations and excuses that tend to get buried and hidden usually, yet have all the power to keep you off track to achieving that outcome you really do desire.

So get as much of an awareness as possible of these excuses, notice how you perceive them, if they have sounds to them, any internal dialogue, feelings and so on. Then, when you really have a feel for them, move on to the next step.

Step Three:

Now we want to assess the excuses and see what they are up to...

The best way to ascertain the pattern of your excuses is to ask yourself some questions. Is it really just an excuse? Do I want to keep this excuse? How does using the excuse serve me? Is there some way that I gain from using this excuse?

If there is some valid value you receive from this excuse, then you can allow yourself to keep those parts of it, you can maintain them should you wish.

With the answers and getting an idea of the purpose of your excuse, move on to the next step.

Step Four:

Did you ever say the expression "Hell NO!"?? Did you ever deeply refute and refuse something with a strong sense of "NO!" ??

Now is the time to recall a time when you said or felt like saying "Hell No!"

Maybe it was an occasion when you were absolutely disgusted at something, when you totally refuted something, or maybe when something was utterly and completely unacceptable to you. Get in to a state of "Hell No!" and the more disgusted, the more you mean and refute with that sense of "Hell No!" the better!

Imagine that you spread this state throughout your body. Imagine it as a colour. Imagine the sense of it connecting to every cell in your being. Spend as much time as you possibly can to ensure you get a very deep-rooted sense of "Hell no!" running through every cell of your being.

Step Five:

Imagine your excuse in front of you.

Tread on it.

That's right, stamp on it. Stomp on it. Jump and down upon it. Use all the mustered up power of your "hell no" state and bounce up and down on that excuse.

115

Pick up and throw it to the ground. Tear it in two, cast it to the floor again and stamp ferociously upon it.

Keep stomping. Keep stamping. Unleash every ounce of your "hell no" state upon that empty excuse. Make it sorry! Only move on when you are sure as possible that you have got all that pent-up state unleashed on that excuse and it is fully destroyed.

Step Six:

Have a good test to make sure you did this.

Think about your goal, your desired outcome or that thing that you want to achieve.

Notice what happens when you imagine taking the actions that move you toward that outcome. Notice what you feel right now, what thoughts you have and what images come into your mind as you think about it.

Get a real sense to see if there are any other excuses lurking in the darkness somewhere. If you get a flavour of any, then return to the earlier steps and run through the process again. Think about how any lingering excuses can interfere with the very enjoyment of your life, how they can be hurdles to your accomplishments and leave your life a lot less satisfying.

When you are sure that you are free of those last remnants of excuses in relation to this outcome, then move on to the next step.

Step Seven:

Remind yourself of your state of "hell no" and how you used this with such conviction. Think about a time in your future, ideally the next occasion when you think about going for a run. Just imagine that as you start doing that thing, you smash the last remnants of the old excuse with a massive "Hell NO!" response. Then imagine watching yourself doing that thing, taking that action, leading that life and accomplishing that.

Enjoy the beautiful feelings you get with knowing that you get that done in the end and how wonderful it feels.

Once you have enjoyed enough of that, exit hypnosis by counting from 1 to 5, wiggle your fingers and toes and open your eyes.

Then — and this is important — go and take an action that is undeniably convincing to you that you have gotten rid of all those old excuses and start hatching your plans for a happier life.

With these lighter, motivating initial techniques underway, we'll now move on to some evidence-based cognitive strategies to enhance your running performance.

Chapter Five:
Cognitive Strategies For Runners

"The idea that the harder you work, the better you're going to be is just garbage. The greatest improvement is made by the man or woman who works most intelligently."

Bill Bowerman

There are a number of famous irrational beliefs that tend to reach each and every sports person at some stage:

"No pain — no gain."

"You must give 110% all the time."

"Practice makes perfect."

"Winning isn't everything — it's the only thing."

These kinds of thinking distortions display irrational beliefs of perfectionism, self-worth depending upon achievement and over-personalisation, for starters, and research tends to suggest that dealing with irrational beliefs and overcoming thinking distortions of this kind help the athlete to be appropriately relaxed, focused, positive and motivated *(Zinsser et al, 2001)*.

1984 seems like a long time ago, doesn't it? That is when my copy of the classic Straub and Williams book, Cognitive Sport Psychology, helped athletes and sports people to really engage with a cognitive skill set to enhance performance, and the field of sports psychology has never looked back it would seem.

All the stuff that I have written about in this book so far could in some way be deemed as a cognitive skill set, just as most of the chapters that are coming up could also be deemed as cognitive skills — the mental imagery skills, the relaxation processes, the mindfulness, the goal setting material and so on.

A number of studies have attempted to look at the cognitive strategies of successful athletes and shown a wide number of ways the cognitive strategies help enhance performance. The right use of cognitive strategies can indeed yield impressive results for the runner. Successful athletes do have a different set of cognitive strategies than those that are less successful *(Greenspan & Feltz, 1989; Williams & Krane, 2001)*.

Within my own therapeutic training and work with individual clients, the influence of Albert Ellis and Aaron Beck is obvious and nothing brings me quite as much joy as when I get to bring in facets of their work into other loves I have — such as running.

Running for fun may not necessarily encourage us to have too many so-called thinking errors or distortion, but when we start getting to stages where we want to perform better and race faster, pressure is placed upon our performance and training schedule. This, along with the weight of expectation and defeating beliefs, self-sabotage, as well as distorted and irrational thoughts, can start to find themselves impeding our performance.

Importantly for us runners, we need to recognise that our cognitions (anything that goes on in the head that can be verbalised; dialogue, thoughts, ideas, beliefs, etc.) can and do affect sporting performance, but that our cognitions can be changed and as a result can improve performance *(Dobson & Block, 1988)*.

Gauron *(1984)* identified a number of common cognitive distortions that can and do regularly impede the progress of athletes. Here is a list of the common irrational beliefs and problematic thinking styles Gauron identified:

1. Catastrophisation:

This is something that regularly features in my therapeutic work and when I recently referred to the similar notion of 'awfulising' in my e-zine a while back, my business partner Keith and several of our subscribers took me to task about assuming that everyone understood what I meant by it!

When an individual catastrophises, they tend to imagine the worst case scenario and allow issues or minor adversity to amplify and become a major dramatic issue.

A catastrophising runner may think,

> *"Oh no, I missed my hills session this week due to work, now I am behind on my schedule and I'll never get up to the level needed to run the marathon, and I am now letting everyone down who supported me, and I struggle to live with that and the world may well explode as a result..."*

I am joking about the world exploding bit. The exaggeration hopefully illustrates the point I wanted to make. If we expect the worst-case scenario, it is likely to affect performance and responses to that thought, even creating more unwanted outcomes.

2. Blaming:

This is whereby a runner fails to take any responsibility for his or her own performance. I have met and worked with many runners who blame the course, the weather conditions, the poor advice they received, and all manner of other people and circumstances for their poor performance.

Not taking responsibility for one's own performance can in turn impair good performance. With the right kind of outcomes set and realistic goals developed with the appropriate levels of responsibility accepted, a healthy evaluation of our own running performance can result *(Orbach, Singer & Price, 1999).*

3. Over-Personalisation

On the flip side of that coin, we have **Over-Personalisation.** This is having a self-defeating way of making everything very personal and taking too much responsibility for their own performance. At times, some of the failures and mistakes may well have other valid reasons.

I can remember watching my footballing hero, Stuart Pearce, on his knees crying after missing a world cup penalty for England and shouldering masses of blame for letting the team and nation down. Yet, the team were jointly responsible for not having won the game in the proper 90 minutes and extra time and letting it go to penalties, and the pressure on the shoulders of those taking the penalties in those circumstances is huge and affects ability greatly.

If a runner allows himself to think too personally and take all the responsibility, it can lower the belief in the real ability that runner has and can impair performance, lower motivation and see our commitment dwindle.

A good balance is required regarding the previous two numbered points.

4. Perfectionism:

This is an unrealistic (and often unattainable) level of expectation and can lead to problematic pressure being placed upon the individual. Perfectionism can also lead to the often paralysing 'fear-of-failure' which often prevents people from engaging fully and effectively in the training process or events. If the runner performs or trains in a less than perfect manner or with a less than perfect result, the runner deems himself a failure and can end up fearing more failure.

5. Self-worth depending on achievement:

A lot of athletes in general place value upon themselves correlated to their success in their sport. Realistically, there are very few who can be number one. Many runners I have encountered professionally and personally have used their marathon time as a gauge for their own level of value placed upon themselves.

Runners can be detrimentally affected by this idea of valuing themselves in terms of their running success or achievements. It can demotivate and impair enjoyment as a result.

6. Thinking in absolutes:

When a runner or any athlete thinks in black and white only, it can be problematic. If we are a winner or a loser, with nothing in between, it can be defeating or inaccurate or unfairly representing the performance outcome.

When runners have a polarized way of thinking, they might label themselves in a way that restricts or impairs performance or leads the runner to have detrimentally affected expectancy about future performances.

Within my own therapy rooms, I often use Socratic questioning techniques to dispute, question, look for evidence and rationalise when these beliefs and thinking distortions present themselves. However, it would be inappropriate to write up a full section on Socratic questioning methods here.

Therefore, evaluating thoughts and beliefs by asking the following questions is recommended by Steimetz, Blankenship, Brown, Hall, and Miller (1980)

If you suspect a thought of belief you have is holding you back, ask yourself the following:

- Is this belief helpful to me as a runner?

- Is this thought helping me reach my goal?

- Is this belief based on objective reality? (i.e. is there any evidence for having this belief?)

- Does this thought/belief reduce emotional conflict being experienced?

Potentially even more important to us runners here, though, is the fact that the research into learning to restructure cognitions has been emphatically positive *(Greenspan and Feltz, 1989, is a great example of analysis of such studies).*

In the next chapters, I share some techniques and methods for how to go about cognitive restructuring to enhance your running performance and use a number of strategies to use your own cognitions to improve your running performance.

Chapter Six:
The Belief Of A Runner

"Whether you believe you can or believe you can't, you're probably right."

Henry Ford

Many runners have beliefs that are holding them back from achieving their desired outcomes.

Alongside a very inspiring 25,000 other runners, with a Halloween nightmare of a hangover, and poorly equipped with 4 hours sleep, in October 2012 I ran the Great South Run for the fifth time, and added another finisher's medal to my collection.

Also running that race was an inspiring student of mine, Claire Lincoln. Claire completed the run, it was the furthest she had ever run and she triumphed. The reason I mention Claire here is that not only did she hold herself publicly accountable for her goal (by brilliantly blogging about her progress), not only did she train well, keeping herself driven and motivated, applying her mind to the task as well as her legs; **she had belief!**

She believed that she was going to successfully complete the run. She texted me after the run and one of the things she said in that was *"struggled near the end but wasn't going to walk unless my legs broke."* — Hahahahaha, I love that sort of determination. Beyond that determination, though, is a belief that presupposes she is capable of doing that and getting to the end without walking.

Beliefs fuel runners a great deal.

Many clients (including many runners) have beliefs that are holding them back from achieving their desired outcomes.

My very first therapist said something to me that I have written about many times before in the past: in mid conversation he said, *"Well Adam, whatever you believe to be the truth, is the truth for you..."* As he carried on talking, a lightbulb switched on in my head and stuck with me ever since.

A favourite author of mine, the late Robert Anton Wilson, wrote in **Prometheus Rising**, *"What the thinker thinks, the prover proves,"* meaning that we think a thought and then filter reality to match that thought and thus prove it to be the truth for us. Beliefs do this filtering job incredibly well for us, but not always the most accurately or the most beneficially.

First, We Want to Discover Any Limiting Beliefs:

Your beliefs are explained by many as the rules of your life, well at least they are the rules that you will no doubt be living by at some level. These rules may be what sets you free to achieve things in your life and live the way that you think is important. The beliefs you have about your ability to run, your running skills and how you are as a runner are going to subsequently influence and affect your running.

These beliefs therefore, may be restricting your running and holding you back as a runner; they may even be creating the belief that you are incapable of achieving your running goals. Or as in the case of the previously mentioned Claire Lincoln, make sure you achieve what you set out to.

We tend to form our beliefs as the result of our experiences and then we act as if they are true. In one sense they are self-fulfilling prophecies. If you believe you are a capable runner, you will act that way, dedicate yourself that way, approach your training that way and communicate with yourself that way when running in events. My own beliefs in my running have undoubtedly been forged by years of continuous running proving what I am capable of.

Yet, the belief to run that way in the first instance needed to be there, so which came first? The belief or the experience?

Many think that beliefs are only formed by experiences, but equally experiences are the results of beliefs, which means that you can choose, create and fashion your beliefs.

In any aspect of life, and especially in sporting performance, we all have a personal investment in our own beliefs. When the world confirms them, then they make a lot of sense to us, they are then predictable and give us a sense of security and certainty. We even may take a perverse pleasure in a poor performance, providing we have predicted it; how many of you have used the term, *"I told you so,"* and found it to be a satisfying phrase? Not because you necessarily wanted anything to go wrong, but because your beliefs were proved correct.

Prior to updating our beliefs, it is best to make sure we are aware of any negative and limiting beliefs.

Limiting beliefs are a major offender stopping us from achieving our running goals. They act as rules that stop us from getting what exists within us as potential and we all have so much potential as runners that we do not tap into nearly enough. Limiting beliefs hold us back from achieving what we are actually capable of.

So have a good think about this question; *"What is stopping you from achieving your goal?"* and know that the answers are very often your limiting beliefs.

Further to the phrases I mentioned earlier in this chapter, here are some typical limiting beliefs that are amazingly common among runners;

> *"I am too heavy to run."*
>
> *"I do not have a runners build."*
>
> *"I'll never be a great runner as I started so late in life."*
>
> *"I am too old to run an ultramarathon."*
>
> *"Other people are better suited to running than me."*
>
> *"I do not deserve to be a successful runner."*
>
> *"I have reached my limits."*
>
> *"I need to work very hard to just run a mile."*
>
> *"Successful running takes a very long time."*
>
> *"Running is painful."*

This is important: These and similar beliefs are only true if you act as if they are. Suppose they are mistaken? What difference would that make? Is the difference worthwhile? What if you held other, more progressive beliefs?

In the process of achieving your goals, sometimes just being able to articulate any existing limiting beliefs and in turn noticing their effect is enough to alter or dissolve your old unwanted belief and therefore change and update your own reality.

It has certainly been my experience that the majority of people are not usually aware of their limiting beliefs. So the first step is to put them into language or to write them down. Then they are exposed and can be examined and ideally let go of.

One way is to simply ask yourself what the reasons are that you are not currently achieving your goal. What do you think is holding you back? Or ask yourself what the reason is you are struggling in some way? Ask yourself that question and answer as truthfully and thoroughly as you can. The answers will reveal what it is that you perceive to be limitations. More often than not, these limits will be more about you than about the world. When they are about you, they are something that can be changed or updated.

A good principle to work from is the following;

Whatever you state is preventing you from achieving your goal is a belief and comes from you, not reality.

Barriers to success are created in the outside world from limiting beliefs in your mind.

Reason with yourself intelligently and objectively and write down and explore any limiting beliefs that you hold that you think may be detrimentally affecting your running.

Now Let's Update Our Beliefs With An 18 Step Process To Be A Runner With Positive Belief:

Having identified a belief that you think is limiting or restrictive or causing you problems, make sure that you write it down precisely. When you get a belief down on paper and look at it in that way, it then begins to dissipate already; it is exposed and vulnerable.

Now run through the following 18 steps to rigorously question and ideally transform the belief. This is a very thorough and diligent process that requires you to take some time, get sat down with a pen and paper and devote some thought, reasoning and conviction. Those that spend the right time on it will reap the rewards and form a solid foundation of positive cognitions that are going to fuel your running performance wonderfully.

Step One:

Ask yourself and write down how true the unwanted, negative belief feels on a scale of 0–100%.

Step Two:

Now ask yourself and write down how true that belief is in reality on a scale of 0–100%.
Be objective here; be as neutral and as honest as you can be.

Step Three:

As you look at that old belief, write down when it feels the most emotionally convincing? Then also write down when it feels the least emotionally convincing.
This is going to give you some valuable information about the kinds of conditions that will exasperate (exacerbate?) the issue and the unwanted belief.

Step Four:

Write down what actual evidence you have for that negative belief.

What evidence is there to support that unwanted, negative belief? Again, be neutral, realistic and objective.

Step Five:

Now write down what evidence you have that contradicts or challenges it.
What evidence do you have, and what evidence can you find right now that proves the old, unwanted negative belief is not necessarily the truth or a fact?

Step Six:

Write down what possible advantages there are to holding the negative belief.
Is it (the negative old belief) serving you beneficially in some perverse way?

Step Seven:

Now write down what possible disadvantages there are to holding that negative belief?

At this stage, before moving on to the upcoming questions, start to recall a time when you doubted a belief?

Can you remember an occasion when you doubted something that you really used to hold as a firm belief? You may wish to reflect on your life, think about the kind of beliefs that you had at certain times in your life, I know that mine have changed and altered a great deal over the years. I remember having solid beliefs about certain things when I was at college and can remember doubting those beliefs as I learned more about life and throughout my studies.

When you think about that period of doubt,

- How did you know that you doubted your belief?

- Did you have certain sensations in your body?

- What were you thinking about?

- How did you think about it?

- What were you experiencing?

Really see if you can get back into that state of doubt, psychologically and physiologically. While in that state, bring to the forefront of your mind the old unwanted limiting belief that you identified earlier and have a think about your old limiting belief that you want to shed; do this while in that doubting state.

Great isn't it? Who would have thought that there are advantages to doubting things? Start to doubt the old unwanted belief.

Continue to do this with some more of the questions that we previously asked, begin picking away at the old, withering belief by asking your self:

"What are the disadvantages to my running of having this old belief?"

"Does it really fit in with what is truly important to me as a runner?"

"In the past, when was having this old belief getting in the way of my running performance?"

"What would it be like to be free of this old belief?"

Just roll those questions around in the mind and then start to get focused again.

Step Eight:

What possible thinking errors are contained in that negative old belief?

- By holding that old belief...

- Are you blaming or personalising?

- Are you discounting the positives?

- Are you catastrophising, or thinking the worst?

- Are you making an over-generalisation?

- Are you engaging in shouldism or musterbation? (If you think you should or must be doing something, for example, it is very different from wanting to do something. Do you feel obliged to do something by having this belief?)

Step Nine:

Having considered all those things, how true does the negative old belief feel now on a scale of 0–100%? Write that figure down.

Get yourself nice and relaxed and breathing deeply and comfortably and then go ahead and imagine that deep inside of you exists a large furnace and if you really want to be free of the old belief forever, then imagine tossing it into the furnace and watch it burn away into nothing.

Now let's update... Think carefully about this: what would be a more realistic and helpful alternative belief to have? Before

135

you write it down on the next numbered step, consider these important points:

Firstly, it has to be stated positively and progressively, remember that you want to move towards goals, not move away from fears with your beliefs, ask for what you want, not what you don't want.

Secondly, you must ensure that you are comfortable and happy with the desired belief, make sure that it does not harm, conflict with or upset anyone to have this belief, that includes yourself!

Thirdly, make sure that it is worded in the present tense, by that I mean phrase it as if it is occurring now. For example if your goal were to achieve your ideal weight, a suitable new belief would be:

"I believe I am able to achieve my ideal weight."

By doing that now, you have made the desired belief relevant and pertinent now and you have gone and given it flow, direction and energy.

Step Ten:

Write down a better, new belief that is going to replace the old one. As you look at it, write down how true it feels right now on a scale of 0–100%.

Step Eleven:

As we did with the old belief, looking at and thinking about the new belief, write down when it feels the least emotionally convincing.

Step Twelve:

Write down when it feels the most emotionally convincing.

Step Thirteen:

What evidence could you possibly have against the new belief? Is there any evidence to suggest a problem with the new belief?

Step Fourteen:

What evidence do you have for that positive new belief?

Find evidence that shows it is correct, realistic and useful to have this new belief. Write it down.

Step Fifteen:

Write down any disadvantages to you for holding that positive new belief.

If there is any kind of downside, objectively write that down here.

Step Sixteen:

Now write down all the advantages to you of holding that new positive belief.

Before proceeding, get into a receptive state of mind now. Think back through your life, just have a think about times when you have been impressionable, willing to learn, open to change and especially open to new beliefs. Remember everything about that wonderful state of receptivity; How did it feel? Where in your body were the feelings? What did you see? What internal dialogue did you have? Really run through as much as you possibly can to achieve that state again for your self right now?

As you recall a time when you were open to a new belief, now really focus on and think about your new desired belief while in this open, receptive state. Now ask yourself;

> *"How would it feel to have your desired belief?"*
>
> *"How is it a better belief than the old one?"*
>
> *"What difference would it make to your life to have this new belief?"*
>
> *"What things would you do that you have not been doing?"*
>
> *"What would you be able to achieve and overcome now?"*

Nothing to write down just yet, simply roll these thoughts around inside your mind as you engage positively with the new belief.

To round off this step nicely, take some time out now to evaluate the new belief. How good does it feel? Is there any tweaking to do? Can you make it even better and even more empowering?

Step Seventeen:

Having run through this, now write down how true it feels now on a scale of 0–100%.

Step Eighteen:

Finally, we come onto the process of taking some action.

Make a choice to take some action. What can you and what will you do differently this very day as a result of having this wonderful new belief? If this new belief were true and you really believed it, how would you act, what action would you take?

How about you set yourself a task, to achieve today, a task that is based on this new belief being true for you and your life now.

Start doing things differently straight away and get that new belief firmly embedded into your behaviour patterns. When you start to do things differently, you then have physiological support and experience of the new belief and it becomes verified and enhanced with each new day.

There you have it. Let go of old beliefs, set up some new ones and your running ability will be fuelled and advanced as a result.

Chapter Seven:
The Mindful Runner

"There are no standards and no possible victories except the joy you are living while dancing your run. You are not running for some future reward — the real reward is now!"

Fred Rohe

As I have mentioned in previous chapters, we are going to move on to cognitive disputation and cognitive restructuring processes for you to engage in soon.

"What actually does that mean, Adam?" I hear you asking me from behind the pages of the book.

Well, evidence (as illustrated earlier) suggests that having problematic thoughts, thoughts that limit us, or that doubt, unduly criticise, put-down, exaggerate and distort can impair our running performance whether they happen during runs, prior to a run or after a run. These are negative or problematic cognitions. We want to have skills and tools for stopping them and creating better performance enhancing cognitions. That is cognitive disputation (stopping those thoughts in their tracks) and cognitive restructuring (generating better thoughts that subsequently start to happen automatically and fuel your enhanced performance).

Before you get on to those strategies, you need to know what you are actually saying to yourself in the first place and what those negative cognitions actually are. Even if there are no negative cognitions, we can still make our cognitions more progressive and beneficial for us as runners, and we can still gain much from some heightened awareness.

Before we do anything else then, it is important for you to be absolutely aware of what you do and how you do it. How do you run? How do you think and feel when you run, what do you do in your mind when running? What do you say to yourself, or believe to be true about yourself when considering going for a training run? How do you feel and think about your run when it is finished? How did you rate your race performance?

One way to learn all of this information and be fully equipped for the cognitive strategies coming up, is to engage in mindfulness.

You run through the following mindfulness protocol and then within the session you expose yourself to your runs, your training environment, or other aspects of your life in order that you can gain a fully informed insight into what you say, think and feel in those situations.

Even if you do not think your cognitions are ever negative, you can use your mindfulness sessions to heighten your awareness massively of how you run, what you think, how you behave and to know yourself in those circumstances very well. Each time you do it, pick a different type of run, whether it is a long run, a midweek mid-tempo run, a speed session with intervals or a race.

The aim of this technique and process is to increase self-awareness. It does this by systematically developing proprioceptive awareness (meaning awareness of bodily sensations) as well as awareness of your thoughts. It is better to remain alert and awake when being mindful, but it is not unusual to drift off from time to time, don't worry if this happens. Resting your fingers on your tummy in a reclined position is helpful in enhancing your awareness of your breathing at the times it is needed.

Self-awareness at this level is going to help you to know how you think, feel and how you hold your body, what your posture is and really develop a very detailed picture of what you do when you run, which is going to be very important as we move forward. Plus when you know what you do, you can change things that may need and require it, you can make subtle adjustments when you notice things happen in your actual runs from having experienced them with mindfulness sessions.

This is going to help you become proactive about your running and is going to form a basis for much of the material we use moving forward. Not just psychologically, but physiologically too.

As an aside, do you remember the Karate Kid, where Daniel-san is told by Mr Miyagi that he will train him in Karate, and Daniel turns up to train but ends up getting whiny and disillusioned because he is being asked to wax on and wax off and paint and so on. It turns out he was developing skill beyond his awareness.

This process being done diligently is going to enhance everything else you do as we move forward in this book and is going to build a strong foundation later on.

Mindfulness has a wide variety of applications for enhancing the quality of your life and this is just one tiny facet of the impressive field of mindfulness. Those familiar with Buddhist meditation will recognise elements of this type of exercise. Here, we are combining mindfulness with the process of exposure, as used initially by Gestalt therapists. You develop a strong sense of mindfulness and then expose yourself to a situation where you are running, about to run or finished running.

Self-awareness brings natural harmony and balance back into the body. Throughout the mindfulness exercises that follow, let yourself be passive, a detached observer, just be content to notice what you notice, feel what you feel. Don't try to change anything and don't try to stop anything from changing.

I have often found running helps me with being mindful as a sort of by-product. In the therapeutic environment with my clients, I often suggest that self-awareness can become a pathway to deeper self- control and self-mastery, here I'd add that it can also result in being a better runner. Later on in this chapter, we'll also learn how to apply mindfulness so that it can be used when you are actually running too.

Mindful Exposure For Running:

Have a good think about a running situation or scenario to use within this session. Make it your goal to become deeply self-aware. To start with, you'll be aware of your body, and then of your mind. Be patient and thorough throughout, when required to do so, contemplate things as deeply as you can.

Practicing this process in a quiet, still environment will serve to enhance your skills for when you use mindfulness during runs.

Take a moment to settle into a comfortable posture and allow your eyes to be closed.

Step One:

Start off by being aware of your entire body as one. From the top of your head, all the way down into the tips of your fingers and toes. Be aware of your entire body as one. Don't try to change anything; don't try to stop anything from changing. Sometimes things change just by being observed.

Take a few moments now to become more aware of your entire body as one. Then when you feel that you have developed a good awareness of your entire body, move on to the next step.

Step Two:

Now use your breath to guide you deeper into self-awareness. Notice the sensations of your breathing. Notice your stomach and your chest as they rise and fall.

Notice sensations elsewhere in the body, all the other sensations in all those other parts of the body that accompany the breathing.

Notice the sensation of the air coming in through your nose and mouth, and be aware of the rhythm of the breath. Don't interfere with the breathing. Just let it happen and observe it happening.

At times, your mind may wander. Just accept that, be OK with it happening and then bring your awareness back and focus it on your breathing again.

This continued cycle of bringing your awareness back and focusing upon your ongoing experience: that is the essence of mindfulness. Once you have engaged with your breathing and watched it for a while, then move on to the next step.

Step Three:

Now turn your attention even deeper, toward your mind.

Start to observe your own stream of consciousness. Notice your thoughts, your mood and the emotional tone of your thoughts as you breathe. Be aware of any emotions you are experiencing in response to your thoughts and just observe and watch them

145

all without trying to change anything and without trying to stop anything from changing.

Don't judge your thoughts or feelings, and don't attempt to attach any meaning or understanding of them right now, simply watch them as a detached observer.

Once you have done this for a few minutes and have really tuned in to them, then move on to the next step.

Step Four:

Now bring this mindful self-awareness with you as you imagine that you are on a run. It can be a training run, or an important race, whichever you chose prior to beginning this session.

Really picture the place that you are running in, as if you are on that run right now. See the sights, hear the sounds, and feel the feelings that you have while you are running.

When you are really engaged in the run, compare and contrast how you think, feel and physically are, compared to where you were a few moments ago.

Notice the contrast in your thoughts, your feelings, the way you breathe, the way you think and how you respond to your thoughts. Notice how you hold your body and how your body responds to your thoughts and feelings as you think and feel them.

There is no need to try to change anything or stop anything from changing, just watch and notice. You might even advance your observations by using your internal dialogue and stating to yourself what it is that you notice, by simply saying to yourself "I now notice…" and finishing the phrase with your observations.

Spend as much time on this step as it takes you to notice as much as you possibly can about everything that you do when you run. When you feel that you have a detailed and informed understanding of all that you do in a wide variety of ways when running, then move on to the final step.

Step Five:

Now begin to breathe a little bit more deeply. Start to imagine and recall the place that you are in, remembering what was to your left and right, above and below you, tune in and start to connect with the room as you slowly open your eyes and reorient yourself.

Bring your heightened self-awareness with you as you go about your day and as you think about running, but then also start to become more aware of what you do when you are actually running. Mindfulness can indeed be that pathway to great self-mastery. So when you are running now, you'll notice the things you do, how you do it, how you think, feel and behave on a number of levels. This in turn can lead to you monitoring, altering and using some of the other techniques in this book to update what you do if you believe it is going to advance your running performance and enjoyment.

This increased awareness is useful in and of itself. With this increased awareness though, we have some material and information that we can use in other ways too. We are going to explore those next.

Spotting Thinking Errors and Self-Hypnosis:

In the previous process, we looked at using mindfulness to gain insight and information on how we think, feel and behave when we are running. That exact same process could also be applied to how we prepare for races, how we prepare for training and so on, so consider using it for those things too.

We are going to advance this process a bit now and use mindfulness to spot thinking errors that could potentially be impairing our running performance.

Earlier in this book, I started to seed the idea of us runners potentially having limiting beliefs and also other thinking errors or problematic cognitions that could impair our running performance. In coming chapters, I will be offering up a number of strategies for employing self-hypnosis for cognitive disputation and restructuring; in simple terms, that is whereby we catch, dispute and restructure negative thoughts or thoughts that somehow contribute to an ongoing problem.

This is all well and good, however many people often are not even aware that they were having the negative thoughts in the first place. Some of the clients that I work with often do not recognize the negative thoughts they have until they have experienced a number of them and looked back upon their day, thinking it was then too late to do anything about them. We are therefore now going to examine ways we can advance this mindfulness process for our benefit and become aware of problematic cognitions in more detail, ideally before or during them happening.

One way to begin practicing becoming more aware of your thoughts is to tune in to yourself at regular intervals throughout your day. For example, as far back as the early 1950s, the book *Gestalt Therapy (1951)*, shared a number of *"awareness experiments"* designed to help build mindfulness and often used as a precursor to more advanced mindfulness techniques.

The most basic of these Gestalt awareness experiments was entitled the *"ABC of Gestalt"* by Fritz Perls. It was as simple as this;

> *"Try for a few minutes to make up sentences stating what you are at this moment aware of. Begin each sentence with the words "now" or "at this moment" or "here and now."*

> **(Perls, Hefferline, and Goodman, 1951 p.31)**

It is incredibly simple, but encourages the individual to start tuning in and being aware of their ongoing experience.

There are many, many techniques and strategies used by therapists of different backgrounds, designed to help individuals spot unwanted thoughts which they can then apply thought-stopping and restructuring techniques to — the likes of which I shall be sharing later in this book.

First of all then, I offer up a self-hypnosis process which draws upon a number of different therapeutic modalities and enables the runner to rehearse the awareness skills within a self-hypnosis session and then apply those skills in real-life. This is going to help you become more aware of problematic thoughts ready for us to then deal with them in a variety of ways later.

Self-Hypnosis For Thought Spotting:

Think about a typical running situation, or training situation where in the past you may have had unwanted thoughts that you wish to be more aware of and deal with in a more thorough fashion. Then keep it in mind, ready to use later on in this self-hypnosis session.

Ensure that you are in a comfortable positive, ideally sat with your arms and legs uncrossed, feet flat on the floor, in a place where you'll be undisturbed for the duration of this session. The proceed with these steps…

Step One:

Induce hypnosis. You can induce hypnosis in any of the ways explained in Chapter Two.

Once you have induced hypnosis, move on to Step Two.

Step Two:

Now imagine being in that target situation. Really imagine being there, seeing through your eyes, noticing the sights, colours, shades of light. Engage with the sounds, those that are near, those that are further away.

Start to feel how you feel in that place, behave as you usually do and engage with this place just as you would any other time. When you really feel that you are fully immersed and you have engaged your imagination fully in this place, then move on to the next step.

Step Three:

Continue to imagine being in this place, and while you are really there in your mind, fully engaged and tuned in, use your cognitions (your internal dialogue) and tell yourself what it is that you feel, think and desire in this situation. Just state to yourself all the things that you are noticing and experiencing about yourself in this situation.

Run a commentary to yourself of everything that is going on inside of you. All the stuff that anyone else would not be able to see from the outside, tell yourself and give yourself an accurate, detailed account of everything

For example:

> *"I am aware of the urge to spit on the pavement."*
>
> *"I am aware of criticising myself."*
>
> *"I feel inferior to my fellow runners."*
>
> *"I want to shout at the driver of that car."*

Start to notice all the things you say, do, feel, and state it to yourself in your mind using your internal dialogue. Run through it methodically and in depth and detail, go through it all thoroughly step-by-step and state to yourself everything that is going on within you.

Acknowledge and label all of these habitual experiences that usually go on beneath the surface. As I said previously, give yourself a running commentary on everything that goes on within you.

As you give your commentary, start to imagine all the words drift away from you. Imagine they take a physical form and the words drift away, they are distanced and float away from you.

Once you have done that in detail, move on to the next step.

Step Four:

Start to imagine that all those words that you told yourself, as they all floated away, all the feelings, old behaviours and associations that used to be attached to them have floated away too and imagine feeling lighter and better. Imagine smiling to yourself.

Realise that by acknowledging and noticing all those things, as you noticed your ongoing experience in that situation, while you commentated on it, you let the feelings all go. When you are sure they are all gone, then take a couple of nice deep breaths; as you exhale you may even wish to sigh.

Remain in that situation, really continue to imagine being there, and then move on to the next step.

Step Five:

Having run through this, having let the feelings go, having tuned in to your thoughts, start to adopt an alternate perspective on the entire situation.

As you look at the situation, explore it intelligently and as you look at facets of this situation, ask what else could that mean? How else would this be viewed by someone else?

See if you can be as flexible as possible, and start to think of lots of different ways to interpret the environment and the situation you are in.

When you have done that thoroughly and well, move on to the next step.

Step Six:

Now you are going to distinguish between your thoughts and facts.

Tell yourself and repeat — *"my thoughts are not facts"*. Really convince yourself that all the previous thoughts, feelings and internal experiences you used to have in this situation are not necessarily an accurate account of reality. Realise and repeat to yourself that those earlier thoughts, feelings are not facts. They were just an old way of you habitually communicating with yourself.

When you think you have drummed that thought into your head properly and diligently (my thoughts are not facts) having reviewed those earlier thoughts, then move on to the final two steps.

Step Seven:

Still in that same situation, still engaging with that place, imagining being there. State some new thoughts, some better thoughts, and deliver to yourself some positive cognitions.

Encourage yourself, state something progressive and positive to yourself, give yourself some better thoughts that support you and nurture you.

For example:

> *"I feel much better."*
> *"I am capable of change."*
> *"I have taken control."*

Or use any words and statements that are good for you and make you feel better when you repeat them. When you have repeated them enough and you notice a better sense and feeling within yourself, move to:

Step Eight:

Tell yourself that the more you practice this process, the easier it becomes to do this in real-life situations.

Then exit hypnosis. Take a couple of deep breaths, wiggle your fingers and toes and open your eyes.

Practice this process as a self-hypnosis session every day for a week, then start placing yourself in those real-life situations and run through that well-rehearsed process.

You'll be spotting unwanted thoughts and removing them before you even realise you are doing it!

Mindful Meditation When Running:

In recent years, my own personal research and study has overlapped with my professional work, in a way that has been both fascinating and thoroughly enjoyable.

Whilst engaging in a course of study in Acceptance and Commitment Therapy with mindfulness, I have been able to apply the skills gained within it, add them to my own existing understanding and the material that I teach and really apply the skills to my own running experience — with some magnificent effects I hasten to add.

Next up then, I thought I would share with you the culmination of my ongoing work and how to bring some of these mindfulness skills into the actual activity of running. It is actually great to be able to offer something different to the usual cognitive strategies and self-hypnosis preparatory skills that dominate most of this book, especially as this is a mental skill that you use when you are actually out running.

This type of process is based upon the classic body scan method popularised in recent times by Jon Kabat-Zinn *(1991)*. I would like to add here though that those exploring the field in depth will encounter other very similar processes within the work of Fritz Perls *(1951)* in the field of Gestalt Therapy, and Cooke and van Vogt *(1956)* wrote too about the same sort of body awareness routine that was used by hypnotherapists back in the 1950s.

The main difference that we are going to encounter though is that most versions of this process are written and done seated or lying down and you tune into yourself whilst absolutely still. We are going to engage in the mindfulness process when very active and are running, so it is very different in that respect.

The main goal of this process though is absolutely the same regardless of where or how you are doing it. You just aim to increase self-awareness. We do this by systematically developing a heightened awareness of our bodily sensations while we are running.

Often, I have found when teaching clients or students mindfulness practices, especially when in the early stages of learning it, they might nod off or drift into sleep as they relax. The beauty of doing this kind of process when running is that you are kept engaged by the natural impetus of your running activity. It is a wonderful level of absorption that you get.

I have written before on my blog about the fact that evidence has shown that elite runners often engage in an associative cognitive strategy that keeps them tuned in to how they are during their running *(Morgan & Pollock, 1977)*. It enables them to tune in and check how capable they are of pushing themselves further whilst running or easing off based upon their awareness of their body, strength and resources.

Therefore, a process of mindfulness is beneficial for that reason. However, the benefits are much more than those simply gained for the purpose of running performance enhancement. There is a large body of evidence that supports the benefits of mindfulness for our physical and mental health in and of itself.

A simple search online will show you how impossible it would be for me to fully exhaust that body of evidence from throughout the years, but it has benefits for specific conditions as well as general health implications.

The runner benefits from good mental and physical health that are advanced by mindfulness and such a practice also enriches and enhances the enjoyment of running, in my own opinion and experience.

A couple of quick notes before you begin with this. Throughout your mindful running, be accepting of the noises, sights and places that you encounter, do your best to allow everything to simply become part of the process for you. Likewise, accept your thoughts and feelings as you run too.

Many times I have spoken and written about what Emile Coué used to refer to as 'the effort error' — that is, don't try to force yourself to do this process perfectly. Accept what happens throughout. Don't try to let go of certain thoughts or feelings, all the time, simply observe it, be interested in your ongoing experience without interfering in it. This is key.

As much as you can, be patient throughout. Enjoy the luxury of the time to yourself, and just be as aware as you can, watch it happening without trying to change anything. If you find that your awareness is distracted or wanders off somewhere else, then accept that too, then bring your awareness back to the process of being mindful.

Simply follow these steps for enjoying mindfulness when running.

Steps For Mindful Meditation When Running:

Step One:

Begin your run and get underway. Imagine that you are smiling to yourself throughout this process. If that brings a gentle smile to your face, then that is ideal, otherwise, continue to imagine it is there.

Once you are running, start to tell yourself what you immediately notice all around yourself. Just offer up a personal commentary of what you are seeing, what you are hearing and noticing about the place you are running in. Accept your surroundings, enjoy them as you tell yourself what it is that you are noticing. Develop and feel a sense of contentment with it all.

Do this for a few minutes and then move on to the next stage of the process.

Step Two:

Now start to move your awareness to your own self, and offer up a commentary on your own body, thoughts and feelings. Tell yourself how your arms and legs are moving, how you are breathing, what sounds you are making, and notice your own thoughts and deeper feelings.

Sense your muscles working, notice your breathing as you run and engage with the experience of running in this moment.

Accept all of your ongoing experiences and as you commentate to yourself on your own condition, develop a sense of self-acceptance, and warmth toward yourself. Remember as you notice your ongoing experience, don't try to change anything and don't try to stop anything from changing, just keep on track with the aim of your run, doing what you set out to do with your run, and observe yourself.

Forget about the past, forget about the future, forget about everything else and rest your mind on the flow of your awareness while you run.

Do this for a few minutes, then move on to the next step.

Step Three:

Now spend some time just zoning in on the breathing as you run.

Notice the sensations of your breathing. Be aware of your stomach and chest rising and expanding as you inhale and notice how they change when you exhale. Become aware of the pace that you are breathing, notice the sensation of the air upon your nostrils and in your lungs, notice if it changes when the terrain of your run changes too.

Observe it, watch it, become fascinated and curious about your breathing. When running, your body knows how to take on board more oxygen as it needs it, so observe that, without trying to change it. Watch it happening, and accept it, enjoy it and even marvel at the simple pleasure of watching your own breathing, feeling it and tuning into it while you run. If you get distracted away from it, accept that too, and then bring your awareness back.

Once you have done this for a few minutes, move on to the next step, unless you want to stay on this step for longer, in which case, move on whenever you are happiest to do so. I have spent many runs just watching the breath and how it changes during runs.

Step Four:

Now start to move your awareness and spread it through your body in even more detail. With each body part that you move your awareness towards, sense the blood pumping through it, watch and observe how it is all feeling as you run and let it all happen, accept it happening as it is. Become aware of the skin surrounding each part, as well as the muscles working deeper within, then here are some other considerations as you scan through the body, focusing for a few minutes on each area at least, tuning into each area and being mindful of each in depth:

Start with your feet — notice how they land upon the ground. Notice the weight and force of them as they impact the ground. Notice the weight of them when they are in the air. Sense the feelings as they move, notice the muscles and bones and sense all the fibres.

Then move up and through the legs — notice the lightness and heaviness that changes (or not) as you move. Notice the sensations within individual muscles, notice how some muscles seem to affect others. Move your awareness into the knee joints, feel them moving, and then all the way up the thighs and hamstrings. All the time move your awareness inside deeply, connect with the muscles, notice them as they move.

Get a sense of your arms as you run. Notice the angle of your elbows, notice the weight as they move, become aware of the muscles and the sensation deeper than that.

As you breathe, sense your chest and stomach — be aware of how it all moves as you breathe, sense the heart beating within, notice the lungs exhaling and inhaling. Notice the muscles throughout and within as they move.

Finally, move your awareness to the head, neck and face area. What sensations do you notice? Be aware of the scalp, the forehead, notice the expression on your face, how are you holding your jaw, where are your eyes pointing, where is the tongue in your mouth?

Notice all of these things, in detail, spend a few minutes on each area, go into detail with your awareness, be absorbed in each area as you run and, once you have completed the scan of the entire body with deep mindfulness, move on to the next step.

Step Five:

With that awareness of your physical body, of the physiological experience of running, now turn your awareness and attention deeper inside toward your own consciousness. As you continue to notice your breathing, become aware of what your mind is doing now.

What thoughts are you thinking? Are you verbalising your thoughts in your head? Is there an emotional tone to your thoughts? Are there unspoken, non-verbal thoughts, sounds or imagery going through your mind? Just watch it all for a few minutes, as if you were watching a film. Be absorbed in your own ongoing experience.

Then notice the feelings within you. Not just physical feelings, but emotional feelings. Notice your general mood and notice how you react to that mood and how you react to your own thoughts.

As you run, notice how your observations influence your thoughts. Notice how your own running exertions affect your thoughts and mood. Engage in it all absolutely, tune in to your own experience in great detail.

Do this for a few minutes, then move on to the next step.

Step Six:

Bring your awareness altogether as much as possible. As you notice your breathing, your entire body, your thoughts and emotions, imagine that you step back and just watch it all. So even though you have been very tuned in to it all, imagine stepping back and observing yourself from a slight distance.

Watch your entire ongoing experience from a slightly dissociated stance, you can re-associate any time, but do your best to have an interlude within this exercise and watch your entire experience of you running, be happily absorbed and engaged to just be... Just be aware, nothing else.

As much as you can, keep a developed sense of calmness and peacefulness throughout your run as you carry on with it.

Do this for a while and then move on to the next step.

Step Seven:

You can choose to rejoin any of the previous steps or interchange between them throughout the remainder of your run. See if you can retain your mindfulness throughout an entire run.

When your run comes to a natural conclusion, or you have got to the end of it, then connect with your surroundings and the environment, breathe deeply a couple of times and go about your day.

At some stage following your run, engage in some post-run reflection — Once you have stopped running, reflect upon the run. How was it? How was the experience of being mindful? How was it different to other runs? How was it similar? Accept it absolutely as it was and be aware of the entire running experience as a whole.

Enjoy that; it'll bring some utter joy to your running when it is done with some regularity and your body and mind will thank you enormously for it, as will your running performance.

Chapter Eight:
The Runner's Internal Dialogue

"It's very hard in the beginning to understand that the whole idea is not to beat the other runners. Eventually you learn that the competition is against the little voice inside you that wants you to quit."

George Sheehan

Following on naturally from our foray into mindfulness and developing self-awareness when we run, are thinking about running and how we approach our training and races, how can we start to update our thoughts?

Let's start by looking at our internal dialogue in a bit more depth.

Many evolution theorists believe that our advanced development as a species is in part due to modern speech or, to be precise, the ability to internalise speech and so create internal dialogue. How we use that internal dialogue and our cognitions is central to much of the modern therapeutic interventions used within my own work and proliferates the fields of talk therapies and the personal development field today.

The suggestion that your internal dialogue could be the key to understanding the special attributes of the human mind is hardly new though.

The Ancient Greeks, Stoic philosophers and the 17th-century philosophers of the Enlightenment — particularly Thomas Hobbes — all made reference to the use of internal dialogue. In **The Descent of Man,** Charles Darwin wrote:

"A long and complex train of thought can no more be carried on without the aid of words, whether spoken or silent, than a long calculation without the use of figures or algebra."

Darwin (1871)

It is now in this more modern era that sports psychologists are beginning to explore how internal dialogue, often referred to as 'self-talk', influences and affects performance.

There are schools of thought that believe every thought and utterance that occurs in our head is affecting our physiology. Whilst working with the UCLA medical school, Norman Cousins *(1990)* conducted research whereby he had blood drawn and his blood levels and immune levels measured. Cousins then immediately meditated peacefully for an hour. He filled his mind with a simple meditation technique, engaging with ideas and thoughts of everyone around him being peaceful and finding peace.

At the end of that hour had blood drawn again and it was shown that some of his immune factors went up 200% in his blood. His work was scrutinised and even criticised by sections of the scientific community but the work does illustrate the point of our self-talk affecting us on many levels.

If this does not stand out as the most credible of evidence, then allow me to offer you some more.

Evidence for Effective Use Of Internal Dialogue:

The reference to internal dialogue or self-talk here within this book, then, is any statement that the runner thinks, whether it is just said internally or if it is said aloud.

As runners, we benefit from being aware of and influencing our self-talk in ways that help us to develop and utilise our focus, the way we perceive and judge our abilities and performances, as well as anything that could impair or obstruct a good running performance in a race, event or during preparation and training.

You'll be aware already from us looking at ways to update limiting beliefs, that such beliefs and thinking errors are often apparent within our internal dialogue. Therefore, our internal dialogue is a great way for us to access our beliefs, our cognitions and the way we think. Our internal dialogue can become a tool for taking control of our thoughts, beliefs and perceptions *(Zinsser et al., 2001)*.

There have been a number of studies that have explored how internal dialogue is used within the field of sporting performance. Highlen and Bennett *(1983)* found that successful divers tended to use more progressive self-instruction within their internal dialogue when competing than the divers who failed to qualify for competition. In a study conducted on successful Olympic athletes, Orlick and Partington *(1988)* found that the Olympians often used positive self-statements as part of a structured and developed training schedule leading up to competitions. In particular, when Olympic wrestlers were studied by Gould and colleagues *(1992)* it was found that use of the internal dialogue helped create positive expectation and focused attention effectively when required.

A number of studies have also shown that negative use of internal dialogue can potentially have a detrimental effect on sporting performance. For example, Van Raalte, Brewer, Rivera, & Petitpas *(1994)* conducted a study with junior tennis players and discovered that negative use of internal dialogue was associated with losing matches.

Some studies may initially seem slightly less relevant to runners, but I think they are useful to build the case for the considered use of internal dialogue, and hopefully motivate you to want to learn the best ways to use it. There are, for example, studies that have suggested positive self-statements used by golfers or bowlers may be more effective in enhancing performance than negative ones *(O'Connor & Kirschenbaum, 1986; Kirschenbaum, Ordman, Tomarken & Holtz-bauer, 1982; Kirschenbaum, Owens & O'Connor, 1998)*.

Perhaps more relevant to runners then, are studies exploring simple closed-skill tasks. Closed tasks are fairly standardised skills in a relatively constant environment. That could well sum up some runner's skill of running. Research has indicated that with such activity, positive use of internal dialogue was related to enhanced performance *(Dagrou, Gauvin & Halliwell, 1992; Schill, Monroe, Evans & Ramanaiah, 1978; Van Raalte et al, 1995)*.

Also encouraging for those requiring motivation to train and stick to schedules are studies by Buffone, Sachs & Dowd *(1984)* and Gauvin *(1990)* showing how effective use of internal dialogue can help individuals maintain exercise behaviour.

Importantly for us here then, is the overview indicated by these studies and others that support the idea that positive use of internal dialogue can be associated with enhanced performance. Also, that negative internal dialogue has the potential to impair sporting performance.

In the coming pages I want to show you a wide array of ways that runners can use their internal dialogue effectively to enhance running performance, though there are a good number of methods for effectively using internal dialogue here on the blog already if you explore well.

Overview Of Uses For A Runner's Internal Dialogue:

The ways runners can use internal dialogue are varied. Upcoming within this book I shall be showing you, in more detail, how to use your internal dialogue in a wide variety of ways, however, here is an initial overview of the ways you can start utilising your own control over your internal dialogue to advance your running performance before we get more detailed and specific.

Internal Dialogue Awareness:

As we have done before in this book with our mindfulness and thought spotting exercises, we need to have an awareness of our internal dialogue in order to make any decision about whether it needs updating or changing *(Meichenbaum, 1977)*. So using your internal dialogue to tell yourself what you have noticed is a good way to help you be more aware.

I realise that could sound confusing — *using internal dialogue to be more aware of internal dialogue.* However, if you think of it also as using your conscious, purposeful internal dialogue to notice automatic thoughts that seem to happen all by themselves, then that might help.

As well as those kinds of exercises, keeping a simple log of thoughts and putting a tick in a column of 'negative' and 'positive' thoughts will show which dominates, and I'll be showing how to use thought forms later on when we discuss thought stopping.

Correcting Habits and Technique:

Runners can use internal dialogue when trying to correct their running technique, form or habits picked up throughout life. For those fortunate enough to be coached or advised on technique, or just those that are self-correcting their running posture, progressive use of internal dialogue can help to purposefully "override" old automatic habits if they occur.

I recall attending a *chi running* workshop a number of years ago and my stance in those days was a muscular, powerful one whereby I lifted my quads up from the thigh to run. At the workshop I was encouraged to raise my lower leg towards my backside by squeezing from the hamstrings. It was so much more efficient and effective, yet I would keep drifting back to the old way of running. My use of my internal dialogue started with actual instructions telling myself to lift the leg differently and moved to a single word advising me to "lift"; I knew what it meant through repetition.

It is important that you focus on what you want to change about your technique, and do not talk yourself away from the wrong move. For example you really won't benefit from telling yourself, *"Don't pull up with the thigh."*

Once you build a new habitual style or technique, you can stop with such use of internal dialogue.

As an aside here, I am not a technical running coach with qualifications in biomechanics and orthotics and the likes that are required for helping individuals with technique. As far as I can see also, the evidence base with regards to the *Chi Running (Dreyer, 2008)* I have mentioned here is not substantive or impressive. I found personal gain to be had with this process during my own exploration throughout the years, but I am not promoting its use universally. It was just my way of illustrating this point.

Focus, Attention and Arousal With Internal Dialogue:

We'll be examining ways of getting the correct levels of arousal and focus in later chapters. For now, know that runners can effectively use internal dialogue to appropriately and beneficially focus attention during training or races.

This can be done with mental imagery or by using words inside the mind that stimulate and hold focus. Likewise, both imagery and trigger words can be used to boost arousal and stimulate energy levels as well as relax the body and calm the mind when needed.

Confident Internal Dialogue:

As I mentioned previously, a runner's internal dialogue can directly affect belief and confidence in a detrimental or progressive way.

If the internal dialogue is dominated or heavily punctuated with negative expectations and too much doubt, this will adversely influence the confidence of the runner.

Runners can all be prone to outside influence, but all are responsible and in control of their own internal dialogue. There are rare occasions when negative internal dialogue can motivate, but it is incredibly rare for dominant negativity to have any beneficial use.

It is wise for internal dialogue to be accurate and grounded in realism. Offering up an honest critique to ourselves of our performance can be useful. In fact, using internal dialogue directly after a training run or an event or race to reflect upon the performance is seen as beneficial and is encouraged.

However, simply blinding ourselves with unrealistic praise and shrouding ourselves in sickly sweet positivity could create illusions that impair performance. For example, a study by Kirschenbaum, O'Connor, and Owens *(1999)* showed that golfers who were unrealistically optimistic with inaccurate positivity about their skill level, tended to make poor decisions and shot selection.

Updating Internal Dialogue:

With the awareness of our thoughts in place and developing an ongoing attitude and internal environment of awareness, the runner's internal dialogue can then be adapted, changed and updated if necessary. We have a wide number of ways of doing that, most of which we'll focus on in more depth in later chapters.

Thought Stopping:

Stopping certain thoughts in their tracks can help limit and prevent unwanted internal dialogue *(Meyers & Schleser, 1980)*. Thought stopping shows the runner how to interrupt and stop unwanted thoughts as they happen, or prior to them happening. Sometimes this might involve using the word "stop" or imagining a stop sign flashing in the imagination or it could involve a number of ways of getting the internal dialogue to be quiet or turned down.

With frequent and persistent use, the unwanted thoughts tend to lessen.

One very practical way to do this and incorporate some of our previous themes, is to start using a thought form.

There are many, many types of thought forms from within and outside of the field of cognitive behavioural therapy that I use within my therapeutic work to help clients update their cognitions and internal dialogue. Here with regards to our running, a very simple form can be used to heighten awareness of our internal dialogue and also help restructure internal dialogue.

You simply divide a page into 3 columns. You keep the form with you throughout your days, and keep vigilant and aware of your thoughts. If and when a problematic thought is said within your internal dialogue, you write it down unabridged and unedited in the first column. You get to see it exactly as it is and the thought becomes exposed and vulnerable. It is also moved out of your head by doing this, which ceases the way the brain makes it worse and amplifies it by letting it rattle around in your head.

In the second column, you then write down how you think that thought can detrimentally affect you and your running performance. You are refuting the thought here and applying some rationale and intelligent reasoning, showing yourself it is of little value to continue with such thoughts.

Then in the third column you write up a replacement, progressive, beneficial thought that you say to yourself with meaning, purpose and volition. You then repeat it inside of your mind a few times for it to start restructuring your thoughts.

For example, a runner may catch himself thinking *"I can't be bothered to run today."* The runner writes that down exactly as it was said, in the first column. Then in the second column, he writes that, *"By thinking this, I am talking myself out of training which could negatively affect the goal I want to achieve of running that half marathon in June."* Then, having given it some thought, he writes in the third column, *"I really want to get out and enjoy a run today, I know how good I'll feel afterwards."* He then repeats that with a sense of conviction and belief a few times to really get it registered.

The negative thought in the internal dialogue has been

1. Spotted.

2. Disputed.

3. Restructured.

Some forms will encourage you to measure your level of belief and assess the ownership you have of your thoughts and you may wish to explore and investigate other more comprehensive thought forms to monitor your internal dialogue should you wish. However, this method here is going to be useful, effective and simple.

Turning Negative Internal Dialogue Into Positive:

With this type of approach, we aim to allow positive thoughts to dominate and prevail in our internal dialogue. However, we don't really just want one set of thoughts to be shouting over another set of thoughts.

Increasing the use of positive internal dialogue may well help runners reduce the negative or limiting internal dialogue.

A favourite process of mine that I use in my therapy rooms very often has it roots in cognitive behavioural therapy and is referred to in the field of hypnotherapy as the **'cognitive mood induction'**. The process encourages you to accept the negative thoughts if they happen, not resist them or fight them and let them simply lead into more positive and progressive thoughts. This process is explained in depth later in this book.

Understanding Negative Impact of Negative Internal Dialogue:

Whilst I love the previously mentioned process, sometimes just changing negative internal dialogue into positive may be rendered impotent if we do not believe in the positive statements and in fact still attach belief to the negative internal dialogue *(Bell, 1983)*.

We need more than to simply be nice and civil to ourselves.

As you saw within the thought form, we learned to understand the negative impact of the problematic thought. This reasoning and understanding of the unwanted thought helps the runner to let go of and cease having belief in the unwanted thought and serves to counter the unwanted thought.

Bell *(1983)* recommends that when athletes believe in negative internal dialogue, they benefit more by building a case against that belief or negative thought and giving themselves proof of it being non-useful. This advances the change.

We have the belief-updating process already at our disposal from an earlier chapter. We also now have the understanding of doing that with or without a thought form; there should be no excuse for not applying some rationale against negative thoughts and really aiding your internal dialogue.

This can be advanced with the use of Socratic questioning techniques, namely those of the empiricist ilk:

"What evidence do I have for that?"

"Is there proof of this being true?"

Prior to a race, a nervous runner going for a personal best time might think: *"My breathing is going too fast. I'm tiring myself out before I even begin. I'm not going to be able to run at my best."*

Another example might be a club runner thinking, *"I can't keep up with the others on the group runs, therefore I am going to come last in the upcoming 10k race."*

The runner can look for evidence for this negative internal dialogue:

"OK, my breathing may be faster than when I get out of bed in the mornings, but that's natural, and happens to most runners prior to a race, especially when they place extra demands on themselves of a personal best. It shows me that this is important and exciting to me. I have run personal best times before, and I can do it now."

This is better than simply saying, *"I'm not nervous really,"* for example. Especially when they are actually nervous. Our club runner could think:

"These are good, dedicated club runners in the advanced group. I have not finished last in a race before and enjoy

the challenge of finishing further up the field. It inspires me to perform as best as I can."

The runner benefits from intelligent reasoning as well as offering up a new thought.

Altering The Framework Of The Internal Dialogue:

Those in NLP (neuro linguistic programming) refer to this as reframing. Some runners can be a bit hard on themselves and others can be very limiting in the way they perceive themselves and their ability.

Gauron *(1984)* recommended the technique of reframing for changing an athlete's frame of reference, or view, of the world. Often, athletes can change negative self-statements to positive by changing their perspective.

If we go back to our previously mentioned club runner, concerned about coming last in a race and perhaps thinking, *"It's going to be embarrassing to come last,"* they can reframe this thought and turn it into a progressive opportunity to measure their progress by instead thinking, *"I'm going to see how all this training has affected my running ability compared to my previous race."*

You saw how we did the same with the previous fast breathing runner, who reframed to be aware of himself as excited with this important race, not just nervous in a negative fashion.

Further research support for the positive effects of reframing comes from a study that compared the mental preparation of teams who met or exceeded their goals in the 1996 Olympic Games with that of teams that failed to meet their expectations

(*Gould, Guinan, Greenleaf, Medbery, & Pederson, 1999*). Gould and colleagues found that members of the more successful teams reported that they were able to reframe negative events in a positive light

Likewise, using reframing to keep perspective is used by lots of professional sports people, though I tend to find it disappointing when footballers who have scored a hat-trick in a match say, *"Well, the three points was most important and we have to now focus on next week's important game against United,"* when I want them to say, *"Yes! I scored a hat trick, I'm going to call my Mum and celebrate at the pub with my mates tonight!"* I do understand the importance of not getting carried away though.

Runners will want to use the crest of a wave gained in a good race and let it propel the ongoing training or goal setting for the next event instead of getting complacent.

There is an entire chapter coming up focusing on the use of mental imagery which is going to require the orchestration of the internal dialogue. I hope this has begun to get your juices flowing with regards to how to use your internal dialogue and cognitions. Now let's move on and get more specific with the applications of how.

Chapter Nine:
Specific Techniques For
Advancing Internal Dialogue

With an understanding of the implications of the evidence, and with an initial overview of how to start taking control of internal dialogue, in this chapter we are going to offer up ways to use your self-hypnosis skills in conjunction with some of the afore-mentioned principles to give you an array of specific step-by-step processes.

Ending Catastrophisation:

Catastrophising and/or awfulising is where we have an irrational thought process of thinking things are worse than they are. When faced with challenge, a catastrophiser may see the worst kinds of problematic outcomes. A runner may think one bad run means he will never get back to the same performance level he was at before, for example.

If you ever think the worst, catastrophise, create unnecessary drama, then this first process is for you. It is also going to be helpful if you just sometimes let your thoughts take control of how you feel when you train or compete.

On my blog a while back, I wrote and confessed to partaking in some catastrophisation. When you teach Socratic questioning techniques as I do each year on my therapy diploma training courses, you do tend to find yourself able to fairly calmly dissipate any tendency to *awfulise* or *catastrophise* by asking some of the classic questions aimed at doing just that (dissipating and overcoming catastrophisation):

"What makes the situation so terrible, awful or horrible?"

"Are you making a mountain out of a molehill?"

"Are you exaggerating the importance of this problem?"

"Do you have any reason to think you might be blowing things out of proportion here?"

The rational consideration of these questions and looking at the truth of the situation by answering them, does tend to help us to get a grip.

However, if the feelings themselves have taken hold, then feeling a particular way can create a cycle within us that makes us continue to think the worst!

"What if this terrible thing happens?"
(Start to imagine that thing happening and then start to feel bad… The bad feeling makes us feel worse.)

"Oh no, it is going to happen…"
(Imagined scenario starts to be perceived more vividly, turning the bad feelings up.)

"If this terrible thing happens, then these other terrible things will happen as a result and (more imagery, more unwanted feelings) *then something else will happen and my entire life will be ruined for ever and there'll be no way I can ever be well and happy again…"*

This exaggerated and non-specific example is one way of illustrating what I mean by catastrophisation.

For some runners, they imagine the worst thing happening, or think about what could go wrong immediately when competing or training, or think of the negative potential of minor injuries, lapses in training, lack of motivation, or any other temporary blip that can in fact be easily overcome.

This could be useful if you were on Royal Security duty, or if you were coming up with a strategic business plan. But if you have simply been invited out for a training run with friends, or are thinking about making a decision of which race to run in, then such thoughts of the worst thing happening — catastrophising — can prevent us from taking action and can also result in us feeling unhappy, uncomfortable and living in a darker, cynical or unsatisfactory place.

It can be useful to assess situations and make changes if we ever need to, but if we continue to catastrophise with no let up and heap pessimism on our thoughts on a continual basis, that habitual thought process can lead to it becoming second nature and in turn this could lead to worse things; including detrimentally affecting running performance and lowering motivation.

One of the other issues with constantly thinking the worst and awfulising, is that if we continue to think those kinds of thoughts, we may well even be increasing the chances of it happening. Such persistent thoughts can sometimes become self-fulfilling prophecies, can't they?

Our minds are incredibly amazing fantastical things. The depth of complexity and realism that can be created inside our heads is immense. Instead of keeping things real, offering up some intelligent reasoning and balanced thinking, sometimes we catastrophise and our mind draws us in to drama and our physiology responds accordingly.

As our imagination creates those awfulised scenarios in our minds, our body responds with all the feelings that go with that scenario, and those feelings get us on guard and we feel that way

181

more often. So we catastrophise more as we scare ourselves in a particular direction.

That cycle I referred to earlier happens with runners and athletes of all kinds.

This can be a very stressful way to live. It can mean we end up with a negative outlook on life. All roads lead to disaster…

In behavioural cognitive hypnotherapy, one of our stock processes to teach our clients is to dispute thoughts that lead us to catastrophise, and we ideally then learn how to restructure our thoughts in a number of ways.

Here though, I am simply going to show you how to dispute the thoughts effectively with self-hypnosis, and other upcoming techniques are going to help with developing some thinking skills to enhance what we do and develop cognitive restructuring.

With this process, you are simply going to run through typical situations in your life, training and racing, where you have had negative thoughts leading to thinking the worse, and you are going to interrupt the thought process mid-flow with an alarming method of disputation.

So before starting with the process, get a good idea of the typical situations where you might have negative thoughts that lead to you catastrophising or expecting a negative outcome. Then also it is important for you to accept the idea that negative thoughts are not useful and can cause problems and that you intend and expect them to stop as a result of this session — frame things in a progressive and positive way, develop expectation and then get stuck in the step-by-step process that follows:

Step One:

Induce hypnosis using any of the processes taught previously. Once you have induced hypnosis, move on to Step Two.

Step Two:

As vividly as you can, imagine yourself in the kind of situation where you would typically experience negative thoughts. This might be prior to training, the day before a race, or during your working day when weighing up whether to attend the running club that evening.

Really imagine being there. See the sights of the place, the colours, the shades of light and details. Hear the sounds of the place, notice the distinctions of the sounds around you and just engage in this place.

Allow being in this place to take you deeper inside your mind and when you are really engaged and tuned in to this place, move on to the next step.

Step Three:

Start to take the actions you usually take in that situation and then pay close attention to your thoughts and how you think in that situation.

Talk to yourself and describe to yourself what your thoughts are in that situation. Start to translate your feelings into words and describe to yourself the kind of mental imagery that happens in your mind in this scenario.

Really explain to yourself all the thoughts, ideas, imagery and feelings that you have in this typical situation. Run through the situation in its entirety.

When you have done that in detail, then move on to the next step.

Step Four:

Here comes the fun.

Run through the previous step again in your mind, but this time as soon as the unwanted, negative thought and accompanying feelings starts to happen in the slightest, you imagine wild, loud sirens going off in your head and there right in front of your eyes pops up a bright and large **STOP** sign flashing noisily before you.

As soon as the old negative train of thought starts, you create the most alarming noise in your mind, the most vivid, bright **STOP** sign that fills your entire imagination — fills it entirely. It dominates the mind.

Practice this step over and over, making things more vivid, more real and encourage yourself to make if more forceful each time you practice doing this. Take responsibility here too and be as creative as you like in making the stop imagery as alerting as possible to really interrupt the negative thought before it gets started.

When you feel that you have really got a hang of stopping the old thought as it starts, then move on to the next step.

Step Five:

Following on from that rather frenetic step... Take a couple of minutes out now and engage in some progressive relaxation. Just imagine relaxation spreading through your body; you can do this with colour, you can simply imagine muscles relaxing, you can tell them to soften, you can imagine tensing muscles and letting them relax thereafter, you can just spread a relaxing sensation through your body using your intention and imagination. Spend some time to get your body really deeply and beautifully relaxed.

When you are feeling really relaxed, move on to the next step.

Step Six:

Think of a progressive, positive, encouraging statement that you can say to yourself in that same situation in the future.

Word it in the present tense, make it be something you want, not something you don't want and let it be supportive and using the words that appeal to you, get them set up in your mind.

Now run through the same situation that we began with, while you are wonderfully relaxed, run through that same scenario and repeat this new internal dialogue statement to yourself. Say it with meaning and say it in a way that is undeniably convincing to you, say it in a way that makes you feel that you believe it to be true.

Run through the scenario 3–5 times while relaxed, repeating your new positive thought, your positive statement to yourself in your mind. When you have repeated it all those times, move on to the next step.

Step Seven:

Tell yourself that you plan to bring the benefits of this session with you into real-life situations from now on. Tell yourself that you are going to **STOP** negative thoughts, relax and replace them with positive statements in your mind if they ever occur again in the future.

This is going to stop catastrophisation, for sure.

Bring yourself up and out of hypnosis by counting from 1 to 5, take a deep energising breath, wiggle your fingers and toes and open your eyes.

Practice this process daily for a week in your mind using self-hypnosis. Then go and place yourself in those situations and start to practice using this skill and enjoy taking control and stopping awfulising in its tracks.

Cognitions to lift mood: Modifying your internal dialogue:

Now that we have looked at a method of disputing unwanted thoughts, let's look at a way to start with our progressive cognitive restructuring and updating our thoughts.

Maybe we expect more today… It seems that increasingly more people are currently lacking satisfaction as far as their moods are concerned. Therapists of varying kinds that I encounter are reporting that more people are coming to see them and reporting being depressed or having a withering level of positivity. If a runner lacks a progressive mindset, it may be difficult to train, or build the inclination to get working towards a running goal of some kind.

Now for some, a dip in mood could well be some sort of biological issue in the brain, the chemical make-up of the individual or hormones of the body, so I always make sure people are consulting with their GP as well. That said, the health benefits of running are numerous once it becomes a regular, integral part of life and we benefit physically and psychologically from it.

Mastering your cognitions and internal dialogue can vastly alter mood and perspective and get the runner in a driven frame of mind. If a runner is already driven, then knowing how to take control of cognitions and internal dialogue is going to help advance and enhance performance, which makes this a very important technique.

As a reminder, when I refer to cognitions, I am talking about anything inside of your head; such as ideas, thoughts, beliefs, etc. that can be verbalised. Those are your cognitions. As discussed in the previous chapter about internal dialogue, this process shows you how to change negative thoughts into positive ones and start getting the inner workings of the runners mind filled with progressive, performance enhancing belief and instruction.

Before you actually run through this process, work out, create, design and write down a statement (a positive cognition) that you think will be undeniably convincing to you to say to yourself to enhance your internal dialogue in certain situations and circum-stances of your running life. You'll need it later in this exercise, and ensure it is in the present tense i.e. it is happening now. With that written down in your own words, run through these set of steps:

Step One:

First of all, get yourself into a comfortable position where you'll be undisturbed for the period of this exercise. Then start to think about typical situations where you used to either lack positivity, doubt your running ability, feel unmotivated, fear the worst or just criticise yourself.

Ideally, pick a single situation in relation to your running, where you have negative cognitions that accompany the doubt or worry.

Step Two:

With that in mind, with your eyes now closed, picture yourself in that typical situation that you thought of in Step One. Really immerse yourself in it. See what you see, hear what you hear, tune in to the place you are in. As much as is possible, imagine it as if it's happening right now.

As unusual as this may initially seem, repeat the old, negative cognition to yourself like you really mean it. It is likely that this will bring on some of the old unwanted low mood sensation (doubt, lack of confidence, lack of motivation, etc.), and it is OK to tap into that as much as is useful for this technique.

Then just carry on repeating those negative thoughts to yourself in your imagination. When you've noticed the negative feeling increasing within you, start to examine your current experience. Tell yourself how that feels, just explain it to yourself in your own head.

Ideally, you will be noticing, that when you believe what goes on in your head, it can make you feel bad and can dip your mood to uncomfortable and unhealthy levels. When you have got a real sense of this, move on to the next step.

Step Three:

The plan from here is to now undermine that old, unwanted thought process and accompanying unpleasant feeling by gradually removing it from your mind. That is the reason we developed the positive suggestion before we started this. You wrote that down immediately prior to Step One, remember?

Keeping your eyes comfortably closed, continue to imagine that you are immersed in that typical situation. Right now though, start to say the new, positive cognition to yourself inside your mind. Don't just repeat it in a drab fashion. Really mean it. Put some oomph into it! Say it in your mind in a way that you find to be beautifully irresistible, undeniably convincing, that this is who and how you choose to be now!

Keep repeating that to yourself in your imagination. Over and over, with some conviction.

When you say it with real meaning and conviction, you should start to notice that you start to feel different. Tell yourself how it feels different. Tell yourself how it feels better. Start to increase the good feelings you notice and continue to repeat the new positive thought process with meaning.

Just as before, you should also now be learning and noticing that when you think these kinds of thoughts and allow these cognitions to dominate your mind, you feel better. Additionally, when you say it to yourself in a way that makes you believe it, you feel even better.

This can now be reinforced and built upon. You repeat this process over and over until it becomes a habit. That is, it becomes your instant reaction in real-life when you enter those situations — you repeat that cognition and get it lodged firmly inside of your mind.

Step Four:

At this stage, hypnotise yourself using any of the methods you have learned up until now.

The repetition ensures the learning is getting better lodged into your mind and forming a habit that'll influence your feelings more in the future.

As you did earlier, picture yourself in that typical situation that you thought of in Step One. Really immerse yourself in it. See what you see, hear what you hear, tune in to the place you are in. As much as is possible, imagine it as if it's happening right now.

Repeat the old, negative cognition to yourself like you really mean it. It is likely that this will bring on some of the old unwanted low mood sensation, and do allow yourself to really evoke those old accompanying unwanted feelings.

Then just carry on repeating those negative thoughts to yourself in your imagination. When you've noticed the negative feeling increasing within you, start to examine your current experience. Tell yourself how that feels, just explain it to yourself in your own head.

Now you're going to banish those old, negative thoughts and feelings and replace them with the new, positive ones.

As you did previously, start to say the new, positive cognition to yourself inside your mind. Don't just repeat it in a fashion that makes it seem like a chore… Really mean it. Put some welly into it! Say it in your mind in a way that absolutely convinces you, that you believe100% at an emotional level.

Keep repeating that to yourself in your imagination. Over and over, with real conviction.

When you say it with real meaning and conviction, you should start to notice that you start to feel different. Tell yourself how it feels different. Tell yourself how it feels better. Start to increase the good feelings you notice and continue to repeat the new positive thought process with meaning.

Just as before, you should also now be learning and noticing that when you think these kinds of thoughts and allow these cognitions to dominate your mind, you feel better. Additionally, when you say it to yourself in a way that makes you believe it, you feel even better.

As much as is possible, repeat it until you believe in it. Really believe in it.

Repeat this step of the process as many times as you can and until you feel that the positive cognition and new thought process is firmly lodged in your mind. If you are unsure, then do it some more to be sure. Repetition is key here.

Step Five:

Once you have run through that enough times and you feel that you have truly learned the new cognitions and got them installed in your mind, tell yourself that this is going to advance and enhance your running performance, your motivation and your mood in a wide variety of situations and that the good feelings begin to generalise into many other areas of your life.

You may consider running through the process for a number of other typical situations from your running life too. The key learning here is being aware of how to turn that negative thought process automatically into positive thoughts and feelings; which gets easier the more you do it.

Step Six:

Exit hypnosis by counting from 1 through to 5.

Go and take some action that is proof to you that you made this change. Challenge yourself to go and test this and use it. Having practiced this process in hypnosis a number of times, you'll start to find that the way you use your internal dialogue starts to become more automatically positive, supportive and progressive, which is going to advance your running performance and enjoyment.

Tame Your Inner Critic:

Sometimes runners can be their own worst enemy.

In 2012, while I was speaking at a hypnosis conference, I watched the great man Gary Turner (who wrote the foreword to this book) present a lecture. He was quoting a technique he enjoyed using for getting the unwanted internal dialogue in our heads to be quiet. It involved wrapping duct tape around the mouth of the voice of the unwanted internal dialogue.

I rather liked it, and what with Gary being a 13-time world champion at various fighting disciplines, I thought it beautifully apt.

There are so many ways to quiet internal dialogue or to get the internal chatter to shush! Some I have written about here previously. Next up in this chapter, is one simple way for not just disputing thoughts and not just stopping them, but to tame your thoughts if they are being critical and turn them into something effective, useful and beneficial to you. Really building upon the progress and understanding developed in the previous two techniques.

Before we start with this process, think of someone who always wants the best for you, perhaps someone who loves you and even someone who encourages you and supports you unconditionally. If you are really struggling to come up with anyone, then create and imagine what it would be like. Ideally, someone who supports your running or is motivating to you when you run.

Also have a think about a typical situation where you tend to be critical of yourself, or where your internal dialogue tends to talk you out of going running, or doubts your ability, where you might benefit from some more progressive thoughts, or where negative thoughts affect you detrimentally in some way.

Then let's begin. Get yourself into a comfortable position, where you'll be undisturbed for the period of doing this exercise, and follow these simple steps.

Step One:

Induce hypnosis using any of the previously taught methods.

Step Two:

Scan back through your day, or the past week and think of your activities and actions. Think about your runs, your training schedule, your choices made and the way you have reflected upon your running ability. As you think, imagine drifting deeper inside your mind as you consider your recent life.

As you scan through your recent life, notice anything that might be considered an issue or a problem that you are currently working on, or a challenge you are facing, ideally a circumstance where your internal dialogue hindered you or affected you negatively or held you back or was unduly critical. Or you can simply think about some aspect of your running that would benefit from you having more positive thoughts that enhance your performance.

Just start to gather up the details of what happened on that occasion. Recall where you were, who you were with and recall the sounds, notice the sights of the place and be aware of how that makes you feel and just notice enough of those feelings as is useful for this exercise.

As you really imagine that you are there in that place, also start to recognise what was happening inside of your head. That is, what were you saying to yourself, what ideas went through your mind, what was your internal dialogue saying?

Notice any negative elements. Notice any opportunities for better internal dialogue. Notice any unwanted internal dialogue, become aware of the qualities of how it was said as well as the words that were spoken inside your mind and, with a good sense of that, move on to the next step.

Step Three:

As you notice the old unwanted criticising voice, start to build that voice a body or a character of some kind. Maybe it is an animal or a beast or famous person, or even an object. Just start to create in your mind a physical presence of some kind that you think and believe best suits your internal dialogue.

Fashion the voice with a body, a face of some kind and start to create a very particular physical presence and representation inside your head that represents your internal dialogue. You choose, you imagine, you create. Make it detailed and spend all the time necessary to get this in your mind.

As that becomes fashioned and created, also now get a sense of what the underlying meaning or hidden benefit of this inner critic might be, start to frame it in a way that it could be seen as being progressive or positive in some way.

If you feel that the words or sentiments of the voice, the critical voice, were just harmful and had no positive intention at all, then that is fine, there does not have to be… When you have done that, then move on to the next step.

Step Four:

This is the fun part of the process. Start to morph the critic into the person who you thought of prior to Step One: the encouraging and supportive person (or the imaginary person).

Imagine the change happening in the features, in the details of how they look and the colours updating. Notice the sound of the voice beginning to change, the tonality and pace of what is being said. Notice how it makes you feel to see this person.

Really create the change; I love this part because of my penchant for sci-fi and fantasy films where this happens a great deal! Once you have got the old critic transformed into the new person, then move on to the next step.

Step Five:

If there was some kind of positive intention behind the critic's previous dialogue, then now is the time to refer to it and let the new voice start to encourage you and support you with the same positive intention. If there was no positive intention that you could decipher, then let the new person start to encourage and support you — let it say the words to you that are undeniably convincing that they mean well, that you believe unconditionally and let them be words that make sure you take action, or that change how you respond to that situation, or that empower you, or that really put a smile on your face.

You'll know what is most useful for you in this situation, so let that start to happen. Let that be said.

Start to notice the words of encouragement are dominating your mind, filling your mind with progressive sentiments in that situation and notice the words beginning to appear in written form, in bright colours and with more pronounced sounds.

As you focus on the progressive words repeating themselves in your mind, let them affect your feelings. Notice the good feelings growing and developing and even imagine them spreading through your body in some way.

Take all the time you need to spread relaxing and enjoyable good feelings throughout your body while the encouraging, positive dialogue persists in your mind, then move on to the next step.

Step Six:

Now imagine a time in the future when you'll be in a similar situation. Really be there in that place and in that scenario. Then start to let the positive, progressive internal dialogue play inside your mind. Mentally rehearse the new voice dominating your mind in that situation.

Notice how this changes things for you. Notice how you behave as a result of the internal dialogue, how you take action, how you feel good — notice what is different.

Tell yourself that this is how you communicate with yourself in the future and that each time you practice this process you become more naturally inclined to let go of the old unwanted critic and enjoy the new, progressive encouraging internal dialogue.

With that completed, move on to the final step.

Step Seven:

Exit hypnosis by counting from 1 through to 5.

Remind yourself of the new, progressive internal dialogue and think about going and putting yourself in that situation where you can become encouraged by it. Enjoy it, practice it with self-hypnosis a few times and then let that voice inspire you, motivate you, drive you and support you when you are out running, thinking of training and reflecting upon your own running ability.

The processes in this chapter can help you to really utilise your internal dialogue, make it as progressive as possible and start propelling your running performance in the direction you wish. Use the principles inherent within them and in the previous chapter and ensure that your progressive use of your internal dialogue now underpins all the techniques, strategies and processes in coming chapters.

Chapter Ten:
The Relaxed Runner

*"But you can't muscle through a five-hour run that way;
you have to relax into it like easing your body into a hot
bath, until it no longer resists the shock and begins to
enjoy it."*

Christopher McDougall

We are going to start looking at the benefits of being able to
relax when it comes to running. Relaxation is not just important
for your running form, but also for conserving and preserving
energy and enhancing performance and we are going to get on to
that in some depth.

It is possible in hypnosis to teach a runner to be in control of
his own ability to relax. I have worked with many runners who
just needed to be less tense when running to enhance their
speed, attain better times and increase the enjoyment of their
runs. We all benefit from having a good level of arousal to keep
us performing at our optimal levels and we are going to look at
focus, concentration and getting into 'the zone' in later chapters:
for now, let's make sure we know how to relax in a way that
enhances our running.

Introduction to hypnosis and relaxation:

Many people in the field of professional hypnosis and
hypnotherapy get worried, concerned, and sometimes even
frustrated, by the seeming similarity between hypnosis and
relaxation. I say 'frustrated' because some people assert that

hypnosis and relaxation are totally different and how dare anyone suggest they are similar.

There are however a very large number of studies out there, *(Edmonston, 1981 & 1991)* that state that relaxed clients in the therapeutic environment are just as responsive to suggestions as clients who are hypnotised and given suggestions. Like I said, there are many studies that bear out this notion and can be found online or in many good academic books on the subject.

With this in mind, it is understandable then why many professional therapists are worried that they may have been hypnotising their clients without the client or therapist knowing about it, and of course, the flip side, whereby some hypnotherapists have hypnotised their client and neither are sure if it was actually hypnosis that the client experienced, or if they were just deeply relaxed.

In therapy terms, of course hypnosis and relaxation can sometimes be similar, but they are most certainly not the same.

Relaxation can be used to induce hypnosis as well as deepen hypnosis, as I have previously explained, but people can have hypnosis induced and deepened in ways that lead them to remain alert, focused and absorbed and not be relaxed at all.

In fact, in the book *Theories of Hypnosis: Current models and perspectives (Banyai 1991)* Banyai writes about and builds upon his earlier work with Ernest Hilgard, whereby he showed that by having a client exercise vigorously for a period of time prior to a hypnosis session, the client could still be hypnotised, but would not be at all relaxed. In fact, they would be alert and focused and have a heart rate and pulse that was very active and alive. A client undergoing relaxation training in any form of psychotherapy would not gain the benefits of the relaxation in the same way, making the two quite different.

As often seems to be the case, many people wrongly suppose that hypnosis is simply relaxing and many people perpetuate the myth and it comes to be thought of as having relaxation inherent within it. This is not the case, hypnosis and relaxation are not the same and there is much evidence to support that: hypnosis is not merely relaxation. Hypnosis does not have to be accompanied by relaxation, it can be accompanied by alertness and being energised.

The type of advanced relaxation skill we are aiming to use as a runner is something you are going to benefit from greatly.

To begin with, let me introduce **Benson's Relaxation Response**.

It is not just us hypnotherapists and other kinds of complementary therapists who believe in mind-body medicine.

Though we talk about "mind" and "body" as if they operate independently of each other, as I wrote at the very beginning of this book — they do not. They cannot operate so. The fact that you have invested in a book of this nature clearly shows you have some understanding of this.

Today we trace many physical illnesses to emotional stress: ulcers, ulcerated colitis, migraine headaches, arthritis, asthma, allergies and even cancer. In therapy we see people who come in with stomach problems, high blood pressure, headaches and skin lesions and leave without such physiological problems once they experience healing in their mind and with their emotions.

This being a running book, I am not going to spend too much time exploring the mind-body connection with you, though the fact that mind and body are part of the same holistic thing is presupposed throughout this book. Research has been conducted on school children to show that when they were happy and playing, enjoying themselves, the white blood cell count and leucocytes in their bloodstream were higher than when they were anxious prior to an examination. Much research has been conducted on people who meditate regularly, and during deep meditation, to show that the state of mind affects the physiology drastically.

This is relevant to us here when looking at relaxing and focusing our minds as athletes and runners. Due to this fundamental holistic nature of the body and mind, it also becomes impossible for two drastically opposing emotions to be experienced physically at the same time.

Therefore, it is impossible to have over-riding anxiety when one is very deeply physically relaxed.

The subsequent relaxation process we are going to be working on, here in this chapter, aims to produce a relaxed body that allows you to mentally associate a relaxed physiology induced through hypnosis with a relaxed healthy mindset when running and training.

In the 70s, 80s and 90s, a physician named Herbert Benson constructed a process that worked by calming, slowing and relaxing the mind in order to subsequently relax the body.

Benson's work is aimed at health development, rather than with enhancing athletic performance, but his processes have been adopted by athletes and runners, in particular, understand the benefits of this type of process. Much of what we are focusing on here is mental training and the ability to use our mind and our own resources to care for ourselves.

Being able to focus and relax properly is vital to being able to be in control of oneself and care for oneself in such a way that it enhances our sporting performance.

The initial process that I am instructing you about here is heavily influenced by the field of **Transcendental Meditation (TM)** and was adopted from this work by Benson. TM was incredibly popular in the US and then here in the UK in the 1960s and 1970s, with millions reportedly actively learning and applying it.

Benson's Relaxation Response was borne out of the field of transcendental meditation and is a very similar, slightly simplified version of it.

Today, the techniques can be found in many of Benson's books if you'd like to investigate further and there are some variations of it. Basically, there are seven steps that you follow to engage the relaxation response — which is an important precursor to what we are moving on to later in this chapter.

1. Firstly, you choose a word that you are going to focus upon; ideally one that is meaningful to you.
   (Many hypnotherapists use gentle words such as 'calm' or 'relax' or 'soften'. Ideally though, do use a word that resonates well with you that will keep you attentive and enhance focus and relaxation)

2. Secondly, in a place where you will be undisturbed for the next 20 minutes or so, get yourself into a comfortable position with a relaxed posture, ideally with your arms and legs uncrossed. Let yourself be symmetrical and balanced in posture if at all possible.

3. Next up, take a good deep breath and you exhale slowly, allow your eyes to close.

4. With your eyes closed, spend some time imagining your muscles relaxing and suggesting to yourself that the stillness of your body is relaxing your muscles. You might imagine colours spreading through them, sensations moving through them or even imagine the nerves within them becoming quiet. Work your way through your body and relax the muscles of your body.

5. With your muscles relaxed, now continue to breathe gently and naturally, and no longer interfering with your breath, just letting it happen all by itself, let your body breathe as you observe it. Then proceed to repeat the focus word that you chose in the first step on each subsequent breath that you exhale.

6. Again, just observe any thoughts that come in to your mind and do not resist them or concern yourself with them, let them pass and just watch them. Be a detached observer of what goes on while all the time returning with some focus to that word and keeping your mind and attention trained in on that word. You may well wander off from time to time; that's OK, just bring yourself back to that word, having realised what you've done.
Please do not think of this in terms of doing it well or not. There is no right or wrong way, just practice remaining focused on that word as best as you can.

7. Finally, you proceed with this for 15 to 20 minutes or so until you open your eyes and go about your day.

I recommend doing it in the mornings, early. Most people tend to report greater gain and benefits from doing this in the morning and using the benefits for more of the day.

As a result of running through this process, the Relaxation Response (RR) that Benson refers to has been established.

Benson claims that this RR makes the right brain more accessible to suggestions—something that is debated in hypnosis and hypnotherapy circles.

There have been a wide number of different sports taking on this process and applying it to their field. I have tweaked the process very slightly above to suit runners.

Enhanced Hypnotic Relaxation:

Although all kinds of coaches, trainers, psychologists have developed effective techniques for reaching a relaxed state, hypnosis can bring about this relaxation more rapidly and, many believe, more deeply, than without using it.

Being relaxed and knowing how to relax properly is going to help many of the other psychological processes within this book too. Physiologically, being healthily relaxed can help you be more flexible, less prone to injury and there are many other benefits very well documented in research literature.

Relaxing as a runner prior to an event or race is not always the appropriate way to get the best performance. Athletes need a certain degree of tension or energy level to perform well. The appropriate amount of tension is unique to each runner and is best employed throughout training and as a skill to dissipate excessive anxiety when required.

In the therapy field, we tend to identify three main benefits to relaxation skills and therapeutic interventions:

Firstly, generalised relaxation.

This is the simplest and most obvious benefit of relaxation therapy. When people practice relaxation once a day, for example, they usually feel more relaxed in general. There are many documented benefits to physical and mental health from spending time being relaxed.

Secondly, cue-controlled relaxation.

When people regularly practice relaxation skills, they quickly become able to do so at will, with the minimum of time and effort. This can even happen spontaneously on occasion. For example, a runner who has used regular meditation techniques regularly for a number of years often finds he can do so simply by choosing to do so.

With my therapy clients, we often create a trigger to practice accessing that relaxation which can be practiced in various aspects of that client's life. The client can then activate that trigger and learn to be relaxed in situations that may have been a challenge to them previously.

Thirdly, systematic desensitisation.

Borne out of the work of Joseph Wolpe, this process has been used since the 1950s in clinical practice to help people in a wide variety of ways. It is a process that uses relaxation to prepare the mind in advance to overcome adversity.

For some individuals, their ability to relax becomes compartmentalised. That is, they learn how to relax very deeply at the end of the yoga class they attend, for example, but that ability to relax deeply is associated with the yoga class and not usable in other aspects of life where it might be needed.

Systematic desensitisation, then, teaches the individual to relax deeply while mentally rehearsing a wide variety of situations and scenarios in life, in particular ones that made you tense before. As a result, you associate those situations with being relaxed and start to find yourself more relaxed in those actual real-life situations. I'd like to show you how to do that.

Hypnotic Desensitisation:

Some runners get anxious or tense when they think about running and when they actually run, many are not even aware of how much tension they are carrying around with them.

Any slight tension or anxiety you have experienced when running or thinking of running is most likely a learned response, an old habit. Just like any other habit, physical tension and emotional anxiety can be learned over time and become attached to specific trigger events or situations. Running long distances can be pretty stressful in and of itself, especially when your brain releases all that cortisol (the stress hormone) into your body when you run. Any responses that can be learned can also be unlearned. All habits can be broken.

Anxiety and relaxation are two mutually exclusive states; they cannot dominate the same body at the same time, the stronger one tends to progressively cancel the weaker one out. By training yourself to relax very deeply, and by mentally rehearsing your training runs and races at the same time in a systematic way, you can use the relaxation response to cancel out unnecessary stress or anxiety and replace it with feelings of healthy calm. All it takes is a little patience and focus to become a relaxed runner.

You'll begin by patiently rehearsing your relaxation skills while imagining being out on a run or racing. By doing so, you will find that the appropriate level of relaxing feelings remain with you outside in the real world when you are running, racing or thinking about going for a run. Remember to use progressive internal dialogue when you practice this process as that will advance the benefits you derive from it.

When my wife first took in our cat, Spooky, because he had been abandoned by his previous owners and left without food or shelter for a long time, he mistrusted humans. He actually feared people, which we suspect was due to his poor treatment. You see, even animals can learn to be anxious when they do not necessarily need to.

Our own experience, as well as much documented and researched evidence, shows that animals can also be trained to overcome their anxieties. Spooky learned to love the affection and attention of humans and came to love being around people in general.

The following process was first taught to me by Donald Robertson and is based upon what I learned from him. A more detailed understanding of this model can be discovered within his book, *Cognitive Behavioural Hypnotherapy (2012)*.

Prior to beginning, think of a training run, a race or an event that you are due to complete at some point in the future. On a scale of 0–100%, how anxious do you feel about it? With that running scenario at the back of your mind and that number in the front of your mind, proceed with the following process. Get in a place and position that will ensure you are undisturbed for a good period of time.

Step One:

Induce hypnosis using any of the previous methods.

There is no need to deepen the hypnosis as the very nature of this session deepens inherently with the use of relaxation. Once you have induced hypnosis, proceed to Step Two.

Step Two:

Start to imagine that you are tensing various muscle groups in turn. Don't actually tense them. Just imagine that you are tensing them. Of course, if you really imagine that you are clenching your fist tightly, e.g., you may find your hand muscles tense a little as a result. That's fine. Imagining the feelings of tension first makes it easier for you to relax the muscles more deeply than usual, and that's just what you're going to do now. After the tension, go ahead and actually relax each muscle group as deeply as you possibly can, if possible, beyond your usual levels of relaxation. Relax the muscles as you exhale.

Begin by imagining that every muscle in your body is becoming tense and rigid. Really keep that feeling of tension in mind for a few seconds. Imagine all the muscles are growing more rigid. Then very slowly, relax the entire body as much as possible.

Work your awareness through your legs, your arms and the remainder of your body — especially make sure you relax your shoulders deeply, your forehead and tiniest of facial muscles using this process, just imagining that you are tensing them, then relaxing them massively.

Imagine, for a few seconds, you are tensing each of the muscles, then very slowly, relax the muscles as much as you can. You might want to imagine relaxing colours spreading through the muscles, you may want to repeat the words 'relax', or 'soften' to yourself as each muscle eases further.

End up imagining your eyelids are being squeezed tightly shut and relax them, knowing that the entire body is really deeply relaxed. Keep your attention on what you are doing, not allowing yourself to wander from the process. Your relaxation needs to be mindful in order for this to be most beneficial.

Now imagine that even your breathing is becoming more and more relaxed. Relax your body so deeply that your breathing changes all by itself. When the body is relaxed it uses less energy, so the breath becomes more shallow and gentle. Let your breathing gently take you deeper into the relaxation and continue with this until you feel relaxed enough to take the next step in the process.

Please note: It is really important you take your time to do the previous step and are patient with the progressive relaxation. You'll derive much, much more benefit from doing it in a patient, thorough manner.

Step Three:

Now, before we progress to the main crux of this process, scan through your entire body. If you notice any last tiny traces of tension whatsoever, just imagine the feeling turning into a cloud of coloured mist or something similar that appeals to you. Maybe you can just imagine it all relaxing away, melting into nothingness.

So this is really letting go of any last remnants of anything unwanted and leaving you ready to crack on with the next step.

Step Four:

Now imagine the scene of your run, race or the build up to a run, whatever you thought about prior to starting with this session. While you think of it, just remain nicely and enjoyably relaxed. Think of relaxation, imagine relaxation, focus on letting go more deeply. As you relax you are neutralising any tension or discomfort that you used to associate with that running scenario, instead allowing those peaceful feelings spread into your life and into future running situations. Really get that lodged into your mind as you relax and think of that situation at the same time.

Do imagine that you are in that scene: see it through your own eyes, as if it is actually happening right now, make it seem real, all the time remaining wonderfully relaxed. Really believe you are there right now, facing that running situation, being in that place, hearing those sounds and continue to let go and relax deeply.

Then fade that scene completely for a few moments, continue to relax, calm your mind and smile to yourself inside. As we did right at the very beginning, just before Step One, on a scale of 0–100% what was your level of discomfort as you imagined that scene just now?

Tell yourself that number and when you know it, move on to the next step.

Step Five:

At this stage, deepen your relaxation. Maybe count your breaths from 10 down to one and say the word 'soften' again as you drift deeper. Maybe imagine walking down some stairs, or imagining all your muscles relaxing again.

So now, imagine the very same running scenario again and, as you do, concentrate and focus on remaining beautifully relaxed and at ease. Run through the scene in your mind, as you continue to relax, really imagine that you are in that scene right now, as if it is really happening while you continue to let go and relax completely.

Then give yourself a score of 0–100% to rate your discomfort again. Ideally repeat this process over and over until you reach zero. Even consider persisting with it after you have reached zero.

Step Six:

So up until now, you have been facing your runs, races and running scenarios in your mind and associating them with the wonderful relaxation. You can always remember how to do that, can't you?

The more you do this and practice it, the better you'll be at becoming a relaxed runner. You'll find that you begin to feel more relaxed and confident in a wider and wider variety of different races, training runs and in your overall attitude to running.

Step Seven:

When you are ready and calm, begin to get a sense of your body again, take a deep relaxing breath and just let it radiate through you. Let your mind be open to well-being, balance and harmony. Then go ahead and count yourself up and out of hypnosis from 1 through to 5.

Practice it and practice it and you'll be amazed at what a relaxed runner you are and how much you can enrich your running experience.

Chapter Eleven:
Mental Imagery For Runners

"Spend at least some of your training time, and other parts of your day, concentrating on what you are doing in training and visualizing your success."

Grete Waitz

I love the build up to a big city marathon. I love going to those expo events, especially the one for the London marathon.

I love being around fellow marathon runners. All those people that are driven enough to take up such a challenge. All those people who have trained in all weathers, often by themselves, sweated, struggled, found the time to commit to running 26.2 miles on the packed out streets of London or another big city together. I love being around those people who had the discipline, the drive, the courage, the self-motivation and the inspiration to do this — and they all smile with their fellow runners, get excited and start to get social as the big day approaches. It makes me feel good just being around these people, chatting to them, sharing jokes and fun. I could go on and on and suspect I may be already… these events inspire my imagination and give me so much vivid content for my mental imagery techniques.

The London marathon expo event and the race itself always makes my mind drift back to my role as personal development coach in the 2006 BBC1 TV series *'Run for Glory'* a few years back now. I had to devise mental imagery techniques that drew on facets of my work and that were going to help the participants be equipped to overcome psychological barriers throughout the TV series as they journeyed towards their marathon goal.

The participants of the TV series all had very particular and personal reasons for running the London marathon and were running to raise awareness of their good cause. One was a man who was/is HIV positive, two ladies had overcome cancer, one had a son with terminal illness. Despite none of them being athletes, they all successfully completed the marathon with the training guidance of Olympians Steve Cramm and Sally Gunnell, along with a set of psychological techniques from myself.

A paper entitled *See the Ball, Hit the Ball: Apparent Ball Size Is Correlated With Batting Average* published by psychologists at the University of Virginia in the Psychological Science Journal (2005) stated that athletes often say that when they are playing well, be it shooting hoops, hitting baseballs, catching passes — the ball appears bigger. Likewise, they say that when they are in a slump the ball appears smaller. When Mickey Mantle hit a 565-foot home run he said, *"I just saw the ball as big as a grapefruit."* But Joe "Ducky" Medwick of the St. Louis Cardinals said during a slump that he was "swinging at aspirins."

This study found a correlation between batting averages of softball players and how big, or small, they perceived the ball to be. The study documents that when the players were hitting well they clearly perceived the ball to be bigger. And when they were hitting less well, they perceived the ball to be smaller.

There are other similar pieces of research that demonstrate how perception and the images we replay in our minds directly affect our performance.

Everyone these days seems to know that Tiger Woods imagines his shot before he plays it. Boxers often imagine winning and knocking out their opponent. Many Olympic athletes imagine the ideal shot, goal or win before they complete it.

Early on in 2012 I imagined crossing the line at my fifth consecutive marathon, and when it happened, it was almost identical to how I had imagined it...

What do we actually mean when we talk about mental imagery then? Murphy (1994) states that imagery is a process by which sensory experiences are stored in memory and then are recalled and performed when there is no actual external stimulus.

Imagery is used by athletes of varying kinds for a range of applications and, although it tends to get assumed that we'll all benefit from using it, not everyone benefits from using mental imagery techniques. The reason being that not everyone using mental imagery techniques uses them well or with enough persistence to gain the benefit. Research does show us that repeated, persistent use of mental imagery, used properly, will lead to impressive gains for athletes.

Research studies and evidence show that skill development, self-confidence, emotional control, pain relief, and arousal levels can all be beneficially influenced using mental imagery *(Martin, Moritz & Hall, 1999; Murphy & Jowdy, 1992)*.

Mental imagery requires understanding for it to be most effective, it needs to engage as many of the senses as possible and it requires persistence rather than being treated as a one-off quick boost of some kind if it is to be most effective.

The runner using mental imagery in the preparation for a marathon, for example, might imagine himself running powerfully and at the perfect pace. He smells the fresh air around him, hears the crowds cheering and clapping, watches other runners around him jostling and bobbing up and down. When the start gun goes off, he resists the urge to sprint too fast, keeps his cool and gets to his race pace and finds a road position with plenty of room as he gets into the zone. He feels his legs striding strongly and his arms pumping. The senses are engaged and the mental preparation is in detail in the mind.

Two Main Theories Of Mental Imagery:

How exactly does using mental imagery result in gains for athletes then? There are two main theories that are adopted in the majority of the psychology literature on the subject.

Firstly, there is the psychoneuromuscular theory first written about by Jacobson *(1932)*. This theory suggests that by imagining and mentally rehearsing an activity of some kind, the motor pattern of that activity gets duplicated, albeit less so than if actually doing the activity. If we talk in neurology terms, this neuromuscular activation is believed to develop responses in the motor cortex of the brain. This has been referred to as muscle memory by many authors, since Vealey and Greenleaf *(1998)* coined the term.

A 1972 study by Suinn examined the activity of muscles in skiers' legs while they imagined skiing downhill. When they imagined it, the electrical patterns in those muscles was almost the same as if they had actually been skiing downhill. Since then though, attempts to replicate support for this theory have fallen a bit short. Some evidence has suggested that this theory is not consistent across all kinds of muscular activity, with higher levels of activity being more likely to respond to the imagination *(Feltz and Landers, 1983)*.

What's more, other psychological research has suggested that the responses to mental imagery are more to do with the central nervous system operations than actual muscular activity *(Kohl and Roenker, 1983)*. It is the opinion of many in the field, therefore, that the muscular responses to mental imagery may not be the actual reason of enhanced performance.

The other main theory of mental imagery and how it works is that of symbolic learning theory first explored by Sackett *(1934)*. This theory suggests that imagery effects are actually more to do with the athlete having the opportunity to practice symbolic aspects of a motor activity rather than actually activating the muscles.

This theory then suggests that the mental imagery forges a so-called "mental blueprint" which the athlete uses when performing.

Further evidence of this theory has shown that mental imagery works best for activities requiring a lot of cognitive involvement *(Ryan and Simmons, 1981)* which may suggest that mental imagery is likely to suit golfers and darts players more than runners. Also though, this theory suggests that early stages of learning anything new are much more cognitive that the latter stages and so suggest that mental imagery will have more of an impact in the early stages of developing and learning your sport.

There are a number of other theories and alternative notions for how mental imagery is effective, but knowing those theories are not really going to benefit a runner any more than that which I have mentioned already. Some theories contend imagery helps us believe we are capable, and thus advances our belief in ourselves and our ability to master our sport. Other theories suggest that we are prepared for more eventualities as a result of having imagined them; others believe in a somatic response to the imagery which prepares us for the event and helps motivate us by imagining how it feels when we succeed; yet other theories believe our skill levels are enhanced by mental imagery in a variety of ways. Some mental imagery processes are believed to help advance cognitive processes when performing, by mentally rehearsing, and all of these notions are prevalent within the field of therapy that I work in and I see the benefits of these things on a daily basis.

For us, the most important thing is that mental imagery is used by successful athletes and is shown to enhance performance. For example, a comprehensive analysis of 60 mental rehearsal studies by Feltz and Landers *(1983)* found that mental rehearsal was better for the athlete than no rehearsal at all. Weinberg *(1981)* in another similar review of the subject, also stated that mental rehearsal used in conjunction with regular physical training was more effective for the athlete than just physical practice or mental rehearsal alone. It makes sense therefore to include it as part of any training regimen.

There are a number of ways in which athletes can use mental imagery techniques, and not just for mental rehearsal. Many athletes successfully use mental imagery for the development of skills (runners can mentally imagine their technique, for example), for the development of cognitive strategies (mentally rehearsing how you use your cognitive strategies when actually running), building the healthiest levels of motivation for races and training, as well as developing mental resilience (overcoming adversity, being persistent, etc.).

I wanted this to give a good case for the use of mental imagery as a valuable tool for runners. Lots of my blog entries involve mental imagery techniques and lots of the processes coming up in future weeks will involve mental imagery applications of varying kinds.

Next up, I am going to share with you a guide for how to get the very most from mental imagery if you are a runner or an athlete or sports person of any kind.

Helpful Hints and Ideas For Using Mental Imagery To Enhance Your Running:

From the body of research and studies that have been conducted within the subject of mental imagery in sporting performance, there are a number of general ways and means of enhancing and advancing the results gained by using mental imagery and I thought that I would share that with you here before we get on to specific techniques and step-by-step processes.

As I mentioned earlier in this chapter, the more you engage your senses, the more vivid your experience of the imagery is and also, the more effective the mental imagery is going to be for you *(Harris & Harris, 1984; Orlick, 1986).*

When I worked on the previously mentioned BBC1 TV programme, Olympian runner, Sally Gunnell, spoke to the runners about visualisation and I think many people think that mental imagery is purely about visualising. It is far more than that though.

With the processes I have already written about and the ones coming up, when mentally rehearsing facets of your training runs, or races, I suggest that you imagine seeing the environment, hearing the sounds, feel your arms and legs pumping and your feet landing upon the ground, you smell the air, notice the temperature and even taste the water, or energy drink, feeling confident and assured of your running ability — combining the senses to truly bring your mental imagery to life is shown to make mental imagery more effective.

As long as you do it regularly, that is. Which is the next point to make here. Your mental imagery practice needs to be regular to be most effective. As I seem to have said many times on my blog, to derive the most benefit from our mind, we need to practice, and train it as much as our legs and as frequently as the runs we go on each week.

Runners who just engage in sporadic use of mental imagery never get the full benefit and often abandon it as a result. You develop skill with mental imagery in the same way as you do with anything else you practice regularly. Commit to engaging in mental imagery on a regular basis — make it part of your training regimen.

The more runners practice their mental imagery, the more control they tend to develop over the imagery. This is another important point to raise: taking control of mental imagery. It is up to the individual runner to be in control of what proliferates inside the mind. Therefore, always tend to the mental imagery to make sure 'the runner that is you' featuring in your mental imagery is positive, powerful, strong and confident.

If a runner keeps reminding himself of past failures, or having imagery of worrying future failure, then the control of the imagery is being lost and needs to be tended to. This becomes easier with persistence, practice and repetition.

As I have mentioned in much of my writing and I shall be mentioning again, when using mental imagery there is a difference between being associated or dissociated with the imagery. That is, are you watching yourself running (dissociated) or are you looking through your own eyes as you imagine running (associated).

Some of the studies tend to suggest being associated with our mental imagery is better because of kinaesthetic awareness while we perform our sport or event *(Mahoney & Avener, 1977)*. That is, we become more aware of how we are feeling and being. In contrast, a number of other studies suggest that being dissociated is just as important as we learn about our form, technique, about decision making and objectively choosing how to proceed with our event *(Hardy & Callow, 1999; White and Hardy, 1995)*. It is wise, therefore, in my opinion to ensure that you have a mix of associated and dissociated mental imagery within your regimen.

Within much of my extensive work on the subject of self-hypnosis, although we are not required to be relaxed to be responsive to self-hypnosis or autosuggestion, if we try too hard for it to be effective we may encounter what Emile Coué (1922) used to refer to as the 'effort error'. When we try too hard to achieve something within our mind, it becomes more difficult to successfully complete. A classic example to illustrate this would be that if you have ever experienced a sleepless night or insomnia, if you try to will yourself back to sleep, it becomes very hard.

Additionally, a number of studies have also shown that mental imagery benefits from being relaxed *(Weinberg, Seabourne, & Jackson, 1981)*. With the self-hypnosis techniques that I write about here, if you deepen your hypnosis with relaxation or even induce hypnosis using relaxation, that is going to lend itself well to advancing your mental imagery, especially if you are new to using mental imagery. Relaxation has a number of other benefits to the runner also, and when relaxed, we tend to find it easier to focus rather than getting distracted and even agitated.

Within my therapy practice, my clients and I often rehearse coping strategies for dealing with problematic scenarios occurring. For example, the individual who is overcoming a phobia may mentally rehearse successfully dealing with the old stimulus of the phobia. Likewise, although we tend to prefer to base our mental imagery around progressive and positive outcomes, we may also use mental imagery to help us to overcome any adversity that we may face. This may include making sure we train if we are feeling less inclined on a particular day, or it may be dealing with a stitch when running, or considering cutting a run short (unless it is for your own well-being and in your interests to cut the run short), for example.

One way of helping develop good imagery, especially if using modelling processes for part of your mental imagery, is to consider watching video footage. On my blog, I have included 'inspirational imagery' that helps you to get motivated, however it is also useful to have this stimulus to make your mental imagery even more vivid and detailed.

Many professional sportspeople and teams watch video footage of past performances as well as watching others, but here I am really referring to using materials to help you stimulate your mind, make it more vivid and note the details that you can use for yourself.

The only other consideration I want to mention here is the speed at which you play your mental imagery. It may well be useful to speed up or slow down your mental imagery for a variety of reasons. Remember that you do not actually run in that altered way, so it makes sense to play your mental imagery in real-time pace as much as possible, using the pace which you actually wish to perform at.

I think these guidelines are useful for runners to know to underpin the variety of mental imagery techniques that they can use, and certainly the kinds of processes I share here benefit from keeping these principles in mind.

I hope you find that useful with your own mental imagery processes. I feel driven now to go and find a new 'inspirational imagery' clip for the blog.

One way to advance your mental imagery skills is to combine your cognitive skills and internal dialogue when using your mental imagery processes.

Using Cognitions Within Self-Hypnosis Sessions To Enhance Imagery

Recently, in the midst of a discussion I was having with a client of mine who is a runner, we were discussing the importance of being able to engage our imagination.

This particular woman, like so many others that I encounter, stated that she really struggled to visualise or even to get any modicum of stability in the images that were in her mind. She got flashes and had distractions and found it thoroughly frustrating.

That frustrated sense is really going to impede the ability to visualise in hypnosis sessions, and is what we often refer to as 'the effort error' I referred to several times before in this book. This can obstruct us greatly not just with visualising, but in using self-hypnosis at all with any degree of success.

Throughout our hypnosis sessions, we do need to avoid any excess mental or physical effort that can frustrate and hinder our progress, and therefore, using the progressive relaxation techniques discussed in previous chapters in conjunction with self-hypnosis can be incredibly useful.

If we have any anxiety, concern or even a fear of failure, any one of these things can obstruct the progress we desire from self-hypnosis and mental imagery processes. So, practicing relaxing throughout is one particular means of helping provide a solid foundation for the use of mental imagery.

In line with autosuggestion pioneer, Emile Coué, and his law of reversed effect, we want to stop trying and exerting ourselves too much, as that obstructs our progress.

Everyone is capable of visualising and using mental imagery to great effect in conjunction with self-hypnosis. When we have a positive expectancy, correct expectations and we engage our imaginations, the process can and does become smoother with practice.

I thought I'd highlight a very simple, but often overlooked way to simply practice getting better at visualising within self-hypnosis sessions with the use of cognitions to direct, guide and keep on track. You'll be incorporating verbal affirmations that accompany your visualisations and repeat the process over and over. What tends to happen is that the cognitions keep the focus, block out potential distractions and engage the mind so that you learn (with repetition and over time) how to focus on the images, and your mental imagery prolongs and becomes more vivid.

Simply follow these steps:

Step One:

Induce hypnosis using any of the processes you have learned so far.

Step Two:

Firstly imagine yourself in a favourite place. It can be somewhere you have been to before, or somewhere you are creating and imagining in your mind. Let it be a place where you feel safe, secure and at ease. As a runner, and as a means of enhancing many of the other processes we use in this book, you might like to imagine being on a run, ideally in a favourite running environment.

Start to get a sense of the scenery of this place; notice the colours, shades of light and textures of what you see. You can notice sounds too, and enjoy the comfortable feelings, but primarily we are working with your visualisation here.

Get as much detail as you can for now, and then move on to the next step.

Step Three:

Now begin to state clearly to yourself using your internal dialogue the scene that is around you. Use statements that affirm what you are visualising and include the fact that you are seeing and visualising these things within your statements:

For example:

> *"I now picture the trees being blown slightly by the breeze."*
>
> *"I notice the green colour of the leaves of the trees."*
>
> *"I am imagining the trees to be 20 metres away from me."*
>
> *"I am visualising the trees to be in a group, clustered together."*

The above was fairly tree-centred. However, you can then move on to other facets and aspects of the scene around you, just stating and repeating that you are seeing XYZ happening and that you watch ABC in detail. This is not too dissimilar to what we did in the mindfulness exercises.

When you have done this for the entire scene, then move on to the next step.

Step Four:

Now think of some desired outcome that you have for yourself as a runner. Perhaps it is a health and fitness outcome, or something to do with your performance aspirations. Whatever kind of desired outcome you have for your running, start to think about yourself successfully taking the actions required and start to think of that target situation. As you imagine and visualise the scene with you in it, doing that successful outcome, again start to use your cognitions to affirm your visualised scene:

For example:

> *"I now picture myself proudly crossing the finish line."*
>
> *"I see myself holding my finisher's medal."*

And so on…

While you repeat these statements, let your internal dialogue be calming, soothing and enjoyable. Let it enhance your relaxation as you do this. Remember that remaining relaxed and positive throughout, with a peace of mind, is important to help you develop proficiency with this.

Then move on to the next step.

Step Five:

As you continue to describe what you see, using your cognitions to keep your mind focused, gently repeat those cognitions and statements over and over. Keep telling yourself that you can see more detail, and picture things more vividly as you focus upon it and as you use your cognitions.

Step Six:

When you have practiced and repeated the cognitions for this scene to the best of your ability, then take a couple of nice big deep energising breaths, wiggle your toes and fingers and come out of this session.

This depends on repetition for your visualisation to get better. If you practice this process a few times and start to use it within all the other techniques in this book, you'll start to notice distinct results using your own visualisation skills within self-hypnosis.

Right at the very beginning of this book, we focused upon goals and about creating future memories that stick with us throughout our training as we get closer to running events or achieving our desired outcomes.

In the next chapter, we are going to build upon that notion of using the imagination and using mental imagery techniques that combine many of the principles stated earlier in this chapter.

One thing I often do with my hypnotherapy clients, to illustrate how powerfully the imagination can influence our physiology and performance, is explain that if I suggest to you that your mouth is beginning to water, or if I told you to dribble uncontrollably, I might get some slight success if there is a good deep level of hypnotic communication created. If, however, I describe to you a scene involving a juicy, yellow lemon still glistening with a light sheen of condensation, I then suggest that I am cutting that lemon so that you can see all those tangy lemon juices beginning to flow out and then suggest you take a bite and sink your teeth into that lemon flesh…

You see where I am coming from here. Get the imagination engaged and we start to get our running performance enhanced, as we'll look at in the next chapter.

Chapter Twelve:
Imaging Your Run and Performance

Many coaches and academics consider using the imagination to be the most prominent and powerful psychological skill for any sportsperson.

As I mentioned previously when we were engaging in future memories, one runner found a different advantage from imaging success. After experiencing several positive images, he felt as though he had already accomplished the performance, and this gave him the confidence that it was inevitable that he would do it perfectly again.

Though people can engage their imagination without hypnosis, heightened focus and concentration with the aid of hypnosis often makes it more powerful. Before I offer up the first of our mental imagery techniques which will combine with many of the cognitive principles we have discussed already, I want to mention briefly another concept — that of observational learning.

Should We Model Other Runners?

Proponents of the field of NLP might prefer to call it modelling, but in conventional sports psychology, there is plenty of research to support the use of what is also referred to as observational learning. I think it is something that can and should be incorporated into your mental imagery techniques if and where possible.

Observational learning, or modelling, has been researched and examined and shown to help enhance performance by aiding athletes with skill acquisition, enhanced psychological responses and beneficial behaviour change when engaged in the athletic activity *(McCullagh, 1993; McCullagh & Weiss, 2001; Weiss, Ebbeck, & Wiess-Bjornstal, 1993; Williams, Davids, & Williams, 1999)*.

Within sport, athletes often benefit from watching demonstrations or footage of successful, elite or technically ideal athletes displaying proficiency and skill with their sport. Other athletes can then watch and adapt, adopt and take on board those skills and behaviours themselves.

As well as adopting physical skills and behaviours, though, Bandura *(1986)* also considers modelling to be an incredibly powerful way to adopt beneficial values, attitudes and thought patterns too. As this book is about using your mind to enhance your running, it would be foolish for us to not mention the usefulness of modelling to us as runners.

Bandura's *(1977, 1986, 1997)* work on observational learning theory has shown that it is not enough just to pay close and active attention to the behaviours and skills being demonstrated, though it is important to pay close attention. It is also important to remember what was modelled and retain it in the mind in order for it to be used in real life.

It is also important to know what you are looking at — for example, world record-breaking marathon runner Paula Radcliffe has featured in a great deal of my own observational learning. I have modelled her mindset, determination and approach to training by reading a lot of her material. I have also modelled the way she behaves when she races, but I have not modelled her unusual running style as it is not ideal for me and my particular build and physical abilities. I am selective with how I use my attention when modelling her.

We can not always be 100% sure that we are modelling the exact mindset without asking the individual, which is not always possible. So we do our best to intelligently translate what we see in a way that is likely to help us the most.

In addition to paying attention and being able to remember accurately what was being observed, the runner is required to be motivated to emulate what we observe. Without being sufficiently motivated to model the successful athlete, we are unlikely to model them accurately or with enough enthusiasm for the emulation to form part of our own behaviours and actions.

A lot of the work by Bandura *(1977, 1997)* in this field of observational learning does also stress the importance of self-efficacy beliefs. That is, if we believe we can emulate the skills, behaviours and approaches of those demonstrating, then it is going to be more effective. We have already looked at beliefs in this book and making sure you believe in your own ability to emulate facets of that which you are modelling is going to advance it for you. If when modelling you are able to be progressive and positive with your cognitions, support and encourage yourself and believe you are able and motivated to emulate effectively, then it is going to advance your modelling.

When you are selecting who to model, it is wise to observe people who are technically as correct as possible. Others with slight flaws can be modelled, but research shows that it is only really useful if you are given tuition and feedback while watching flawed skills for modelling purposes and so I am not going to go into great depth about how to do that *(McCullagh & Caird, 1990)*. If you have a coach or your club organisers have the time and inclination, then you might consider watching slightly flawed examples; otherwise, stick to modelling excellence.

Some research does tend to suggest that novices will not necessarily benefit (and may even respond negatively) to watching elite athletes because of the great differences between the novice and the elite athlete. So when I refer to excellence, it does not just have to be elite runners. You can model club runners, other good runners closer to your performance level and gradually develop upwards from there.

When modelling, of course the runner also needs to have a sense of what he is doing currently so that effective emulation can occur and changes can be affected thoroughly. Runners can ask for feedback from a coach, a technical expert (shoe sales people, orthotics experts, biomechanic experts, physiotherapists, all have varying levels of useful skills to feedback on how you run) or spend some time running on a machine with a mirror or getting some video footage of how you run and get a real accurate sense of your own style and behaviour before you start to emulate another or make slight changes to your running.

I have previously written about mental imagery and will be focusing a great deal on it later on in this book, but a study by McCullagh and Ram *(2000)* that reviewed imagery studies over a ten year period showed that many of the studies actually included the use of video footage and live demonstrations which showed that modelling was an important part of making some mental imagery techniques effective. There is no real benefit for me to go into much more detail and depth for the purposes of this book, but I wanted to make the point to help impress upon you the value of modelling as well as the wide array of mental imagery techniques you are presented with here. My message is simple — incorporate some modelling into your mental imagery and cognitive skills development and you'll enhance your performance.

The next process I offer up in this chapter then, includes some notions of modelling as well as mental imagery to get you started with combining these notions.

Self-Hypnosis and Mental Imagery For Enhanced Running:

When I was very young, we lived in a road that had a small green in the centre of it and I'd play football on that green for hours with my friends. Every time I went up to head the ball I'd imagine being Trevor Francis (the first million pound player ever in the English league and Nottingham Forest legendary striker, at least according to me) nipping in at the back post and nodding the ball into the goal with my head. I even ran off behind the goal to celebrate in the same way he did when he scored the winning goal in the 1979/80 European Cup Final against Kevin Keegan's Hamburg.

It was great fun to emulate him, but I found that I also took on lots of ability as a result of also taking on a bunch of the star player's attributes.

When I run fast around a bend during a marathon or a half-marathon that is on a road surface, I have a lingering image in my mind of Michael Johnson, the 400m world record holder with his distinctive style. I then hold my back straight, power my arms into motion and feel myself speeding up in a sensible and strong fashion.

There are many kinds of mental imagery processes that are used by sports people of varying kinds. Firstly, I'd like to offer up a lovely way to use a mental imagery technique whereby you as the athlete or sportsperson strongly identify with someone who possesses the attributes that you'd like to behold or acquire.

When you do this kind of thing, you as athlete may find yourself identifying with a famous person; like Michael Johnson, or like Paula Radcliffe. The amount of times I have imagined being Paula ploughing up the roads is great! However, it does not only have to be people that you imagine — you can use animals, machines or objects should you decide they have the desirable attributes you are after.

Being The Star Runner:

You can use this mental imagery technique to help yourself emulate the form and strength of any sporting star. It is a very popular way to use mental imagery.

I study Paula Radcliffe, Haille Gebrasalaisse and other marathon demi-gods. There are loads of English kids being Wayne Rooney with a football on the playgrounds, yet there are also aspiring professionals that study Stephen Hendry's snooker skills, Alistair Cook's batting action, Tiger Wood's gold swing, David Haye's left hook and Usain Bolt's running posture. Even though I mention my wanting to play football like Trevor Francis as a child, this kind of mental imagery, when done properly and diligently, is far, far more than play acting — it helps you, the runner, to develop.

Imagining and emulating the form of the star or leader in the field, and then stepping into that and becoming it inside the mind allows you to understand and sense the correct form in the relevant muscles of the body.

Using self-hypnosis with this kind of process is not essential, though it does enhance the effectiveness of the process and often makes the imagery far more vivid. I say this because, as well as doing this kind of thing in a formalised self-hypnosis session that you invest time in, as a runner, you can use this when running.

Heck, some believe that runners end up self-hypnotised for much of their training anyway and so are going to be suggestible to the right kinds of thoughts and imagery that they engage with during that time.

There are, today, companies that sell visual footage of people expertly demonstrating perfect form in a number of differing sports. There are products out there for skiing, golf, tennis, baseball, and other sports. One part of a tennis programme I have recently accessed while researching for this book, had an expert demonstrating perfect form over and over again, repeated a number of times for a specific top spin shot down the line of a tennis court. The budding tennis player then watches and adopts the positioning, replays the form and imagines himself doing that same motion to the extent whereby it becomes something they feel more confident and more competent of doing on the court.

The video footage then focused in on the knees, the wrists, the position of the arm; it was great. The viewer then imagined it all and emulated it before taking those repeated notions onto the court with them in their head.

Unleashing the Animal Within You:

As I mentioned earlier, it does not just have to be people that you benefit from in your mental imagery. You can also take on characteristics of animals that you deem appropriate and useful. Everyone knows that Muhammad Ali often talked about how he could "float like a butterfly, sting like a bee" and there are many other ways this type of notion can be utilised within your mental imagery.

At the end of last year I was working with a man who wanted to enhance and improve upon his personal best 10km time. He kept falling short of a time he achieved when he was 5 years younger. Of course we worked on lots of other things, including his belief in age-related ability and so on, and his personal trainer got him doing speed-work and intervals, which all long distance runners ought to have incorporated into the weekly running schedule.

He stated that he did not enjoy the speed intervals he was doing and he was clearly tensing up when he did them on the local track, timed with the stopwatch of his personal trainer. In the session with me, I asked him to tell me what kind of animal he associated with speed. He immediately chose a cheetah. We discussed the kind of footage that is often seen on the television wildlife documentaries when you see the cheetah running, sometimes they slow it down for you to see it in all its majesty racing across the landscape. We then followed by doing this type of process in a formalised hypnosis session and while hypnotised, he was encouraged to heighten his awareness of how the cheetah ran with such strength and power, but to see how it's face was loose, limp and relaxed. Also to notice how the legs were strong, thrusting, dynamic and powerful when being exerted, but when they were drawn back for the next step, they also were loose and limp and relaxed physically.

This man was then encouraged and instructed to watch the smoothness of the movements before integrating himself with the movements of the cheetah. He embraced the power, strength and speed and also relaxed while doing it, to let go of the tension he had previously discussed and reported. We ran through it all in slow-motion like on the telly, then got faster and faster and he was tasked to practice doing it all week in the build up to his speedwork track session — which went much better than before. With more practice of this process, his speed sessions became more enjoyable and more beneficial. I have done similar types of sessions with swimmers imagining dolphins and similar types of fast moving swimmers.

238

It is important for me to add here that many runners who learn to relax while running — loose jaw, soft shoulders, easy arms, straight gentle back, etc. — become amazed at how much more energy they have to spend on the actual important running action itself. Often they get faster by using less effort. You have relaxation skills to employ from a previous chapter.

Every now and then, as well as sports stars or animals (or instead of) you can use a moving object such as a machine of some kind. Throughout my own training and competing, and with my marathon-running clients, I have encountered many a runner who ran out of energy or felt as though he or she was flagging, despite the right training and taking on enough food and drink to healthily be running faster.

For these types of people, they get to choose a machine, maybe an engine of some kind with pistons that fire and pump effortlessly, like the kinds seen in many an advertisement for energy drinks or clothing for sports people.

Often when you just tell people to do certain things e.g. *"Relax your shoulders when running!"* they are puzzled and sometimes cannot relate to that kind of instruction. With these types of mental imagery techniques, the runner gets to engage the imagination and adopt that stance as they notice it for themselves.

As I spoke about earlier in this book, relaxing is very important for the runner, and so using correct types of mental imagery becomes equally important to enhance that relaxation within the physical posture, generated by the mind.

Here is a simple step-by-step guide to how to use this kind of mental imagery technique when running.

Step One:

Induce hypnosis in whatever way you prefer. Then move on to Step Two.

Step Two:

Now bring up and into your mind an image of that person, or animal or machine, whatever it may be. Notice all the details of that person (or thing or animal) and observe what tells you that they are performing and functioning so incredibly well. Place that picture in your mind as if you were looking at it on a screen.

These do not have to be perfect cinema screen pictures by the way, just imagine it as best as you can.

Step Three:

As you look at that image, make sure it has motion and so turn it into a film clip of that person or animal or object doing its motion that you want to take on and adopt in some way.

Make it incredibly vivid. Add the kinds of sounds that accompany it well too. Become aware of the places where the feelings of strength are and where the relaxation exists. Make the film clip as sensory rich as you can. Use colours and details as much as possible.

Step Four:

As you look at this image of yourself in your mind, think to yourself, *"I just know that is going to happen for me,"* or, *"I can be that way now,"* and really add some sort of internal dialogue that starts to convince you of your ability to adopt what you need from this.

Step Five:

Finally, you step into that image of you in your mind. Wear it, act like it. When you pretend to be a certain way, you are learning how to be that way at the deeper behavioural level. Mentally rehearse being that way, performing in that way. Let your own physiology merge in a beneficial way with your imagined point of focus. Really, truly associate with it, feel the feelings of it and get it lodged into your mind. How does that version of you think, how does that version of you hold the body? Then do those things and **BE** that version of yourself. You may even choose to mentally rehearse a future scenario (race or training run, for example) in your mind. Importantly, repeat the merging process over and over so that it is available to you without too much though when you are running.

Then you exit from hypnosis by counting from 1 through to 5 and open your eyes and go about your day.

Then when you have practiced this several times — take **Step Five** out with you on your run.

When you are running, you then step into those shoes of that person and you become them with that form in your mind, or you have that machine pumping tirelessly associated with your physiology, or you run smoothly like the cheetah.

Chapter Thirteen:
Building Inner Strength

"There is something magical about running; after a certain distance, it transcends the body. Then a bit further, it transcends the mind. A bit further yet, and what you have before you, laid bare, is the soul."

Kristin Armstrong

Using the types of strategies and techniques that I have described in previous chapters will also help to build self-confidence for you as a runner. The process of setting goals and visualising future memories, relaxing more, being mindful, engaging in cognitive strategies and using the imagery processes all give the runner more inner strength, a strength that promotes your level of confidence in yourself and your running ability.

I do want to mention your internal dialogue here again, because that affects and influences your inner strength massively — the most powerful influence in your life is you. The things you allow to go on inside your head influence you far more than anything I can offer up in this book, so as we look at these ways of building inner strength in relation to running, please be sure to incorporate as much as possible from the previous chapters, and build upon that material.

Discover How You Attribute Success and Failure

Lots of the previous chapters have offered up processes and techniques and strategies that have a by-product of enhancing confidence and inner strength when it comes to running.

When we are looking into enhancing running performance, many runners I encounter are troubled by what they deem to be previous failures, to the point where it is out of perspective and potentially affecting their performance detrimentally.

If we ever perform in a way that is not to our liking, or even make a mistake with some element of our running performance, then the key is to focus forwards instead of replaying it repeatedly and letting the poor performance dominate in any way.

You see professional footballers, golfers, tennis players, as well as runners, who make a mistake and then they spiral downwards, instead of learning to overcome it and deal with it effectively, there and then. Even people at the top of their game struggle with this at times.

Instead of having a simmering notion of failure, we can start to uplift and learn from those so-called failures by framing and perceiving each as a real-life opportunity to learn, and as a direct means to enhance and better our own performance, and, in turn, build our self-confidence.

Some of the mindfulness processes and techniques that we have already looked at can be used to reflect and can help runners to review their performance and their previous efforts.

As runners, we need to adopt a mindset that is always encouraging us to look forward during performances, rather than look back at mistakes. There is time after training and races to review the failures as learning experiences. One of the best ways to help encourage this type of solution-focused, progressive thinking and adopting an internal environment of this kind, is to adapt the work of Martin Seligman *(1990)* and his formulation of how to increase optimism.

Seligman found that, upon measuring the levels of optimism that athletes had, the ones that were more optimistic tended to perform better and more strongly. The way optimism is explained in his work is in terms of the way people respond to their own success and failure.

It is this attribution theory that states that humans need to explain why events happen. So we explain to ourselves why we performed well or badly and we attribute things to our success and failure. We find or invent causes for things that happen to us. It is not necessarily the real reason the thing occurs, but it is the way a person interprets the cause of the thing that happened. For athletes or sportspeople of any kind, there are three ways in which we apply these attributions to our success and failure.

Firstly, we have the ***permanent-temporary*** example. Something permanent is quite absolute and tends to lead to people thinking along the lines of, *"I can never run a 4 hour marathon."* Whereas a temporary type of thought would be, *"I couldn't run a 4 hour marathon on that occasion."* The permanent ones are thought of as immoveable and unable to change, whereas the temporary ones may change over time.

Secondly, we have the ***pervasive-specific*** example. A pervasive example would be, *"I don't do well in any running races."* A specific attribution would be, *"I don't do well in 10k races."* The pervasive attributions apply to all aspects of a situation, and the specific ones apply to only one or a few aspects.

Finally, we have the **personal-external** example. A personal example would be, *"I wasn't feeling my best that day,"* and an external one would be, *"It was such a hot day, making the race really tough."* (I said this after the 2007 London marathon, which was scorching hot.)

Do examine your own thoughts and see how you attribute certain reasons for your success or failure. Some people think they are lucky when they have done incredibly well — to go through all the training for any long distance running event is surely not down to luck, is it? This is very much a temporary, specific, external thought process. Others might say they did well because of all that effort, hours of training and dedication which is a far more permanent, pervasive and personal way to attribute success.

The simple way to enhance your awareness of how you attribute failure and success is to do the following simple steps:

Step One:

Induce hypnosis by using your preferred chosen method.

Step Two:

Deepen the hypnosis by running through a successful running event. Imagine being there, running or performing in that way and run through it in detail, engaging as many of your senses as possible. As you think about the event, reflect upon it and ask yourself the reasons for your success and notice your thoughts without editing them at all, trust what you came up with initially.

Step Three:

Deepen further by running through an event that did not go as you wanted, just observe the event, without getting into it too much; note what you did and then ask yourself the reasons for the results you got, and notice what your responses are. Again, make sure you do not edit your thoughts, let them be as authentic as possible so that you get an honest account of what you do inside your mind.

Step Four:

Exit hypnosis and make a note of what the thoughts were. Note how you attribute success and failure.

Step Five:

Finally, you now think of the kinds of thoughts that you can affirm to yourself and dominate your thoughts with as you go forward, in order to be more progressive and truthful about how you attribute your success or failure and ensure that you are not getting things out of perspective.

This is a nice and simple process to help you understand how you attribute success or failure, which is really important for developing a progressive mindset to advance our running performance.

Using Rational Emotive Therapy For Enhanced Optimism:

Having looked at how optimists and pessimists attribute different things for their success and failure, I want to share a process that could easily fit into virtually any other chapter in this book, but I think warrants being used to build our inner strength as runners.

The previously mentioned Seligman *(1990)* does not, of course, endorse total optimism. A total optimist would have trouble seeing and correcting problems in a poor performance. As discussed earlier, analysing a failure for its true causes can be of great help in overcoming problems. It is important for self-improvement to maintain a balance between optimism and taking responsibility for your performance. Neither a totally optimistic nor a totally pessimistic attitude leads you to examine your problems realistically with any hope of improvement.

Using Ellis' Rational-Emotive Therapy To Be More Optimistic:

We looked at how you identify the way you attribute success or failure. Then, once any individual is armed with that information, we are in a position to work out how to best enhance our optimism — and being more optimistic about our performances enhances our actual performance, according to the research.

It was Seligman *(1990)* who took the theories of Albert Ellis, and applied them to his optimism work in order to help sports psychologists help athletes. For athletes who attribute a variety of pessimistic reasons for the success and failure, Seligman suggested building upon Ellis's **Rational Emotive Therapy** in order to override the falsely pessimistic thought processes and enhance the more optimistic thought processes.

Using self-hypnosis, we identified what our own approach is when it comes to how we explain and attribute a cause to our good and bad performances.

When working with personal clients in my consulting rooms, on the occasions whereby the runner is leaning towards being pessimistic, then the following process based upon Ellis' **Rational Emotive Therapy ABCDE Framework** provides us with a way to enhance optimism and move towards more successful, progressive thoughts.

This **ABCDE** framework states that each of us experience **Adversity (A)** or an **Activation (A)** of some kind each and every day. This can vary from seemingly small things to deal with, such as a light bulb needing replacing, to much bigger, more profound things such as dealing with the loss of someone close to you, or a change of career. As a runner, a relevant example may be a poor training run, or even a skipped training run, or a race where you failed to achieve your desired outcome or set goal.

Whether these experiences are major or minor, they get us thinking about the reasons for things occurring, which then results in us developing a **Belief (B)** about the situation, the circumstances, and how we relate ourselves to that situation and occurrence. Now that we have a firmly rooted belief set up inside of our mind, there are now emotional **Consequences (C)**, which result in response to our belief. If we develop irrational beliefs about life events, then we generate irrational emotions. These are beliefs though, not necessarily the truth and in order to deal with any irrational beliefs, we subsequently **Dispute (D)** them using disputation methods, and once they are successfully dealt with by disputation and seen as they are, this in turn **Energises (E)** you.

With all this in mind, let's apply this to a runner who is problematically being too pessimistic about his or her performance and needs to move towards being more optimistic so as to enhance subsequent performance.

- **A is the Activation** that appears to produce C, a Condition or an emotional consequence.

- After a poor time in a race (**A**) for example, a runner might be disheartened (**C**) and even think about not running anymore. (**C**) is the emotional consequence and condition that is created by (**B**).

- **B is the belief**, often created in response to **A**. Rational Emotive Therapy suggests that it is not actually the poor performance that has caused the runner to be disheartened but **B**, the Belief of the athlete.

- If this belief is a negative, pessimistic type of belief, the runner is now shown how to dispute that belief and is encouraged to **Dispute (D)** the pessimism and negative belief and thereby **Energise (E)** themselves to move forward to better performances, and be energised to change the way they perceive the poor performance.

There are many ways to dispute thoughts and dispute our reasons for pessimistically thinking about our success and failure. One way we did this was explained in a previous chapter; you were asked to stop (**STOP!**) certain thoughts in your mind if they were negative.

One way is to use a thought form as previously explained. That is, charting the thoughts occurring and noting them down when they occur, noting down how they contribute to the negative belief and then writing down a better thought and belief to have.

Another way is to simply ask empiricism styled questions of the belief, as we did previously too — do you have any evidence for this? What proof do you have that this is the case? Another way is to mentally rehearse success as you have been doing with our future memory creation. Another way is to develop mindfulness which you've also been doing.

The other way is to enjoy some progressive and positive self-hypnosis sessions that encourage and help to build your inner strength, which is what I have for you next.

Building internal encouragement:

"My legs are a tad sore, I have a red forehead and shoulders due to the very hot sunshine, but I took 30 minutes off my London marathon time from last year... If I carry on as I have been, I am certain I can take another 30 minutes off at next year's marathon! I am going to be signing up again..."

This is what I wrote at Facebook and on my blog following the London marathon in 2010. I give a lot of praise for a particular approach that helped me achieve what I did in 2010; self-encouragement.

So, with regards to building our inner strength, I want to show you how to make the most out of encouragement and how I encourage myself in my training for events, such as I did for the London marathon 2010.

The marathon running bug hit me the year before I decided to run my first. I watched the TV coverage of all those people running together throughout the streets of London for the London marathon. The City was just about closed. In addition to the thousands of people that were running in the event, there were many more thousands lining the 26.2 miles of the course.

When I first started participating in races and getting into marathon training and running, someone said that it is a great idea to write your name on the front of your running vest and throughout the race the crowds will keep on shouting your name and giving you personal encouragement. It is such a wonderful tonic on busy races.

It is amazing how different it is to run on a street lined with thousands and thousands of people shouting and encouraging you, compared to running alone on a rainy, cold, dark evening or a grey, windy morning on your own, with only your own internal dialogue and MP3 player for company.

I also remember when the world record-holder marathon runner, our very own Paula Radcliffe, ran the London marathon for the first time — every inch of the course, she was greeted with cheers and encouragement that was unparalleled to anything I had seen before at a marathon event. She led within the first couple of miles and destroyed the field. She made the world's greatest marathon runners look ordinary and herself look superhuman. You just know that everyone watching at home was cheering her on and encouraging her too.

So much is said about being the home team in a football match too, for example, as the crowd supports and encourages their players so much more. The home team are said to have an advantage as they are playing in front of more of their own supporters.

You know what? I believe that we all need some of that kind of encouragement from time to time. This is especially true when we want to make positive and powerful changes in our lives for our own betterment.

In previous chapters, I have written a great deal about internal dialogue; I recommend your own internal dialogue supports and encourages you. Take a moment out to imagine this scenario. First of all, think of someone that you love: a child or your spouse or best friend or any other dearly beloved person in your life. Imagine that they were really trying to achieve something; I mean that they really wanted a particular thing to happen or wanted to create something or achieve a goal. Now imagine that a total stranger came and belittled their efforts. The stranger told them that they could not do it and they might as well give up!

Imagine the stranger said that they should not have tried in the first place and their efforts will amount to nothing!

How would that make you feel? To understate it, I guess you would feel annoyed at the stranger's sentiments, wouldn't you? You are likely to defend your loved one, aren't you? Maybe you'd like to box the ears of the stranger!

In contrast, what would you say to that loved one to encourage them and support them? Really take a moment out to think about that. How would you encourage them to successfully achieve and apply themselves?

You see, so often the kind of thing that the stranger was saying is the kind of thing that people say to themselves. You would not tolerate that sort of thing being said to a loved one, as you have just demonstrated, yet you may well be just as guilty and harmful in the way you communicate to yourself. Not just with your internal dialogue, it could be with your belief about yourself and your actions in life.

Encouragement should not just be reserved for sports stars, or babies learning to walk. You never hear anyone saying to a baby, *"That was a pathetic attempt to walk, you are rubbish at walking, just give up and get back in that Moses basket!"*

We all need encouragement as often as we can. Even if we are not getting as much as we should from others, we can encourage ourselves.

My brother still jokes about the time he and I ran the Bristol half marathon together a few years ago. We were going for a personal best time at this race and in the last few miles we were battling ourselves, our aching legs and our lungs that were readying to burst! We encountered a steep hill that most runners were groaning at the prospect of scaling at this late stage in the race. As we got over the hill and carried on speeding along the flat road, trying to catch our panting breath, my brother was laughing at me and I asked him what he was laughing at.

He said, *"I was just laughing at you shouting and swearing at yourself."*

I had not realised that I was so determined and was encouraging myself so much inside my head, that I had said my words out loud! I shall not repeat them here as they are far too blue.

As of this very day, begin to think about what you would say to someone else in certain situations in life if you wanted to encourage them. How would you encourage a loved one? What language and tone of voice would you use? Consider writing it all down and repeating it to yourself inside your mind so it becomes your new, progressive internal dialogue. How do you encourage others?

Ensure that you are convincing and sincere, make sure that you really mean what it is that you are saying. When you then communicate with yourself in that way, notice how that makes you feel. Notice what it is like to have that kind of progressive, encouraging internal communication instead. It can be like a breath of fresh air for your brain because you are now nurturing it.

As a result of encouraging yourself so much more, each time you create some internal communication with yourself, as you are more and more supportive, this is going to naturally increase your self-esteem and your self-confidence too! In turn, that builds a stronger foundation for your success and grows your ability to achieve more as a runner.

Over the course of the next week, maybe consider allowing yourself to relax and deliver this kind of dialogue to yourself for 10 minutes a day and become aware of how good you feel as a result.

The way in which you behave and the feelings that you have affect each other. Your behaviour often shows what your feelings are and your behaviours also affect how you feel (and vice versa of course). Very often, people think that they have to feel different before they change any of their behaviours. However, it is often far, far easier to do it the other way around.

Follow these simple encouragement steps to start really helping yourself to achieve more:

Step One:

Induce hypnosis in whatever way you prefer. Then proceed to Step Two.

Step Two:

Have a good think about a running success that you have experienced or a run that went really well. If you are really struggling, you can instead think of any other significant achievement in your life or any everyday achievement. As you think about it, think about what it was that has been so successful about it and also notice that thinking about it makes you feel better.

Notice what you thought, what internal dialogue you had, where in your body the feelings were, what you saw and heard and how you behaved. With a full, sensory rich idea of your successes you can learn from them and replicate them.

Step Three:

Run through that entire process again using another occasion. Repeat it a couple of times for both times. Really do this. Invest some energy into your success here. These are things that are indicative to you that you are on the right path in certain areas of your life.

Step Four:

Give yourself some praise. Go on, go ahead and praise yourself. Pat yourself on the back! This is nourishing, it is nurturing your relationship with yourself and rewarding and leads to you building your sense of self. Have some laughs as you do it, I know I find it hard to keep a straight face when I am doing this.

Now, start piling on the encouragement, as I have been writing about throughout this chapter. Give yourself some really good encouragement. Encouraging yourself gives you more and more resources for the challenges and difficulties that may lie ahead. As we did earlier, think about how you would encourage someone else and then deliver that encouragement to yourself.

Step Five:

Next up is comfort. Now I am not talking about the kind of comfort that I get when I sit in my lovely reclining chair, although it is very nice. Comfort yourself about something that may not have gone as you wanted. Heal those old wounds that used to be there. Take some time out to nurture yourself and heighten your own personal awareness of self.

Accepting and heightening your awareness of these things, rather than resisting and fighting past things, will allow you to start to take yourself to a new place in the future. This is a different flavour of encouragement.

Step Six:

Create a time in the future when you have a darling loved one encouraging you. Imagine them telling you how amazing you are and how proud they are of you — maybe someone that motivates you or someone you admire.

You can take it up a level and imagine a small crowd of people that you know and love all encouraging you and loving you and telling you all those wonderful things that make them sure that you can achieve what you want to achieve.

Then, you can even take it higher than that. Imagine the sights, sounds and feelings of running past thousands of people, or standing on a stage in front of thousands of people, or whatever you want to imagine, and those people are cheering you on, applauding you and showing you how much they believe in you. Soak this stuff up and enjoy the encouragement of the masses!

Step Seven:

When you have soaked up enough of these combined encouraging processes, exit hypnosis by counting from 1 through to 5 and opening your eyes.

This is fabulous stuff. Having practiced this process in hypnosis, start to encourage yourself when running, prior to runs and after runs in real-life too. Apply encouragement to yourself and observe what a fabulously enjoyable effect it has on your running and your life in general.

Using Performance Enhancing Hypnotic Drugs:

This book does not have enough space and it is not really relevant for me to write in depth about the placebo effect. My favourite book explaining and detailing the placebo effect is *"The Emperors New Drugs"* by Irving Kirsch, though I'll give an overview here because I want to show you how to build your inner strength as a runner using the placebo effect to your advantage.

Last year, I had the worst cold and flu bug of my life and the cough that followed seemed to hang around forever. It just would not go away and I could not run as a result. I was so miserable. I kept coughing in the middle of talking, which is not ideal if you are a hypnotherapist, right? It woke me up at night and so my sleep was affected. I tried every single cough medicine available, even the super power plus, guaranteed to beat any chesty cough linctus stuff from every brand known to man. Wondering whether it would ever desist, I called my GP's office and arranged an appointment.

Upon arriving at his daytime surgery office, in his usual authoritative, informed and dynamic manner, he enquired about my symptoms and proceeded to tell me that a persistent cough was common following this recent flu strain and that in most cases it gradually cleared within a few weeks. He prescribed another medicine which I picked up at the neighbouring chemist, he told me I should notice some improvements within a week, and to get back in touch with him if my symptoms persisted.

That week my cough dissipated, bothered me far less and the following week, was just about gone. As soon as I had left his office, I had felt in control of it and it got better.

I really have no idea how much the medicine helped or if my illness would have disappeared eventually anyway. However, as an evidence based practitioner myself, I do know that the mere fact of seeking and receiving medical care, contributed to me feeling better; more in control, more at ease and gave me optimism.

The benefit I received from this scenario is in some part due to what is known as the placebo effect. On many occasions, when subjected to scientific scrutiny, many, many treatments of varying kinds are proven to derive their benefits from the placebo effect.

Much of our modern treatments and interventions do actually undergo rigorous testing to prove their effectiveness. There is certainly a movement demanding that treatments be based on evidence; I am one such person making those kinds of demands in the field of hypnotherapy.

With that said though, there are many academics and experts who estimate that as little as 20% of the treatments routinely used by our doctors today have actually been proven effective in careful studies. Doctors and their patients continue to ascribe healing powers to certain medications, psychotherapies, and medical procedures that may well be impotent.

Most people think of a placebo as an inert tablet or capsule. It is that kind of idea of a placebo that we are going to use to advance our running. Study after study does indicate that expectation undoubtedly makes an important contribution to the healing power of placebos. Across a wide range of issues and ailments, clients who expect to improve are more likely to improve. Bear that in mind when using any of the self-hypnosis processes offered in this book — they'll be enhanced by positive expectation.

Up until very recently, it has continued to be inherent within understanding of placebo, that in order for the placebo to be effective, the clients or patients using them need to believe they are something else — that they are real medications that are going to help them. This leads to big ethical issues meaning that a doctor or therapist, for example, would have to lie about that which they are giving as a placebo.

Therefore, dealing out placebos has meant very few doctors actually use them… And why would I mention such a thing in the lead up to a particular self-hypnosis process I am about to share? Let me explain.

A very recent study by Kaptchuk and colleagues *(2010)* examined whether the placebo effect would still occur when patients suffering from irritable bowel syndrome were told that the pills they were being administered were inactive, it was like a sugar pill which had no medication in it.

Those in the study that were administered the placebo, were educated on the benefits of the placebo effect. They were advised that placebo helped with mind-body healing processes. The results of the research showed that the placebo effect still occurred.

One way to build inner strength, optimism and encourage yourself as a runner is to use the power of placebo.

Create Your Own Performance Enhancing Hypnotic Drugs:

The day before I wrote this chapter of the book, I ran 22 miles in the morning; I felt out of my usual shape having not slept well for a few nights previously, though I was so happy to have the wind in my hair, the sea air in my lungs and the sun shining on my face.

Once indoors, I started my recovery process by taking my protein shake, then, later, my cherry juice and having showered, stretched diligently, used the foam roller I have and got my compression stockings on, I got my feet up for a short while.

I also did something that I have not done for a very long time indeed... I took an ibuprofen tablet. Shock. Horror! It relaxes the muscles, reduces inflammation and I thought of it as an easy option. This confession is an interesting one that so many of us use in varying ways.

It represents that notion that is so prevalent in conventional health care — that well-being is just a tablet away. One of my favourite musical bands is a group called The Jam who were big in the 70s and early 80s here in the UK. They sang about 'The Bitterest Pill' they had to take. Isn't it funny what that expression is referring to: That you are having to swallow something that is for your good, yet it tastes bitter and is not palatable. Yet, we find it so very, very easy to take a tablet, don't we?

I can't stand that culture of taking a tablet if we have a headache, taking a tablet if we are depressed (in my therapy rooms, I encounter people who have been taking tablets to feel happy for years and years), a tablet if we have indigestion, if we have a cold, if we have pretty much anything — there are companies out there who make fortunes by telling people that they have a miracle tablet that will make you thin! It is not proven to work by any credible authority, yet we cling on to the notion because it might just work for us.

So I was a tiny bit guilty and decided to revisit my own exploration on the subject of hypnotic tablets, because it would be far more effective to get your mind and body in shape with proven methods — though they require more concerted effort than taking a tablet.

Even I think that once in a while taking a rare tablet for pain and inflammation is not a big, big problem. However, what about performance enhancing drugs? Rather than using tablets for after an event (when we are sometimes too tired to use self-hypnosis, God forbid!), we take them before we perform to make us excel!?

Many pieces of research about the placebo effect have shown how much faith we truly have in tablets. This self-hypnosis process then is going to show you how to create your own legal, performance enhancing drug. This process allows you to create your own hypnotic tablet that you can take and allow your body to respond accordingly. You may be amazed at just how your mind and body respond to taking a hypnotic tablet and how your running performance benefits.

Before you engage in this session, you may want to have a grape, orange segment, sugar lump or any other thing that could take on the role of your hypnotic tablet, or you may simply choose to imagine taking it in your mind later on. Whether you opt for imagining consuming it later, or if you need a bit more reality in your mind, then prepare accordingly at this stage. As you get settled, have a good think about the effect that you'd like your hypnotic tablet to have on you and then follow these simple steps.

Step One:

Induce hypnosis using your preferred method. When you have induced hypnosis, move on to Step Two.

Step Two:

Get some sort of outcome in your mind. Have a think about the effects you wish your special hypnotic tablet to give you.

To help with this, using your imagination, think about if you had a miracle drug of some kind, then what would it be for? What would it do? What is the effect that you wish? Would it make you feel fitter on your run, would it make you faster, stronger or endure more discomfort when running?

Once you have the effect in mind, also think and ask yourself — what would that be like? If it could create that outcome, then have a very good think about what is going to tell you that you have achieved that outcome. What are the signs that are undeniably convincing of the success of your hypnotic tablet?

With those things in mind, move on to Step Three.

Step Three:

Tune into your body. By that I mean, get a real sense for how you are feeling physically throughout this technique, this is important because you want to benefit physiologically and psychologically from this process.

Now is the time to imagine that tablet. Create it in your mind. Imagine that you have it in front of you or actually hold your grape, sugar lump or whatever you may be using if you are going for a real life thing to use with this session — charge it — insert all your hypnotic abilities into it.

By that, I mean, imagine that you are enchanting it with all the desired effects. Maybe you imagine the effects that you have had before and empty them into the tablet. Maybe you imagine it changing in colour as it becomes enchanted. Maybe you imagine it vibrating or pulsing as you add all the specialist elements that you wish.

Imagine the effects pouring out from you and from all nature around you: Filling it with magic, health, well-being, joy and more and more of the things that are going to make this so wonderful for you.

Once you have completed creating it in your mind, ensure you perceive it correctly and move on to the next step.

Step Four:

Now, as you look at your completed hypnotic tablet, just think to yourself, *"I know that is going to work."* Just trust that it is going to have all the desired effects that you created. Believe in it with conviction.

Secondly, recall a time that you have taken a tablet for a similar type of effect and ask your own mind for an enhanced version of that experience. An experience that is even better.

Connect with your body all the time. Tune in to your own physiology throughout each step of this process. Really allow your body and mind to feel a sense of togetherness with this as you really want your hypnotic tablet to communicate its effects physically and mentally. Then move on to the next important step.

Step Five:

Take the tablet. Pop your tablet. Gulp it down, swallow it, consume it in whatever way is right for you. Imagine the tablet's journey. Imagine it dispersing its effects as it enters your body. You may want to spend some time just imagine it spreading through your system for a while.

Imagine connecting with all the cells in your being and that tablet having the desired effect. Maybe you can imagine the tablet spreading a performance enhancing colour throughout your system. Or an energy or vibration or just a renewed sensation of well-being.

Bask in the healing sensations and enjoy the effects spreading and multiplying. Turn the tablet over to your mind — by that I mean, make a request of your mind to truly allow this tablet to have the full desired effect. Feel the difference in your body and start to think about how this is going to feel when you start your run.

Tell your mind what you want to happen and what to expect — add some suggestion to your hypnotic tablet. Whenever you feel that you have truly absorbed all that you need to and are ready for the tablet to do its own thing from here onwards, then you move on to the final step.

Step Six:

Now think about engaging in your sport or that performance and how you are going to react and respond, decide on taking that action as you imagine what is going to happen. Then bring this session to an end by counting yourself up and out from 1 through to 5.

Now go and take some action, go and make the most of this tablet and its effects upon you. Notice how much it helps you and how it enhances your performance. Maybe consider repeating this session and taking a course of tablets hypnotically that serve to advance your desired running outcome.

The variety of processes and themes in this chapter have been with an aim of building your inner strength. We are now going to build even further upon all the previous chapters, incorporating everything we have done so far and getting very specifically focused on running strategies.

Chapter Fourteen:
Runner-Specific Cognitive
Strategies And Mental Imagery

*"Most people run a race to see who is fastest. I run a race
to see who has the most guts."*

Steve Prefontaine

We have already looked at a wide range of cognitive strategies
and mental imagery techniques. In this chapter, we get more
specific and examine cognitive strategies and mental imagery
techniques specifically to enhance our running performance. The
entire chapter is just techniques and step-by-step processes for
you to engage in, enjoy and reap the benefits of.

Altering Our Perceived Level Of Effort When
Running:

In all of my explorations of methods and strategies for using
hypnosis to help advance sporting performance, one of the most
impressive uses of hypnosis within studies has been that,

> *"Perception of effort during exercise can be systematically
> increased or decreased with hypnotic suggestion even
> though the actual physical work-load is maintained at a
> constant level. Furthermore, alterations in effort sense are
> associated with significant changes in metabolic responses
> and brain activation as measured by SPECT and MRI."*

Morgan, 2002

This is incredibly good news for us runners.

Additionally, my friend, hypnotherapist, writer of the foreword for this book, and multi world title-winning fighter, Gary Turner, has been writing a lot about running while he is spending just 12 weeks preparing and training for a 40 mile ultra marathon. Here is what he wrote as his Facebook status update earlier this week:

"Heard on the radio earlier a DJ talking about his London Marathon entry talking about what a massive hurdle it is to overcome.

It isn't.

In a couple of weeks I'll be doing a marathon a week for my ultramarathon training. Long runs for me now seem normal. Yet this is only my 4th week of preparation. Impressive? Nope. Just know what I'm doing and expect to be able to do it.

Eddie Izzard did 43 marathons in 51 days on just 5 weeks of training. Think about what our military do in training as a matter of course.

Many people do far more impressive distances.

Your body can do 1,000 times more than you think it can. You just have to vote with your feet, and have a strong mind."

Gary Turner, 19th September, 2012, Facebook

Gary sums up nicely my own sentiments and there is evidence to show that we are more capable than we sometimes think, and also that we can alter our perceived level of effort to enhance and advance our running performance.

In the early 2000s, Williamson and colleagues *(2001, 2002)* showed how hypnosis and receiving suggestions in hypnosis could alter the level of perceived effort by the athlete, resulting in them being able to perform better — and actually having a cardiovascular response from the brain believing in that perceived effort level. It sounds like the stuff of fantasy, but evidence repeatedly supports this notion and it makes complete sense when you consider it fully.

This next self-hypnosis technique and process is a cognitive strategy to engage in while running, but to implement with mental rehearsal in self-hypnosis sessions.

Our bodies respond to the message of the brain and we really do tend to respond to effort, pain, discomfort in a very sanitary and self-preserving fashion, which does not really stretch and push us.

Elite athletes and sports people know that they can go further and have conviction and belief that they can push themselves further. This is not the central theme of this particular technique (we do have a technique for that coming up though), but that belief in our perception of our own level of effort is what this is all about. You'll be able to run further, faster and also enjoy your training runs much more as a result of learning this process. Just follow these simple steps:

Step One:

Induce hypnosis in whatever way you prefer. Once you have induced hypnosis, move on to Step Two.

Step Two:

Imagine being out on a typical run. (You can start doing this with training runs, ideally your long runs where you are on your feet for longer periods of time, then start to use this process for racing and competing and practice it for use during those crucial events.)

Imagine being on that run. Engage with surroundings. See the sights, hear the sounds and just tune in to what you notice around you.

Tell yourself that each imagined step, each sight and each sound all take you deeper into hypnosis. Spend enough time on this step to really get a good receptive, deeply perceived level of hypnosis.

When you have fully engaged with the run and the environment and have it all vividly in your mind, move on to the next step.

Step Three:

Now move your awareness inwards and tune in to how you are feeling while running.

Be mindful. Notice your breathing and the movements attached to your running and breathing. Become engaged with your level of perspiration and really notice how hard you are working at this stage of your run, according to how your body feels and the kind of thoughts you are thinking and having while running.

On a scale of 0–10 rate what your level of effort is at this stage of your run.

Think of how much further you have to go, how far you have gone, and weigh up how much effort it is for you to continue going at this pace; gauge and scale how much effort it is for you to continue as you are doing.

Then just ascertain one number on a scale of 0–10 of what your level of effort is currently at this stage of your run.

Once you have that number in mind, move on to the next step.

Step Four:

Now start to think of reducing that number to a level where you think you'd be more comfortable, more capable and would be enjoying your run further still.

So if you felt that you were struggling to maintain your pace at mile 10 of a 20 mile run, you might have gauged that you were at an 8 or 9 level of effort. You might think that you'd prefer to be at 4 or 5 for things to be more comfortable. (I sometimes yearn to be at a 4 or 5 when I am running a fast 20 miler!)

Simply change the number in your mind to a 4 or 5, for example.

Superimpose that number in your mind, imagine a sound that goes with it, and as you look at that number in your mind, look at it as if you believe it. You might colour it, you might make it incredibly large, do whatever you like to have that new number inside of your mind and at the forefront of your awareness — representing your new level of effort.

Look at it and encourage yourself to believe that this is actually the true representation of your level of effort. Do all you can to convince yourself.

Once you have that new number there in your mind, and you are looking at it as if you believe that is your actual effort level, move on to the next step.

Step Five:

As you carry on running, now start to run *as if* you are at that effort level. Hold your body *as if* you are at that effort level. Think in your mind *as if* you are at that effort level. Behave, act and run absolutely as if you are at that lower effort level — convince yourself that is where you actually are.

Adopt the behaviour of how you would be at that actual level of effort.

Once you have done so, move on to the next step.

Step Six:

Now engage your internal dialogue and affirm powerfully to yourself. Use your cognitions to advance your belief and response to your effort level. As you run, repeat to yourself something along the lines of;

> *"This is easier and easier."*
>
> *"I am so much more comfortable."*
>
> *"I am more capable than I realise."*

Or whatever it is that suits you and your preferences. Use language that is in the present tense (i.e. is happening NOW) but that you feel comfortable with and that inspires and drives you onwards.

Importantly again, though, say it in your mind as if you truly mean it. Say it with purpose and volition. Say the words to yourself as if they are the truth and you believe it 100%. Be determined and driven.

Repeat this for a while with real meaning and keep doing all you can to believe, then move on to the next step.

Step Seven:

Continue to repeat the positive cognitions, continue to believe in the new number, the new effort level you have set in your mind. Then imagine a sense of comfort is now spreading through your body. You can do this in a number of ways;

1. Imagine a colour of comfort spreading through you.

2. Imagine a sound resonating comfortably through you and spreading.

3. Imagine a feeling of comfort moving gently and surely through your body, especially your legs.

4. Imagine your muscles relaxing and softening.

You could easily engage in a version of progressive relaxation here if you have a good understanding of it.

Notice how it feels and enjoy the ease of running at this new perceived level of effort. Remind yourself that this is affecting and influencing your brain's response to your body. Once you have spent enough time on this step, and you are really noticing the level of comfort, then move on to the final step.

Step Eight:

Exit hypnosis by counting from 1 through to 5.

Run through this process a few times in a self-hypnosis session, get it all set up, loaded so that you remember it all, and then go and start using this strategy when on your runs, and start to influence and affect your perceived level of effort when running — because you'll really be able to run further, faster and better as a result.

The Mountain of Strength — To Keep Going and Enhance Endeavour:

Sometimes people need to have the courage of their convictions. Sometimes we need an enhanced sense of purpose, belief and endeavour. This is so true in running performance.

In marathon running, as you may have gathered already, my own hero is Paula Radcliffe, not just because she holds the world record of 2 hours 15 minutes and 25 seconds (at the time of this book being published), but because of her strength, mentally.

In her earlier career, despite being tipped for great things, she suffered from injury in the early 1990s and seemed destined to always come 4th, 5th or 6th in the mid 1990s at the 5km distance and although she got a silver medal at the 1999 World Athletics championships, she was out of the medal positions in the 2000 Olympic games and 2001 World Championships. She did of course win plenty of stuff here and there too, but I think many lesser people may not have gone on to do what she did in 2002 where she began to take the marathon running world by storm. She ran the fastest time in the world that year, then went on to achieve the fastest time ever run by a woman later that year.

The following year she did not just break her own world record. She smashed it out of sight. Also in 2003, she set the world record time for a road 10km race. Of the 7 marathons Paula Radcliffe has run, she has won six and set records in five of them. Awesome.

I admire not just her extraordinary achievements, but also her strength to carry on against adversity. To keep plugging away and achieving greatness eventually. She inspires me and helps me to keep plugging away at running marathons.

The personal development world often tells stories of people such as Colonel Sanders, Abraham Lincoln, Thomas Edison and many other remarkable individuals who kept on despite many set backs. So I wanted to offer up a process that can be used to train ourselves to keep on, to be persistent, to keep putting effort in even when we feel deflated or feel like giving up.

What better metaphor to use than that of a mountain which is a symbol of strength all of itself? People have climbed mountains, which is recognized as some feat, and mountains are used as metaphors in a wide array of ways. Here I am using that mountain both as a symbol of strength to draw upon, but also as something that requires continued effort and endeavour to reach the summit of.

Prior to starting this process, have in mind what it is that you wish to achieve and keep on doing. It may be training for a race, it may be developing new running skills, it may be joining a running club, or any next logical step in the process of progression for your running. With that in mind, get yourself in a comfortable position, sat upright with your arms and legs uncrossed, and then proceed to Step One.

Step One:

Induce hypnosis using whatever method you prefer. When you have induced hypnosis move on to Step Two.

Step Two:

Engage your imagination in whatever way is best for you. Imagine walking along a path, notice what the path is made from, hear the sounds of your feet upon it and sense the feel of your feet upon it.

Each step that you take along the path, imagine and tell yourself that you are going deeper inside of your mind too.

Notice the surroundings, the weather around you is just right for you, it is absolutely comfortable and easy to be here in this place. Off in the distance you can see a mountain.

Spend as much time as you require to truly get a sense of this place, walking along the path and getting more and more comfortable and at ease, drifting deeper inside your mind. Once you feel that you are at ease and comfortable, then move on to the next step.

Step Three:

As you continue walking and drifting deeper, and getting nearer to the mountain, notice the scenery, notice any landmarks and absorb as much detail as you can; focus on all that there is to notice about this place.

Notice the sounds being made around you, allow them to soothe and relax you and enhance your experience. Notice the colours and shades of light as you continue walking and going deeper inside your mind, all the time keeping comfortable and at peace.

Once you feel that you have really studied the details of the surrounds and got them in your mind, then move on to the next step.

Step Four:

Notice now that the pathway is changing. It is becoming narrower and more difficult to walk along with so much comfort. The surface seems to be getting rougher and uneven and it is starting to develop an uphill slope. You manage to keep your balance, but it is becoming increasingly more difficult to do so.

You start to think that perhaps it is time to head back to the comfort of the pathway away from the mountain now, but you notice a sense of strength as you take your first steps up the mountain side. Almost as if the mountain is developing and building within you some inner strength and courage and installing a sense of resolution to keep on.

Get a sense of that and when you feel it, move on to the next step.

Step Five:

The pathway is deteriorating in quality even more now and the slope is getting steeper, each step you take, it seems to be getting slightly steeper and is more challenging. It is actually tough to press onwards any further.

The surroundings have changed too, trees and bushes and shrubs stray onto parts of the pathway and often obstruct smooth passage, the vegetation is getting thicker and blocking out more of the light, the surface of the path is slippery in places and even verges on being treacherous and you perhaps find at times that you slip or miss a step.

You start to think rationally, you try to talk yourself out of carrying on... *"This is getting problematic and I really ought to head back now."*

Such sentences are soon replaced with a growing sense of strength that the mountain seems to emanate and is filling you up with a sense of courage and you feel something deep within you urging you onwards.

Again, feel that sense and, when you feel it, move on to the next step.

Step Six:

As you now walk up the steep climbing pathway, you start to notice a change in the air. That is, as you step higher, you find yourself in amongst an increasingly thicker fog that hangs in the air. It obscures your vision to the point that you cannot see where you are going and you are unsure as to where you are. It gets thicker and surrounds you and you keep thinking that you should head back, yet something deep within you keeps you stepping forward and moving onwards. You feel your footsteps on the pathway and vaguely make out the edges of the path and keep on walking onwards, with purpose.

It is increasingly challenging and part of you keeps nagging at you to give up and turn back, but you enjoy the sense of strength that the mountain seems to give you as your senses begin to numb and all you are left with is this deep inner sense growing within you, keeping you moving onwards and upwards.

When you sense it, move on to the next step.

Step Seven:

Just at the point where you really start to question your actions, the fog begins to lift, in fact, you are leaving it behind. You notice that each step is becoming easier and the air is becoming clearer.

The fog thins and clears and you rise up into the sunshine and the pathway starts to level out and you start to see more of the scenery around you again. You notice colours and so much more. The world opens up again, you hear the sounds of new life, new beginnings, and each sound seems almost triumphant.

You notice below you and behind you is the pathway you came up on, you notice the scenery that you had paid such close attention to earlier and you breathe the clean fresh air and it fills you with a sense of contentment and satisfaction… It also feels like victory and it is a glorious sensation to enjoy spreading throughout your entire body.

You find a rock to sit upon and absorb the deeper lessons and learnings that have occurred to you and for you as a result of you overcoming the adversity represented here, and keeping on to discover the beauty and awe that exists at the top of the mountain and that existed within you all along.

Celebrate being you. Celebrate your victory.

Think about how you now plan to make changes in your actions and attitudes in that particular area of your life. Think about how elated you are going to be once you have achieved your desired outcome and let that fuel even more of your ability to press on and build your sense of courage and endeavour.

Enjoy this victorious feeling and when you feel you have admired the view and basked in your feelings for long enough, move on to the final step.

Step Eight:

Once you have spent enough time reflecting upon your achievement and your inner strength and endeavour, bring this session to an end.

Take a couple of nice deep energising breaths, wiggle your fingers and toes and open your eyes, once you have counted from 1 through to 5.

Now start to plan your next steps of action on your journey towards achieving that running goal that you want to achieve.

Going The Extra Mile:

Last year I watched a reality TV series on a random satellite channel about an overweight family who were being given lots of resources and training by a famous TV broadcaster here in the UK, to lose weight and make some changes in their lives.

In one episode, they went on a fitness walk around some beautiful scenery and hills, but after a while they convinced themselves and each other that they were all far too tired to carry on. Note I say 'convinced themselves'. They absolutely could have carried on for hours and hours if they had to.

The youngest daughter of the family was given the chance to work out at a gym and, throughout her personal training from the instructor, kept insisting that she *"could not go on"* and *"could not possibly keep on"* — she insisted on it, she used a very negative tonality when insisting on it and despite the protestations and the energy displayed by the instructor, her own belief that she was too tired prevailed.

Shame.

They are not alone with this type of behaviour. I have found that during marathons or other races, I have felt tired at mile 10, doubted myself and got weaker, but when I started to dispute that and drive myself on, or got some encouragement from the crowd, or thought about my wife, etc. I have overcome that wave of seeming fatigue and run for another 16 miles with more gusto than the first 10.

We are all far more capable of going on for longer when it comes to exercise, physical activity and running. I was so certain of this that I adapted an idea using self-hypnosis that I use for all my long runs and that can be applied by any runner.

You just need to be able to imagine an old-school graphic equaliser that used to be on stereos. The youth of today may not know what I mean, but it was a panel on the stereo front that showed you how the sound was divided and what the sound levels were like while music played. If you are a proper youngster who does not know what a graphic equaliser looks like, go Google it and it'll help you have some imagery to work with for this process.

You could turn graphic equalisers up and down to affect the sound and you could get a visual interpretation of how loud certain parts of the music were. My initial point here is that sometimes people think they are using all their effort and have used all their energy and simply cannot go on, yet you always see good athletes pushing themselves to do more and alter their own perception of what they are capable of. Those ripped guys in the gym always squeeze out another rep on the weights and other athletes put in that little bit extra throughout their schedule — it makes a great deal of difference.

We all recognise a certain level within ourselves that we reach, but we are often able to go much further than that. This next self-hypnosis technique is designed to help you go further and literally go that extra mile, get your mind focused and believing that you can do more, or go faster, or stay for a while longer.

Step One:

Induce hypnosis using your preferred method. Then when you have induced hypnosis, move on to Step Two.

Step Two:

Imagine a graphic equaliser or a visual measurement gauge of some kind in front of you.

Each breath that you breathe, the gauge pushes up to show the amount of effort and energy that you are using.

Take a few moments and just watch the lights going higher, brighter and longer with each breath that you breathe and then dissipates between in breath, so it is going up and down in time with your breathing.

As the gauge moves up, notice that if you breathe out really fast and hard, the colours move and just touch upon the red zone. As you breathe typically it stays green, barely turning amber or orange, but a hard breath gets into the red zone and the lights reach red for a brief moment.

Spend some time to get it absolutely synchronised with your breathing. As you watch it moving in time with your breathing, rising and falling, tell yourself that you are going deeper and deeper inside your mind.

When you feel as though you have spent enough time deepening your experience in this way, move on to the next step.

Step Three:

Keep the colourful gauge reflecting your breathing while you now imagine that you are exercising. Imagine yourself engaging in your choice of exercise and, as you exercise and breathe, notice how this affects your gauge; it starts to go up and move towards that maximum level. The colours start to encroach upon the maximum level: the red zone that indicates the upper levels are being reached.

In your mind start to slide the gauge controller downwards and imagine yourself feeling fitter, stronger and more energised, at a healthy and safe level of course.

Bring the colourful indicator graphics downwards using the sliding switch and notice it coming back down into the safe and comfortable zone.

283

Step Four:

Start to notice that you are able to keep the levels of exertion and effort being displayed on your gauge at a constant, easier, comfortable level even as you exercise yourself harder and for longer.

Imagine that you are now reaching a point of exercise and exertion that is the most you would have done, and the time that you'd then have chosen to stop in the past. This time however, you keep the graphics of your gauge at a comfortable level, and you start to affirm your belief in yourself to go for longer.

Affirm to yourself in your mind, in time with your breathing, something that resonates well with you, for example:

> *"I feel more and more capable of going on for longer."*
>
> *"I am healthier and healthier, fitter and fitter."*
>
> *"This is easier and easier."*
>
> *"My body loves this exertion more and more with every step I take."*

Choose whatever resonates best within your mind and that you like the sound of most. As you say those words to yourself, keeping the graphic gauge at the right levels… your breathing responds well, your muscles respond accordingly and you feel wonderful.

Keep imagining this happening in your mind for a while, get tuned into it, so that when you are actually out exercising, it works powerfully and effectively just as you are imagining it will.

Once you have spent a while on this step, then move on to the next step.

Step Five:

Start to tell yourself that you can use this process when you are actually exercising too and that it starts to have the same effect as you imagine it having now.

Spend some time and get it absolutely synchronised for you, get the control absolutely as you want it and can affect it, then bring this session to an end with the final step.

Step Six:

Exit hypnosis by counting from 1 through to 5.

Practice this process. The more you practice it in your mind, the better it becomes and the more usable it'll be during your actual runs; allowing you to alter your perception of how you feel in response to exercise and also helping you to run faster for longer.

Use it with self-hypnosis a few times, then start applying it when out running and make sure you really do go that extra mile.

Getting and Using The "Runner's High" With Self-Hypnosis:

Over the years, I have read a lot of information, opinion as well as some utter nonsense, about something referred to as the "runner's high". Popular running blogs, and non-academics in the running community refer to this "runner's high" as a sort of euphoria-type of state that results in the body being flooded by endorphins and feel-good chemicals when we engage in running.

I certainly experience this, particularly after a run, though according to the research and actual evidence, there is speculation about what it is and how it happens. There is very little evidence to suggest it happens as a result of increased endorphins in the brain, and we really need more research and well-designed studies to be sure of what is happening physically within us to cause this.

The fact of the matter, though, is that the vast majority of runners, especially when certain levels of fitness have been achieved, do report that they enjoy a general sense of well-being after they have been running, and way back in 1979 Mandell wrote in the *Psychiatry Annals* about such a thing as the "runner's high" existing.

Mandell *(1979)* wrote at a purely theoretical level and considered neurochemical literature illustrating the effects of various drugs on the central nervous system, drawing parallels to what goes on in the brain when we exercise. Mandell also suggested the role of serotonin was more important and this has since been confirmed in a study conducted by Chauloff *(1997)* which showed the importance of neurotransmitters such as dopamine, norepinephrine as well as serotonin (feel-good chemicals known to effect mood), as much more present following exercise.

So although there is discussion to be had about the real chemical production in the brain when running, we can be sure that it happens to make us feel good and also that if it keeps on feeling good, we are going to be more inclined to persist with our running. Heck, when we enjoy something and it makes us feel good, we are going to carry on and do more of it, right?

The evidence may not be of much interest to you, or of much use, but I hope the process that follows is one that you'll use for great effect as I certainly have been doing. Once I had read the paper by Mandell *(1979)*, I also read the personal account and seeming cognitive strategy that was chartered within it and having read about how exercise and our thoughts can influence feeling, it made logical sense to use our self-hypnosis skills to develop and purposefully engineer our very own "runners high".

Mandell's account even stated these cognitions when charting the runner's high subjective experience:

> *"The running literature says that if you run six miles a day for two months, you are addicted forever."*

Our aim is not to get you addicted of course, but this is the kind of suggestion that the researcher reported whilst engaging in the "runner's high".

Make sure you are in a place where you'll be undisturbed for the duration of this session. Ensure you are in a comfortable, seated, receptive posture and position yourself with your feet flat on the floor with your arms and legs not touching each other, then begin.

Step One:

Induce hypnosis using your method of choice. Once you have induced hypnosis, move on to Step Two

Step Two:

Imagine being out on a long run. See the sights, hear the sounds. Be in a typical place that you run regularly and engage with it.

Be well into the run. That is, imagine that you have been running for a while and your exertion levels have been impressive.

Notice your breathing rate, notice if you are sweating, notice your body temperature and really feel how you are.

Tell yourself that with every step you run, you go deeper into hypnosis. Then continue on your imagined run, tuning in to your physical self, noticing how you feel when you have exerted yourself on a good run and, once you have that, move on to the next step.

Step Three:

Notice the way that your running exertion has affected your brain. Imagine that deep inside your brain, it is responding to the exertions and releasing and producing those feel-good chemicals.

Imagine deep inside your brain the running exercise is causing it to produce serotonin and other feel-good chemicals, and use your imagination, in whatever way is right for you, and imagine how they are being spread from your brain and through your body.

If you need to encourage more production of those chemicals, you can increase the volume or the depth of the movement as you imagine it spreading from the base of your brain and throughout your body.

Maybe imagine the good feelings as a colour, maybe imagine them as light, maybe you just follow the actual physical sensation, maybe you imagine it as a sound resonating and moving... Represent the good feelings generated by your brain in whatever way best suits you.

Spread the good feeling around and go deeper into hypnosis as you do that.

When you realise that those good feelings are building and developing notably, then move on to the next step.

Step Four:

Engage with the surroundings of your run again. This time in much more detail, almost as if your senses have come to life and are sharpened, like everything is fresh and new and exciting.

Notice how the colours are brighter and more vivid, spot more of the details of all that is around you. Notice and tune in to the sounds being even more harmonious, clearer and sharper, and enjoy the feelings developing within you as your senses enliven.

As you do this, imagine that your body is flooded with a deep-rooted sense of contentment that spreads from the base of your brain, the seat of your mind and works its way into your physical body and even nourishes your soul — whatever that means to you and who you are: let it uplift.

Imagine it as a warmth, not in temperature terms, but as a contented warmth and a soothing sense that spreads through your body, glowing and easing, almost as if it is in your blood, working throughout everything that is you.

Get a real sense of this and move on to the next step.

Step Five:

Imagine and allow all/any thoughts to simply bubble up through the mind and out of the head to be dissipated and enjoy some moments of mental calmness as you run effortlessly and enjoyably with a peaceful mind.

Imagine a connection with your surroundings, enjoy feeling connected to the environment of your run and if you want to have any thoughts simply affirm to yourself that, *"Running feels good,"* or, *"I enjoy running."*

Continue that sense of warmth spreading through you, develop that connection with the surroundings and bring it all together and just exist within all of that for a while.

Continue with this step for a healthy period of time and really connect and engage with the good feeling and associate that good feeling (even if it is just an imagined good feeling for now) with the run and the process of running.

Once you think you have spent enough time on this step and you have really associated running with that good feeling, then move on to the next step.

Step Six:

Tell yourself that each time you practice this, it works better and better for you and that when you practice this process during your runs, it becomes increasingly more noticeable and beneficial and that it helps you remain motivated to run and that you enjoy your running experience even more.

Spend a bit of time bringing those thoughts together and then move on to the final step.

Step Seven:

Take a couple of deeper, energising breaths. Wiggle your fingers and toes and open your eyes.

Practice this using self-hypnosis a couple of times, then with some mental rehearsal under your belt, start using this process during your runs to develop and build your own "runner's high" which will serve to enhance your enjoyment of your runs and keep you running.

The Association Cognitive Strategy Of Elite Runners — Using Psychological Profiling:

Later on in this book, I write about using dissociation as an evidence based process for enhancing endurance as a runner. Throughout my own research and exploration on how to use the mind to really develop our running ability, I have also found that related to the research on hypnosis and running, there is much on the cognitive strategies used by runners and a fabulous amount of information about the psychological profile of marathon runners and elite runners for long distance running.

I have been reading a fascinating paper entitled *"Psychological characterization of the elite distance runner"* by Morgan and Pollock *(1977)* and, along with a number of other investigations of a similar ilk, it would seem that elite marathoners in general tend to be introvert — which was initially something I read with sadness because my own psychological profile tends to move in the direction of extroversion. However, this is not universal and several winners of Boston and London marathons have rated as extroverts on the Eysenck Personality Inventory and so there is hope for me yet!

This technique is not about exploring personality or psychological traits though, and that is not really what this entire chapter is about or aimed at. The reason I mention it at all though is because those introverts do tend to be very well skilled with their own active cognitive strategies, that aid them with their running in a wide number of ways.

Whenever I read **Runner's World** magazine or a running blog I subscribe to, I am often barraged by pieces of research showing that runners listening to music tended to recover quicker or run more efficiently in some recent study. I listen to music a great deal when running, particularly on my longer runs, it helps me pass the time and I enjoy the absorption in the music — this is dissociation. It is me classically distracting myself from the detail of how I am really feeling, like when you are battling through fatigue or aches at mile 25 in the marathon and using whatever you can to get you through to the end. Music has other ways it helps us, being uplifting and inspirational and having emotional association that aids us, but it also can distract and aid dissociation.

However, the earlier mentioned study by Morgan *(1977)* showed that despite the prevalence of such, these dissociation strategies were not the main "cognitive strategy" among elite runners. In fact they tended to use an associative strategy.

These elite marathon runners stated that they actually paid very close attention to their own bodies and especially noticed what happened within their legs and feet as well as monitoring their breathing closely.

They also did keep a note of time; heck, these are elite runners. I watch my Garmin a great deal, but these guys are watching it with more interest than I am! However, they generally stated that the pace they adhered to was dictated by how their body felt.

When marathon racing, these elite runners also tended to instruct themselves to relax and keep the muscles loose throughout the race. They tended to be people who dealt with anxiety very well outside of running and though there was much, much more to the research, these are the bits that are relevant to what I am writing about here.

It is far more common to think of runners using dissociative strategies, but these studies all highlight the fact that runners who excel are mentally actively in some shape or form while running. I hope you have realised that by now and at the very least can see the benefits of that.

One such cognitive strategy then, as already suggested here, is that of 'association' and this is particularly prevalent with introverted elite distance runners. I suspect that most of you readers are not elite runners, and so we may not have as much awareness of ourselves when running. Those of you that have only been running for a short period of time may not know your own limits or how to spread out your exertions within your longer runs as successfully as elite runners who rely on such an awareness.

This next process aims to help enhance your ongoing capability awareness when running, as well as use an associative cognitive strategy when running to get a good sense of whether to really push on with your pace, or whether to ease back during a long training run, or a race with a specific desired outcome where it is particularly pertinent.

When I write about an associative strategy, I am referring to one whereby you tune in to how you are: how you feel, how you think and how you are generally. This awareness is often considered unhelpful as it reminds us of pains and aches and tiredness, so many tend to favour dissociative strategies such as those I write about later on in this chapter. I know people who count, who listen to music, who recall lists, who imagine past and future runs and all sorts of things as means of dissociative strategies.

The study suggests that too much dissociation, especially running through considerable pain using dissociation, can cause injury and cause us to ignore real-life issues and problems.

It is shown in the research that having an associative strategy is what helps many elite runners thrive and we'd be foolish not to learn from them. So simply follow these simple steps and develop your own associative cognitive strategy using self-hypnosis, and you can enhance your long training runs and race more effectively.

Get yourself into a comfortable, seated position where you can be receptive, with your arms and legs not touching each other and your feet flat on the floor. Ideally, somewhere that you'll be undisturbed for the duration of this session, then follow the steps outlined here:

Step One:

Induce hypnosis using your method of choice. When you have induced hypnosis move on to Step Two.

Step Two:

Imagine being out on a run. It really needs to be a run you regularly go out on, ideally a run that you will be going out on, whether that is a race or a longer training run.

Be thinking that you are in the first half of this run somewhere and no later.

Take a couple of moments and spend them on developing the scene, the colours, the sights and sounds, and imagine that each step on the run takes you deeper into hypnosis.

Also, think about the outcome for this run. Do you want to complete it in a certain time, or is it a distance to complete, or is it part of a training programme in which you hope to complete a race, or build endurance or reduce weight, or any other desired outcome. Have that in your mind while engaging in this run in your mind.

Continue running, engaging with yourself on the run rather than the environment and when you are really tuned in to how you are on this run, then move on to the next step.

Step Three:

Be mindful and enhance awareness of your body while running.

Notice what sensations you have in various parts of your body. Of course, being a runner, you'll want to check your feet, your calves, your hamstrings and glutes, as well as your lower back, shoulders, stomach muscles and so on.

Notice your breathing. Is it heavy, is it automatic and gentle? Get a sense of whether you are grasping for air or if it is a comfortable means of breathing. Are you breathing from the tummy or the chest?

All of these things you can notice and be aware of, but don't try to change them, just notice them and be aware of them. Also don't try to stop them from changing; if they do, just tune in to how you are during this run.

Be aware of the thoughts you are thinking. Are they comfortable and relaxed, are they quiet, or are they loud, are they stressful and/or doubtful? Get a sense of how they are without changing them.

295

Finally, get a sense of how you are emotionally, note your mood and how you know you have that mood, note it, watch yourself and really ensure you feel tuned in to exactly how you are in this run.

With all that information, particularly awareness of your physiological feelings, use your own cognitions and internal dialogue to tell yourself in your mind what you notice and what you are aware of, almost as if you are giving yourself a report.

Once you have completed the full, in depth report of how you are at this stage of your run, and fully advised yourself of how you are, then move on to the next step.

Step Four:

Assess your ongoing exertion levels and think about how much further you have to go in this run.

Using your internal dialogue and your own cognitions, now make an assessment of how this run is going, based upon how you are feeling physically, psychologically and emotionally. Note how much further you have to go, how you are feeling and what it is going to take to achieve that distance, and how fast you'll be capable of completing that in (taking into account how you feel at this moment).

Report back to yourself on your thoughts and feelings about this run and the remainder of the run.

In accordance with your desired outcome for this run, whether it is a training run, or a race, start to adjust your pace in line with the way your body feels.

Use your own internal dialogue and tell yourself your assessment of the run, then adjust your pace accordingly to ensure you complete the run in the way that is best for you and your desired outcomes, but not necessarily forcing the desired outcome at all costs, just getting as close to it as you possibly can, again, according to your assessment of yourself.

Once you have completed your assessment and delivered it with dialogue to yourself in your mind, then move on to the next step.

Step Five:

Adjust your pace and exertion levels in accordance with your report. Adjust your thoughts, mood, emotions and physical exertion levels in whatever ways you know of, in accordance with your informed report that you delivered to yourself.

Continue with your run, and then repeat Steps Three and Four (as well as the first part of this step) at a latter stage of the same run.

Tell yourself that each time you practice this within a self-hypnosis session, the better you become at doing it within your actual runs and that you do it within your actual runs with more and more ease and fluency.

Then you can move on to the final step.

Step Six:

Exit hypnosis. Take a couple of deeper breaths, wiggle your fingers and toes, open your eyes and think about making plans or taking action to get out on that very run you just imagined.

Practice this self-hypnosis session a few times and then start to apply the associative strategy during your own longer runs and races. When out on your run, you monitor, assess and adjust according to your rehearsed processes.

Remember though, the mental rehearsal is to practice the cognitive strategy and assessment process, not to mentally rehearse the run itself. Your runs will not be (and should not be) dictated by this particular process.

You'll probably want to run through the process more than twice during your runs; I tend to have it ongoing and do it formally 5–10 times during a 20 mile run or a marathon, however, the fluency is such that I can do it fairly quickly more often if I need to.

Many elite marathon runners within the research have an associative strategy as part of their ongoing cognitions throughout a marathon; they continually assess and adjust in just seconds of time.

It is certainly something you can do within a race or long run as well as your dissociative strategies, but just make sure you do not get so dissociated that you never tune in and get the benefits of the associative process, if you want to adopt the same sort of processes of an elite runner.

Using Self-Hypnosis To Raise and Advance Endurance For Running:

To be really, really honest, the results of using hypnosis to enhance muscular performance are not that impressive and do not actually show any real gains.

Reviews by a number of key authors, including Hull *(1933)* and Barber *(1966)* and the very influential (in the field of hypnosis and sports performance) Morgan *(1972, 1980, 1993)* — mostly showed that suggestions given in hypnosis were just as effective as suggestions given to a non-hypnotised, but motivated individual when it came to muscular performance.

However, the really great news for us runners is that numerous studies show that the gains made in terms of endurance and aerobic power are significant when it comes to the use of hypnosis. And I have an evidence based strategy to share with you next.

Most of the research concerning muscular performance and aerobic performance also suggests that hypnosis helps to motivate individuals much more and finds them exerting more effort as a result. This really does assure me as a lot of my own work is focused on those areas.

OK, one of the pieces of research that I have been reading in relation to the next process is by Morgan et al. *(1987)* Facilitation of physical performance by means of a cognitive strategy, in **Cognitive Therapy and Research**, which shows a 32% marked improvement in endurance performance as a result of the strategy employed, compared to the control group. I don't think the nitty gritty details of the study are going to make for compelling reading, especially not for this book, but for anyone wanting to find out more about the methodology and the way in which the study beautifully isolated the maximal aerobic power to be measured, then go read the study.

I thought I'd share a self-hypnosis process that all runners can engage in that is founded upon the evidence based cognitive strategy used in the study, but I have added various facets of other evidence based processes to make it less dry and academic and more usable, in my opinion.

A number of studies that I have encountered (as mentioned previously in this chapter) show that elite athletes often use association techniques for enhanced performance, but that real elite athletes tend to utilise dissociation strategies to enhance their performance with their mind; this process has a dissociation leaning. Long distance runners from Tibet have run 300 miles nonstop in 30 hours using this type of dissociation technique, and many accomplished marathon runners are known to successfully employ similar techniques.

With this process, you are going to mentally rehearse the steps with self-hypnosis and then, ideally, go out and adopt the cognitive strategy when you are running. With practice, your endurance is enhanced as a result, though you have to run some actual miles too, of course.

The idea behind dissociating in this particular way is that you will not perceive the same amount of fatigue, pain, or discomfort while running. You are dissociated.

Get yourself comfortable and in a place where you'll be undisturbed for the duration of this process, ideally sitting in a receptive position with your arms and legs uncrossed, then follow these simple steps:

Step One:

Induce hypnosis using your method of choice. Once you have induced hypnosis, move on to Step Two.

Step Two:

Imagine being out on a run along one of your usual running routes.

Get as vivid a scene as possible inside your mind. Notice the surface of the ground, what it is made of and imagine hearing the sound of your feet stepping and running upon it.

Get an awareness of how you are moving your body as you run along your route. Then start to engage with the surroundings, the colours, the details, notice the sounds all around you, those near and those in the distance and get a general sense of how you feel as you run this route.

Whilst imaging this, tell yourself that you are going deeper and deeper into hypnosis with each step and spend a little while doing this process. Once you have really engaged in the scene and feel that you have deepened sufficiently, move on to the next step.

Step Three:

The next few steps of this session are for you to rehearse the cognitive strategy that you are going to adopt while you run.

Firstly, as you run, you do not speak. You run silently and strongly. You keep a straight face, a blank (almost stern, if anything) expression on your face, relax the facial muscles, letting them be vacant and blank. With this posture and expression, imagine that you are 'psyching' yourself up for your run while you are running.

Practice this internal, blank expression and psych yourself up, and when you start to feel psyched up, yet sure you are not communicating outwardly, move on to the next step.

Step Four:

Secondly, you ensure that you look straight ahead of you only.

While you run, you pick a spot or object in front of you and concentrate on it until you reach it or get sufficiently close to it, then pick another spot to focus on. Think of yourself as aiming for that spot or object, all the time heading for it with determination.

Spend a few moments, imagining that you are focusing on a spot, chasing it down and then chasing down the next in a continuous process of keeping focused ahead of you. When you have done this and are still imagining doing this, move on to the next step.

Step Five:

Thirdly, with each step that you take with your legs, say the word "down" to yourself with real meaning and vigour.

So that as each leg moves to the floor, followed by the other, you are almost repeating a mantra of the word "down-down, down-down" in a rhythmical fashion that matches your footsteps.

Get that steady rhythm occurring and keep it going while keeping the previous two steps instructions going too — blank expression, psyched, looking ahead on a focused spot and repeating the word "down" with each step you run.

Once you have all these elements combined, and are comfortably and automatically continuing, then move on to the next step.

Step Six:

Once you have spent some time practicing this process in your mind and imagination then tell yourself that you are going to include this process in your running, especially your next long run designed to enhance endurance while training.

Then, when you are sure of it, exit hypnosis by counting from 1 through to 5 and bring the session to an end.

I recommend that to get maximum benefit from this process, that you get it practiced in self-hypnosis a few times and really be sure you have the cognitive strategy down to a tee. Then get out there on your long run and start using it to enhance your running endurance.

Overcome The Wall:

Back in 2011, when my race pack for the New Forest marathon had arrived, which included my race number and the course map, there was a lovely section in the brochure for the race where the course is described mile by mile and, within the sentences of beautiful description for the stunning villages, countryside and forest trails that are run through, were subtle mentions of the course being 'undulating' and frequent mentions of 'uphill climbs'.

Therefore, this race is not likely to be anyone's first choice of marathon for achieving a personal best, but I was using it as preparation for 2012's spate of successive marathons that I was running for charity.

In the early days of being a runner, one of those things that used to affect me was the promise of a tough, hilly race such as the New Forest marathon. These days things are different though.

Remember right at the very start of this book I wrote about Roger Bannister achieving the four-minute mile? As soon as runners considered the four-minute mile possible and saw it achieved, it was swept aside as more runners believed themselves capable.

There is a metaphor often told in personal development circles about a circus that was training a baby elephant to perform. From day one, a heavy chain was tied to the baby elephant's back leg and the chain was attached to a strong metal stake that had been fixed and drilled deep into the ground. However much it struggled, the baby elephant could not move beyond the range of the chain's length and stopped trying to escape after a while. Despite growing big and strong, the elephant always assumed that when the chain was attached to the leg, it would not be able to move. Even when later in life, it just had a chain affixed to the leg and not attached to anything else at the other end, it stayed tame and within the distance it had learned, never challenging it further despite being more than capable of walking away.

Many hypnotherapists use similar ideas metaphorically and I often use a notion with my sporting clients that I learned from a 1989 book by Havens and Walters whereby a similar notion is used, but about horses.

The horses are enclosed by an electric fence that gives them a very light electric shock when near and so they learn to stay within its boundaries. Then after a while, the electricity can be disconnected and ribbon used to fence the field they are in and the horses remain within those barriers.

Yet if one horse were to run and jump or power through the ribbon, many others may well follow, much the same as Roger Bannister and the four-minute mile. The focus then becomes more about the beliefs of the individual in relation to what they believe they can achieve.

I can remember when I first knew I wanted to be a hypnotherapist. I had enjoyed the benefits of hypnosis myself to create some well-being in my life. It had a profound effect upon me. I had only met one hypnotherapist and liked him, but he did not run courses of any kind and so I muddled around trying to find the right course for me to train to be a hypnotherapist myself.

I allowed that to be a barrier until I got off my backside many months afterwards and found someone who I liked and resonated well with. This wasted some time that I could have used to be living the life I wanted, the life I created and discovered for myself a few years later.

Often, marathon runners refer to a particular phenomenon and, following a couple of 20 mile races during my last marathon training schedule, I overheard some fellow runners discussing this thing that is known as 'The Wall'.

In running terms, 'the wall' is whereby your body has used up most of its readily available fuel (glycogen) and is trying to find it from your muscles and other resources and, if you have not been replacing that fuel throughout the race, your body can scream and shout and cause the runner a lots of issues — possibly leading them to stop being able to run at all. There is lots of TV footage of people writhing in agony because of this phenomenon of 'the wall'.

Why am I mentioning this then?

Well, of course, the wall is simply a metaphor for such a physio-logical occurrence. A wall is a powerful metaphor in many other aspects of personal development too and that is the metaphor for your benefit with this hypnosis technique.

Many, many runners that I encounter or work with seem to get stuck by the same things in their training or racing. It is amazing. We all experience obstacles, barriers and things that impede our progress towards our goals and sometimes we simply give up instead of breaking through.

When diets fail us, or we lose motivation to exercise, or we do not reach a target set for a race, or we cannot seem to go faster, or we can't let go of a fear of failure that we keep having, or whatever it is that we seem to keep running up against — this next process is designed to help deal with that.

Step One:

Induce hypnosis using your method of choice. Once you have hypnotised yourself, move on to the next step.

Step Two:

Just have a think about something you wish to overcome in relation to your running. Keep that thing in your mind. In my earlier example, I'd wish to overcome the potential fear of running a marathon that is described as very hilly and undulating!

Now as you relax, just reflect on your inner thoughts, not directing your thoughts, just observing them for a few moments.

Become aware of what you are thinking and become aware of how you think. This might seem unusual, just observe yourself and let your beliefs, your abilities roll around in your mind for a few moments. Then have a little think about how wonderful it is going to be to overcome limitations or blocks that may have been getting in the way of achieving that outcome.

Comfortably expand your awareness and allow yourself to be receptive to what is coming up.

Step Three:

From here onwards, allow yourself to use your imagination.

Imagine that there is a barrier or a wall of some sort out there in front of you in the distance. As you get closer you can sense the details of the barrier; the colour of it, the texture, the material it is made of. Be aware of the size of it, which might be parallel to the size of the issue at hand.

Allow this barrier to appear in front of you in whatever way feels and seems right for you.

Here is the key: Imagine that the barrier in front of you symbolises anything that has been impeding your progression toward the running outcome you want for yourself.

Ask yourself what the real reason is that you want to overcome this barrier. A great way to do that is to think again of your desired outcome that exists beyond the barrier and remind yourself of how things are going to be when the barrier is gone from your life and your mind.

Once you have a really vivid idea of how things are going to be once the barrier is gone, then move on to the next step.

Step Four:

Imagine reaching deep inside yourself and finding the determination and inspiration you need and then symbolically and metaphorically get rid of this barrier in your mind.

Really imagine reaching deep inside of yourself to that special place within you where your inner resources are. That place where you know you can achieve wonderful things.

In your mind, go ahead and bash it down. Smash it, destroy it, scrub it out, zap it and erase it in any way that feels right and satisfying to you. Have some fun here and discover how good it feels to have the freedom to move forward and be free of that old wall.

Use whatever power, whatever thoughts, whatever abilities or information you need and remove that barrier. Maybe you blow it up with explosives! Just release it in whatever way feels most suitable and satisfying for you.

Now look out into the clear horizon and see what is there now that you are free of that old wall. Imagining that your running dreams are coming nearer now as a result of your actions.

Inside your mind, celebrate. Shout a few "*Woo-hoo's*" inside your mind. Get some fireworks going off. Maybe you remember other times when you really accomplished something you were proud of. Get that feeling and spread it throughout your body and let yourself feel really good. Get some excitement inside your mind and feel really wonderful to have removed that barrier from your mind and from your life.

Step Five:

Exit hypnosis by counting from 1 through to 5.

You see, with marathon runners, there is no actual physical wall. With the right preparation, the right training, the right attitude, the right actions, the wall is simply avoided and does not exist when you run a marathon.

Any wall or old barrier that may have existed in your mind in the past is just the same. It exists only in your mind. Just as Roger Bannister showed us all.

This chapter was aimed at providing you with a range of techniques and strategies to use in order for you to develop your running specifically. We now alter our focus slightly.

Chapter Fifteen:
Getting The Runner Focused

"Running should be a lifelong activity. Approach it patiently and intelligently, and it will reward you for a long, long time."

Michael Sargent

The appropriate level and depth of focus is not the same for us runners as it is for other sports. Good football players, when playing, often seem to have a broad focus that enables them to be aware of what other players are doing on the pitch and it helps their decision making and passing ability or where to make a run to. Different to that, when taking a penalty kick, the good players manage to block out the whistles of the fans, other players' attempts at distraction and narrow their focus to the part of the goal that they are going to put the ball into.

In his 1992 book, **Psyched to Win**, Nideffer writes about making this distinction and that it is healthy for all athletes to have a variety in their ability to focus. For example, with a broad, external focus the runner can examine the environment and be aware of cadence, the incline and decline in hills, the variety of the surface being run on, the wind and the traffic and other things in the environment that are important to notice. Whereas a depth of internal focus means you react and respond to the environment and how you think during your runs and how you deal with discomfort or slight pains at times and how you make decisions about whether to speed up or slow down at certain times, etc. Focus also helps us to be aware of how we are performing and whether we are keeping to our desired timings, but without it becoming a distraction. We keep our goal and outcome in mind in a healthy way and look to attain that. How we relate to the goal when performing is going to affect our ability to perform.

Nideffer says that good athletes learn to shift rapidly from internal to external and from broad to narrow. This ties in nicely with us having associative and dissociative strategies as discussed in the previous chapter. Effectively dealing with all aspects of focus is important in enhancing performance.

Focusing When Running:

In his 1998 book, *The Inner Game of Golf,* Gallwey suggests that when performing their sport, an athlete should make sure they have three main points of focus. These three points to focus upon are:

Firstly, making sure you give your best every time. Giving the best account of yourself, as much as is possible. This area of focus is all about delivering as good a performance as you are capable of, not just in races and competitions, but also when training, making sure you hit your targets for each session. The effects of training are diminished if that training session is not approached in the best possible way, with the same vigour and enthusiasm as when you are involved in a race with crowds and lots of runners. Don't let anything you do become a chore, get focused and engaged with it.

Secondly, that you pay close attention and fully analyse that performance. This focus is whereby you examine your performance and do all you can to learn from it, use the experience and insight to move forward with more effectiveness. When you run a fabulous race, or get a personal best time at 10km or a half marathon, you can look at the conditions and observe in great detail what you did and how you made that

was depleted. The desire to succeed in business had grown and dominated his life to the exclusion of all else.

The work that we did together in my hypnotherapy consulting room centred around getting him to change his focus. He was to stop worrying so incessantly about his business, because the evidence was there for all to see: his business was being run brilliantly and did very well; even when he was not around, his partner ran the business wonderfully.

He was then to properly attend to the three foci recommended by Gallwey: to give the best performance of which he was capable; to learn something each time he ran by analysing his successes and errors; and, particularly, to enjoy the runs he went on, thus regaining the joy and love for running he had previously.

With the first focus, and in line with the sort of mindfulness techniques we have already examined in this book, he noticed how much his attitude change had affected his performances. Imaging successful outcomes from his runs and races helped him to focus on the enjoyment he could still get from running too. He decided that unless he could enjoy his training, he did not want to race the following year. By being able to relax, to get rid of the tension he was under from his own very high expectations, and to focus on the fun of running in some of the most beautiful parts of the country, he approached his races and runs with a very different attitude.

His running times did improve, his race performances also improved. However, he also decided his future was his business and he wanted to make that more fun too and applied lots of what he did to ensuring his business approach now matched his renewed zest for running. He decided he did not necessarily need to be the best runner in the county anymore either and eased off the pressure he put on himself, enjoyed his runs with less emphasis on winning. It ended up not being all about succeeding on those terms.

If it is not fun, performance suffers. Making an athlete aware of this often rejuvenates an outlook and thus a performance.

I recommend you run through Gallwey's three foci and apply it to your own training and running in some depth.

Jar of Concentration:

I was chatting to a good friend a while ago and we were having one of those "Men are from Mars, Women are from Venus" type conversations. My friend married a girl that we both went to school with and we have all been friends for many years. She would tell us that when they had girls' nights together as teenagers that they would gossip and discuss the boys and talk about every other subject under the sun.

Now, my friends and I often had hearty discussions as teenagers though they were not as lively as the girls by the sounds of it. There was one particular time when we boys did not chat about much at all, when we went to the snooker centre together and played snooker.

Yes indeed, we would be chatty and catch up, order drinks, set the balls on the table, and then communication stopped. We all just concentrated on our game at hand. We studied the table, the balls, the colours. We 'tutted' if someone on a neighbouring table was too loud.

The snooker centre in the town where I grew up was amazing. Lots and lots of tables as far as the eye could see. Smoky halls, little booths where you flicked on a light for someone to come

and take your drinks orders. Wall mounted score keepers…
aaahhh, the memories of it.

We all had our own cues, brought our own chalk for the cues
and we were fiercely competitive with each other. Once the game
was over, we would go into the bar and talk and talk and share
some laughs and have fun and meet with other players, often
the older men that had been playing for years that loved our
enthusiasm for the game, we would have lots of banter and we'd
all communicate again. It is a strange thing to think about.

So is snooker a deeply hypnotic game? I know that it can keep
a group of 18-year-olds in a trance. Have you ever seen a more
hypnotic sport? I know that some people would argue that it just
sends them to sleep, though it is extremely hypnotic and at times
I have found it to be extremely relaxing and exciting and I am
amazed at what those professional players can do with the balls.

Snooker players sum up a lot about what I think you need in
life to be successful — they have to practice and practice and
practice to get to those levels, they have to be focused on what
they want to the exclusion of all else at times, they have to learn
from their mistakes and learn from each other. I know you can
get metaphors to the same effect from most sports, it is just that
back in 2007, I was inspired by one particular young man in the
snooker World Championship.

The hero of that year's tournament, for me, was the losing finalist
— a 23-year-old man by the name of Mark Selby. They call him
'The Jester from Leicester'. Not only was he wonderfully exciting
to watch play snooker, he actually smiles during games! He has
fun, he makes jokes, he entertains, he has a look about him that
is extremely endearing and I really warmed to him, despite that
year being the first time he had broken into the top flight in the

Snooker World championships. Mark Selby seemed to really enjoy what he was doing and I found that so inspiring.

What really amazed me was this guy's stamina too.

First of all, because he was not in the world top 16 rankings prior to the 2007 tournament, he did not get an automatic place in the tournament, so he had to qualify by playing several matches. In the first round, he came from 5–0 down, to win 10–7. In the second round he beat former world champion Peter Ebdon, having trailed 6–2, he won 13–8. In the quarter finals he won 13–12 in a last frame decider. Then in the semi final, he beat another former world champion Shaun Murphy in a gruelling match: having trailed for much of it, he won 17–16! A last frame decider again. Each of these games were hours long and the individual frames were often going on for very long times. The final, which he lost to John Higgins 18–13 went on until the early hours of the morning!

Wow. To maintain that level of mental endurance and concentration for such intense, pressurised lengthy periods of time is just incredible.

I get asked very frequently about how we can increase our powers of focus and concentration and so to round off this chapter on focus and concentration for improving running, I thought I would offer up a simple self-hypnosis technique with you to help you do just that.

If you need to learn how to concentrate when running and develop your focus more as a runner, then here is a simple technique to help you keep focused for longer periods of time.

Step One:

Induce hypnosis using your method of choice. Once you have induced hypnosis, move on to Step Two.

Step Two:

Deepen hypnosis using whatever method you choose or prefer. Once you have deepened sufficiently, move on to Step Three.

Step Three:

As you feel more relaxed, noticing the rhythm of your breathing, maybe it slows down slightly. Allow your breath now to move to other parts of your body. Imagine breathing in to muscles and parts of your body and releasing them, relaxing them and imagine the muscles softening and the nerves in those muscles just becoming still and quiet. Not having to do anymore than is absolutely necessary.

Relax your body in the way you have learned in previous chapters. Once relaxed, move on to the next step.

Step Four:

When you are sure that you have sufficiently relaxed your body and are still focusing on your breathing, now move your awareness to your mind. This is where the key to this technique exists.

Using your imagination, imagine that in front of you is a clear glass jar. The jar is clear, it is clean, even shiny, and it is well and truly empty. Really imagine details of the jar, the textures, the way light reflects off it, the top and bottom of it, what kind of lid it has — really get a good idea in your mind of how this jar is.

As you have been doing, observe yourself now. While you continue to observe yourself, imagine that you unscrew the lid of the jar and remove it for now.

Look closely at this empty jar, become aware that it is waiting to be filled. Imagine it inviting you to put something inside. So this is your chance to let go of any burdens, any distractions, any unwanted thoughts and aspects of routines from your day. Whether they were generated by your activities, your work, any tasks you are wanting to perform, any errands, your travels, your apprehensions, any anxieties, your cares, any discomfort you may be experiencing or any other thing.

Observe carefully now as, one by one, you place them into the jar. Imagine that your mind pours it all from inside of you and places it into that jar. Continue now to fill the jar with any remaining distractions, burdens or unwanted thoughts or feelings.

You can have fun here and be creative. Maybe you can imagine a string of things pouring out from you, or a cloud with all these things inside, all travelling into the jar. Empty it all out in to the jar. Once you have done that thoroughly, move on to the next step.

Step Five:

Carefully and deliberately now, replace the lid on the jar. Give the lid one extra turn.

Breathe deeply now and observe that you stand and begin to carry the jar toward a door. Open the door. Outside, on the front step is a large bin of some kind. Open its lid now and place your jar inside. Know that you may dispose of it now and forever, or return for it at another time if you wish. Put the lid back on the bin, turn away from it, walk back through the door. Lock the door and return to your starting point.

Affirm to yourself something along the lines of, *"I have true clarity of thought and supreme concentration and nothing can interfere with it until I have achieved ___(...)___,"* or something along those lines, using language that appeals to you and resonates with you.

Imagine that you have a focused vision, a level of concentration and focus now that is going to serve you really well with whatever you want to begin focusing on now. Feel it, experience it, imagine brimming over with this focus of mind and imagine generating a state of being focused.

Step Six:

Exit hypnosis by counting from 1 through to 5.

Hold your body in the way you would when you are focused. Hold your thoughts in a way that says, *"I am focused,"* and go about your day or the upcoming run or approach your training with focus. Spend some time getting yourself really focused and engaged when you choose to run and notice how much more you excel — though you may communicate with the outside world a little less!

Chapter Sixteen:
Getting In the Zone For
Running and Racing

"Remember the feeling you get from a good run is far better than the feeling you get from sitting around wishing you were running."

Sarah Condor

When I talk about getting in the zone, it may well be different to what you think I am going to talk about. Here as I mention getting into the zone before a training run or a race, especially a marathon, I am referring to the level of anxiety or arousal that you have before and during the run. We have looked at curbing too much anxiety with the use of relaxation in an earlier chapter, however we are now going to look at developing the optimal levels of arousal.

I am going to illustrate the issue that can sometimes occur when it comes to arousal. In their book, **Foundations of Sport and Exercise Psychology**, Weinberg and Gould *(1999)* describe a piece of research whereby an athletic coach asked his 400-metre runners to run all out, and to exert themselves and give it 110 percent.

Then a few days later, the same runners were asked to run exactly the same distance, but this time to run at 95 percent. The times for the 95 percent run were better than those for 110 percent.

The results of the research were interpreted to suggest that trying to run at 110 percent effort, which may well be considered an over-the-top amount of arousal, resulted in the runners tightening up more than was necessary, including muscles not needed for running. At 95 percent, the muscles not needed for the run remained relaxed, which allowed those muscles that were required for a fast run to function without as much resistance. They became more efficient and effective runners at 95% effort and, as a result, ended up running faster.

This chapter is now all about getting to the optimum level of arousal and practicing getting into *that* zone so that we run faster during our training and races.

Way, way back in 1908, in their work entitled The Relationship of Strength of Stimulus to Rapidity of Habit Formation, Yerkes and Dodson explored the effect of arousal and their work has been a bench-mark used by many throughout the last century.

Their various studies and pieces of research led to the idea of an inverted-U theory when it comes to optimum arousal. It always reminds me of the law of diminishing returns I learned in a college economics class — if one man works in a field, the work gets done slower than if 2 men work the field. If 3 men work that field it gets done quicker and likewise for 4 men. However, if you put 10,000 men in that field, there would be too many and it would not get done effectively or as the field owner might wish. Likewise, our inverted-U theory means that you get better performance as you exert more effort and have more arousal, but then when there is too much arousal, the performance is mal-affected and diminishes.

Throughout the years, as with most long-standing and pioneering theories, there have been several modifications and challenges to this theory, though the basic idea of the inverted-U has general acceptance, which is that performance increases with arousal up to some level, but arousal beyond this level interferes with performance. More modern research has gone on to indicate that different athletes have various best arousal levels, and it has also been confirmed that each runner has a unique optimum amount or level of arousal for their own best performance, and performance is diminished when arousal is under or over this level. This optimum level is now viewed as a range, that is, a zone.

The zone varies greatly throughout various sports, as you'd expect, and it also varies within individuals. Many theorists and researchers suggest that you do not just need moderate levels of arousal to achieve best performance, but all this debate and discussion is not what you are after.

I want to help you find out that optimum performance zone for yourself and teach you how to spend more time in it, so that you can train and race in that zone. Follow these simple steps for getting in that optimum zone.

Step One:

Induce hypnosis using your method of choice. Once you have induced hypnosis, move on to the next step.

Step Two:

Imagine an occasion when you performed really well. Ideally, an occasion when your arousal level prior to a run was spot on; maybe this is a time when you ran at your optimum level or a time when you felt you were really in the zone. If you struggle to think of an exact occasion, you can imagine and create one, or you can choose a time that was very close to being perfectly in the zone.

When you have engaged all your senses in this, seeing, hearing, and feeling this occasion or instance in your mind, start to examine how the body feels and become aware of what your mind is doing — what are your thoughts, ideas, internal dialogue?

In most people, when asked to explain this in words to me in a hypnotherapy session, they'll use words along the lines of relaxed, strong, focused, concentrated, confident, and smooth.

It does help to express in words what the feelings are, so tell yourself what words best describe your feelings when you are in the zone — you may even find the feelings themselves start to become more noticeable as you mention them.

Once you feel that you have imagined the optimum arousal as best as you can and even started to feel some of those accompanying feelings, now imagine a large scale of some sort, perhaps like a thermometer, or a large dial or scale of some kind that goes from 0 to 200. Get the colour of it clear in your mind and notice the variety of details to have it vividly in your mind.

Notice that when you are performing at your optimum level of arousal, the scale sits nicely at 100. That is what we aim for as often as possible; 100. This is the arousal level that we now refer to as your best performance level.

Step Three:

Next up, now imagine an occasion when your level of anxiety and arousal was too high for you to perform to your best. Maybe this was an occasion when you experienced an excessive amount of anxiety that impaired your performance.

As you imagine that, notice what you see and hear and start to notice how the body and mind feel. As we did in the previous step, start to explain this, using words to yourself. When I do this with my own hypnotherapy clients, the kinds of words that are typically used are words like tense, worried, distracted, uncertain, weak and unfocused.

Now look at your scale so that you can see that the scale is now reading somewhere in the region of 130, 140 or even 150; just see where it is for you and really notice the difference. Once you have spent the right amount of time on this anxiety-laden experience and have a good, clear idea of how the scale is different, then move on to the next step.

Step Four:

Now it is time for you to practice how to bring the scale down. You can of course just imagine bringing it down using your imagination and letting the scale alter your feelings. This might work better when you are practiced at this. However, we want you to get a real physiological sensation and physical evidence for the scale coming down in the first instance.

Start to practice bringing the scale down to 100 (the optimal level) by using your breath. Each time you inhale, say the word 'strong' or 'focus' to yourself — use any word that you can then go on to associate with optimum performance.

When you then exhale, start to say the 'relax' or 'smooth' or 'soften' to yourself and imagine the scale then goes down 10 or 15 points or so. As the breath goes out, the scale will come down 15 or 20 points, about halfway back to 100.

So when you inhale, you gain poise, strength and focus and when you exhale you relax and ease yourself towards that optimum 100 mark.

Aim to get yourself feeling strong and confident, while letting go of excess tension.

When learning to breathe effectively, breathing using the rib cage and the diaphragm will ensure that you bring in much more air. Push the tummy out when you inhale and draw it in when you exhale and use the lower torso to breathe more deeply and effectively. As you practice using this breathing technique to get the arousal level to 100, once you have practice lots of times, you find that breathing this way prior to a race, helps you do that when you are not hypnotised too.

Allow a few breaths to help you get your scale to 100, and ensure that you feel that you have achieved a controlled and optimum state of mind and body. When you are sure of that, move on to the next step.

Step Five:

Now we are going to test rigorously!

So now imagine being in another troublesome and problematic, over-anxious experience once again. Practice running through the previous steps and reducing the scale and get it to 100. Practice doing this with another 2 or 3 examples to really get confident on how to do this.

You'll start to find that when the scale reads 100 more often inside your mind as you think of these previous experiences, optimum performance will come much more naturally and you are almost starting to reframe previous poor experiences.

Remember also, this does not have to be experiences of only being nervous or anxious before an event. It can also include reducing anxiety and creating optimum arousal during an event of some kind too; in the middle of a marathon or a race when the crowds are cheering you or you are feeling a certain way about your current time, for example.

Step Six:

Exit Hypnosis. Open your eyes, wiggle your fingers and toes and start to practice your breathing prior to training and any races you run. The more you do this, the more easily it'll start to happen by itself too, as a matter of course.

There you have it, a self-hypnosis process for developing the right level of arousal when running. Practice really does make perfect with this process, so get practicing.

Chapter Seventeen:
Recovery and Recuperation

*"We may train or peak for a certain race, but running is
a lifetime sport."*

Alberto Salazar

Some of the earliest recorded uses of hypnosis-like 'states' used
in Greek and Egyptian sleep temples, as well as the precursor to
modern hypnosis, Mesmerism, were all focused on the ability to
heal and recover. As we have explored in previous chapters, the
ability to self-heal is demonstrated with the placebo effect as well
as many works of varying kinds in modern health science.

When I put on my compression stockings after my long run,
whilst sipping my cherry juice, massaging my legs on the foam
roller or whatever other process I have found to be fashionable
and convincing at that stage in my running career, I always
engage my mind to enhance my recovery too.

Ievleva and Orlick *(1991)* demonstrated that positive internal
dialogue, mental imagery focused on recovery, and goal setting,
all enhanced recovery from injury. Within this chapter, I offer
you a number of mental imagery techniques combined with
hypnosis to mobilise your inner resources to speed and enhance
your recovery from races and training runs as well as injury.

Using Self-Hypnosis To Aid Recovery and Enjoy The Benefits Of A Massage:

Whenever a runner has started getting into the first few weeks
of a training schedule working towards an event or race of some

kind, that runner may have gotten a few aches and pains as the mileage starts to increase.

First of all here, then, I am offering up a process to aid your recovery after your runs. Your long runs in particular. You can continue to use the upcoming hypnosis session throughout your training as an ongoing part of your training for after your long run or any other time you feel you need it; but to get it working really well for you, it requires some practice.

In the summer of 2010, when my miles were increased greatly in the middle of my training for that summer's two marathons, training in the heat for those two multi-terrain marathons, I started aching more than I usually did in my marathon preparations.

One of the biggest challenges I faced was recovering. I am no longer a twenty-something whose body responds to exertion with the greatest of ease. I am at that age where I get up to use the toilet in the night, and yes my legs tend to feel sore after my weekly long run and they scream at me during my speed sessions.

Added to that, I had incorporated some weight training aimed, at the muscles I use when running, to enhance my speed and strength, and it is that which I was feeling at that stage of my training schedule. Especially in my lower back following sessions aimed at my core.

I do go and see a sports massage therapist, though not as often as I would like and do see other great people who tend to me, though I never lose track of what my own mind is capable of, and use self-hypnosis at any and every opportunity to help along the way.

In previous chapters here, I have offered up a range of processes aimed at helping enhance performance when running. Now, I thought I'd offer up a couple of really simple and basic self-hypnosis process that anyone can run through to help ease aching muscles, speed up healing and advance recovery. Which of course also aids performance.

It is not a strategy or a technique borne out of a deeper therapeutic process, it is more of a mental imagery technique which any runner can apply to himself. Many therapists sometimes look for underlying psychological causes to physical problems, but that is not an approach one can adequately administer by oneself and not one that I hold much stock in anyway. Follow these simple steps for a hypnotic massage.

Step One:

Induce hypnosis using your method of choice. When you have induced hypnosis, move on to Step Two.

Step Two:

You are going to engage your imagination in a number of ways now. Firstly, we want to warm you and your muscles up.

Imagine you are in a natural environment of some kind: a favourite place in nature. Notice the sights, colours, sounds, and how wonderful it makes you feel to be in this place of your own choosing. Really get a vivid notion of the surroundings.

Imagine lying with a balanced and comfortable posture, in a position that you feel relaxed in. Start to imagine the sunshine naturally and gently warming your legs, your back, your shoulders. The heat is so softly warm, at exactly the right temperature for you.

As a side note, you may have seen what my own colouring is like: I am a red head. When people ask me to imagine lying on a beach, I tend to think, *"No! When I am at a beach the sun burns me!"* So you need to adapt this notion at this stage to your own level of comfort and suitability.

Just imagine and feel the sun warming and easing your muscles. Take some time to let the sun's rays work their way into your muscles, imagine them relaxing and softening and do take some time to consciously let go of any lingering tension.

As you relax deeper, imagine and sense that the rays of the sun are directed to those places within your back, shoulders and legs (and/or any other place where they are needed) that need it the most.

You might start to notice that as you focus your attention on relaxing and warming the body, that you start to develop some mental calmness too and notice your breathing relaxing.

As the sunshine continues to warm and soothe you, imagine that it is slowly and deeply easing and allowing you to let go of any discomfort. You might imagine a change in colour to represent this happening, you might imagine a sound soothing it, you might just notice a change (however subtle) in actual sensation in those areas.

Spend as much time as it takes for you to notice something tangible as you imagine being warmed, soothed, and letting any discomfort ebb away. Once you notice that difference occurring, then move on to the next step.

Step Three:

Now imagine the goodness and benefit of the sunshine is moving deeper and into your bones. Imagine them moving into place and soothing and feel a shift in how you hold your body in the most optimum and balanced posture. Imagine this happening beneficially and gently enhancing your comfort.

Let the light move towards the sources of any previous discomfort, warming and soothing and working into those places, relaxing and loosening.

This is the start of the healing. Let yourself relax and warm-up deeply and allow your mind to become more clam and focused. Allow yourself to smile as you heighten your awareness of how much good you are doing yourself and getting ready for the next, even more progressive step.

Step Four:

Continue to engage in the surroundings, smell the air, let it soothe your senses and enhance your calmness, notice the sounds and enjoy basking in the relaxing position you are in.

Now imagine that a number of beautiful looking hands appear directly in the space above your back and legs. Sense that you are comfortable with them, let the numbers be the amount that will help you the most. Imagine them to be magic, healing and beneficial to you and your recovery and healing.

You can watch and feel what happens now as the hands start to gently and deeply work on your back, legs, shoulders and anywhere else that requires it. Notice the hands going to the areas that need it the most.

Notice them massaging gently but deeply: it is almost as if they know the perfect pressure to apply for you to sense that it is really doing you some good.

You might imagine each warmed muscle now feeling as if it is melting and letting go of any tiniest traces of tension and discomfort. The heat remains and helps the process.

Imagine that the hands are absorbing any discomfort, removing it and letting it go. Imagine a sense of relief as the hands move along and through the muscles. Let the massage benefit each muscle, tendon, fibre and then let every bone get a sense of relaxing and letting go.

Spend as much time as is necessary for you to notice a difference in sensation as you engage your imagination with this step. When you are really noticing the benefits, then move on to the next step.

Step Five:

Now you let the hands start to manipulate a bit more, not just the soft tissue of the body, but also flexing the joints and allowing everything to slot into its correct place, making any beneficial adjustments. Allow each muscle and bone to find its correct place and enjoy the sensation of knowing things are healing.

Imagine repairs starting to happen more rapidly than usual, and notice a continued sense of relief and letting go of old, lingering discomfort.

All the time, you enjoy this calming your mind, and allow yourself to continue with a satisfactory smile that tells you and your mind that you are benefiting from this process beautifully.

Let any last remnants of tension leave the body, let the hands continue until that happens and then let them disappear, and spend some time basking in a sense of weightless, soothing, warming comfort.

Bask in that for as long as you feel you need to get the maximum healing and enhanced recovery.

Step Six:

You can return here whenever you choose. Tell yourself that each time you come here and run through this process it works even better and the benefits increase.

Then you exit hypnosis by counting yourself out from 1 through to 5, and go about your day feeling better and letting the feelings continue to be felt.

The Hypnotic Mud Bath:

When I was younger, I lived for a few months on a Kibbutz and have written in some of my other books about some of my experiences during this time and my other travels. After living for a while in Nacscholim, Israel, I got to travel to the Dead Sea in Jordan.

This is not about me reminiscing, but furthering the theme of this chapter about mental imagery processes combined with self-hypnosis, so I shall not indulge myself too much further with my recanting tales of old. But if you have ever floated in the Dead Sea for a while, you appreciate that, whether it is because of the minerals, or whether it is because so many people told you it was good for you, you feel good being in there.

It led me to fancy going and plunging myself into one of those mud baths. So I went to a local one and I have since been to others; one in particular was on the periphery of the volcanic Greek island of Santorini. You get to wallow in mud and minerals and sit with it on you for a while before you swim into the sea and wash it all off.

Again, it feels good, I have to say. I have only fond memories of hanging out in mud.

Mud, mud, glorious mud, eh?

When your weight gets suspended and you firmly believe in the healing properties of that thick, gloopy, gooey, brown stuff you are in, then you respond accordingly. It is that premise that I am relying on for this next self-hypnosis process.

There are all kinds of processes similar to the one I am sharing here, and this is just my own adaptation of such. If you fancy gaining all benefits of a mud bath, without all the actual mud, then this is just the ticket for you. Many believe that mud is good for the skin, good for the joints and for aching muscles and much more besides. Follow these simple steps.

Step One:

Induce hypnosis using your method of choice. Once you have induced hypnosis, move on to Step Two.

Step Two:

Imagine you are in a natural environment of some kind: a favourite place in nature. Notice the sights, colours, sounds and how wonderful it makes you feel to be in this place of your own choosing. Really get a vivid notion of the surroundings.

Imagine that the temperature is just right for you and create in your mind the most perfect day for you. Notice the air around you, how it smells and seems and really tune in to this place in nature. Only move on when you have got that firmly and vividly in your mind.

Step Three:

Look all around you and notice and locate a pool of water. See the light glittering and glimmering on the surface of the water. Watch the surface of the water, notice how calm it is and allow yourself to relax in response to it.

Start to imagine that the water is just the right temperature for you. That it looks inviting, clean, beautiful, revitalising and you anticipate how it is going to feel to get in.

When you are certain that you have imagined exactly how you'd like it to be, then dress accordingly and take a step into it.

Be assured that this is your own creation, your own private place that only you can attend. You can just be at one with yourself here and enjoy it deeply, and imagine stepping deeper and comfortably deeper into the water. It is the right temperature, it feels wonderful on your skin. Engage in this for a while in your mind until you are at a comfortable depth to just relax and be calm as you are supported by the water.

Notice and imagine the various parts of your body relaxing. Spend some time using whatever progressive relaxation technique or process you know here, to just enhance your relaxation while you are in this pool. When you are suitably relaxed, then move on to the next step.

Step Four:

Look deeper down and around you and start to notice that in places there is a soft white mud. Put your feet into it and feel the sensation in your toes, you may even place your hand in and notice how smooth, soothing and nice it is.

With the initial touches, start to notice your body relaxing further. Then in your own time and in your own way, start to allow yourself to sink slowly and easily and comfortably into the mud. Deeper and more enjoyable. It is a delight to the senses as it starts to be felt all over your body.

Notice the feel of the mud around your joints. Notice how your muscles respond and react to the depth of relaxation that the mud instils. Imagine the goodness of the mud starts to find its way into your muscles and joints and it soothes, relaxes and comforts deeper and deeper.

You may even like to imagine being cleansed deeply in whatever way you find to be useful and beneficial.

Now take this relaxation and soothing quality a step further and imagine that the mud draws out any discomfort from your muscles and joints. Imagine that it absorbs any discomfort and takes it away, lost in the pool.

Let the time you spend here be one of healing. Whatever that may mean to you personally, imagine yourself being healed and rejuvenated and bask in this glorious sensation for as long as it takes for you to notice some tangible difference in how you feel as a result of the healing mud.

Relax in the mud. Just be at one with yourself in the mud. Wallow and love it.

Step Five:

Once you have spent enough time enjoying the healing sensation, then start to move up and out and away from the mud, into the clearer water that cleans off all the remaining mud, leaving you feeling more refreshed and invigorated and comfortable.

You might like to dry yourself naturally with the warming rays of the sun, or towel yourself down. Let the sensations of well-being stay with you, notice the difference in how your muscles and joints and body all feel and encourage these feelings to stay with you for longer.

You can then dress and prepare yourself for bringing this session to an end and engaging with the world once again. Remind yourself that each time you choose to do this, it works better and more powerfully and progressively.

Step Six:

Exit hypnosis by counting from 1 through to 5 and go about your day enjoying all those benefits.

Go have a wallow!

The Rejuvenation Tree:

I wrote this part of this book on what was a new day for me in more than the usual sense. I had just run my 4th consecutive city marathon in the space of 3 weeks. I rested, and rested and ate… and ate a lot more… I could feel how all the naughty weeks of eating and far less activity had affected me physically and even made me feel a tad different in other ways too.

I had just started back with my plan of action for getting into prime shape for a holiday due in a couple of months and started training for my next marathon later that year.

Yet all that food and drink seemed to have turned me into an old man. I felt like my posture had gone crooked, and that I was somehow as withered as when my garden plants have not been watered adequately, and I felt in need of some renewal.

Whilst investigating and exploring my own archives for a self-hypnosis approach to get me on track with my training then, I encountered a process that has been used to help deal with osteoporosis, but has also been used for a wide range of applications, and the metaphor inherent within the process meant I got to indulge myself in some fantasy… Lord of the Rings style.

You'll maybe not be as avid a fan of **Lord of the Rings** as I am, so allow me to introduce to you the Ents. In Tolkien's books, the Ents are an ancient species of trees, referred to as the shepherds of the trees and though they look like trees, they are able to talk, reason, feel, understand and possess the wisdom of anyone who lives for hundreds of years, and are pretty tough beings too. Gimli, as with most dwarves, not a big fan of Forests, or Ents, is quoted as saying:

"Talking trees! What would trees have to talk about except the consistency of squirrel droppings?"

Most wouldn't, I suppose, but I found that to be very funny.

Trees are central to our process here, and though I used the imagery I associated with Ents from my early teenage years, you do not have to use the same imagery. In fact, I urge you to tailor this type of session, as with most of the processes that I share in this book, in the way that suits you the best.

Essentially, you are going to liken yourself to, and represent yourself as, a tree within this process and use it to invigorate, refresh, strengthen and enhance. It can be used to revitalise, to rejuvenate and also to get energised and driven, as well as to feel healthier and recover more effectively.

Get yourself into a place where you'll be undisturbed for the duration of this session, sitting or lying down, with your hands and feet not touching each other and then follow these simple steps.

Step One:

Induce hypnosis using your method of choice. Then when you have induced hypnosis, move on to the next step.

Step Two:

Imagine yourself in a private place in nature. Let there be plenty of space around you. Become aware of the colour of the sky, the weather, the temperature and design the environment to suit you.

Notice the colours and shades of light as well as the sounds; sounds that are nearby and those further away in the distance.

Importantly though, as you create this place in your mind, central to this area, ensure there is a tree. A tree that shares qualities that you have, a tree that is representative of who and how you are.

You may choose for it to be a huge ancient Oak tree. Or perhaps a sprawling, draped Willow tree. Perhaps even a fruit tree, or a flowering magnolia, choose and imagine whatever is right for you and whatever suits you and your own preferences best.

Just engage in this environment, tell yourself that each thing you see, hear and feel takes you deeper inside your mind and take some time to get this place just right for you. When you have really created this environment with the tree in the centre of it, then move on to the next step.

Step Three:

Notice that the health of the tree seems poor at the moment. Notice what it is about the tree that demonstrates that to be true currently.

Perhaps it seems weak, perhaps it seems to be drooping, perhaps the colours show this.

Maybe the tree gives off a sense of how it feels right now.

However you notice it, just become aware that the tree is not at its optimum level of health at this time. When you get a sense of that, move on to the next step.

Step Four:

Imagine that you reach deep into your mind to find what it is that this tree needs right now.

You might imagine changing the weather, making it rain powerfully, and then shining the sunshine upon it. You may imagine the perfect tree food, compost, solution and you pour it around the roots of the tree. You may imagine digging around the base of tree and feeding the tree in some way before filling it all back in again. Find all the nutrients and water and other elements that the tree needs right now and begin to deliver them to the tree.

Continue to tell yourself that each thing you give the tree takes you deeper and deeper inside of your mind, and once you have spent a good period of time delivering all this wonderful goodness to the tree, then move on to the next step.

Step Five:

Watch the tree absorb and almost consume all these nutrients and this goodness. Start to imagine it and watch those nutrients now being drawn upwards and inwards into the tree. Imagine the roots drawing it all upwards, imagine the leaves soaking up the goodness and start to notice change happening within the tree.

Notice the leaves changing into a healthier, more vibrant colour. Watch the tree standing upright and looking firmer and stronger. Let that goodness and healthiness be discovered by each and every branch, twig, leaf and beyond. Notice the vibrancy, the rejuvenation and the invigoration spreading through the tree.

Continue to take as long as you require on this step to ensure that the tree is notably different, vibrant, invigorated, stronger and altogether more healthy, and when you are absolutely certain the tree is that way, move on to the next step.

Step Six:

Now imagine that you are experiencing something similar within yourself.

Imagine goodness coursing through your veins. Imagine your bones getting stronger. Imagine colour filling your cheeks and skin. Imagine your hair having a healthy shine, imagine a sparkle in your eyes, a smile on your face and imagine your posture changing, firming up and that the crown of your head is pointing upwards above you.

Adjust your posture, take a couple of good deep breaths, continue to engage in this and imagine the changes happening to you, imagine nutrients reaching you and all the time tell yourself that you are feeling healthier, more energised and invigorated and rejuvenated.

When you start to really notice some difference within yourself, move on to the next step.

Step Seven:

Now start to think about the day ahead of you, or think of things you plan to do. Imagine being there, doing those things with vigour and enthusiasm. Really see the sights, hear the sounds and feel the satisfaction of getting this done and notice how people react and respond to you. Notice how good you feel.

Tell yourself that you are certain this is going to happen, and when you have undeniably convinced yourself of this happening, when you believe that you are absolutely going to do this thing and let yourself get driven, then move on to the next final step.

Step Eight:

Take a couple more big energising breaths and wiggle your fingers and toes, then count from 1 through to 5, and open your eyes to bring yourself out of hypnosis and bring the session to an end.

Practice this a few times to really get it lodged into your mind and then notice how you shook off any old, unwanted slump.

Mind Detox:

In the world of persuasion and influence, there is a much quoted law of contrast — for example, a clever estate agent may show a potential house buyer a run-down, overpriced home before taking them to the one that they have targeted for their client, with the aim of the targeted property then being seen as even more desirable in contrast to the shabby house.

I was once given a demonstration of the power of contrast at a seminar that illustrated the idea well. The seminar speaker brought 3 buckets of water on to the stage: One was filled with hot water, one with lukewarm water, one with very cold water. He asked a couple of volunteers from the audience to place one hand on the hot water and at the same time place the other in the cold water for about 30 seconds to get used to the temperature. Then, they were asked to place both hands in the lukewarm water and say what they felt.

Of course, one hand felt warm and the other cold, yet the water was the same temperature — the contrast to the previous bucket had altered how each hand responded to the lukewarm water.

At the beginning of each new year, lots of people strive to achieve their new year resolutions and set about getting fit and healthy. I notice that when I am out running and training at that time of year, there are lots more people out and about running in very new-looking running gear. Certainly a lot more than there were at the end of the previous year.

Lots of the individual clients I work with at that time of year also embark upon one of many ways of detoxing. They are drinking lots of certain fluids, taking certain supplements and eating certain types of food, to stimulate their kidneys, livers and flush out their body following the excesses of the previous year or just to help kick off their new healthy regime, or maybe it is something they do each year.

Because my work has been so filled with this clean-living detox mentality throughout the years, this is the reason I laugh so heartily at the stark contrast of the big happy legions of people in the crowds at the world darts championships that gets its TV coverage in the new year.

Now, I have tended to pride myself on the fact that I have devoted myself to sports of different kinds throughout my life. I run marathons as well as lots of other races, I have played a high standard of football and make a great armchair pundit and can find myself quite excitable viewing all mainstream sports, events and occasions — live or on TV.

All I have to say with regards to the darts coverage I have seen — hilarious and brilliant. I guess most may think me passé or common, but have you ever seen such consistently happy groups of people having such a fabulously fun time at a sports event?

Maybe it is the amount of accompanying beer-swilling going on, but it seems like a real celebration of human spirit. Each player comes on to loud music, has a quality nickname, before each game everyone chants in unison, "LET'S PLAY DAAAAARTS" — it is wonderful. And when someone scores a 180, well, I have run out of words to describe the noisy joy that fills the rafters in Frimley Green's Lakeside establishment! I have found myself watching it and laughing and also enjoying the sporting and co-ordination skills of the players.

The reason that this was such a contrast to the healthy, detoxing band of people that I encounter each new year, is that if you gaze around the room filled with darts fans, they were all swigging beer, smoking cigarettes aplenty (prior to the smoking ban here in England) and to attempt to say this in the most diplomatic way; there are very few 'waif-like' waistlines in the place. This seemingly care-free group of people make me laugh as I enjoy the contrast between them and many other people that I encounter during the first couple of weeks of each new year.

Don't get me wrong, I am not championing one over the other. I have encountered many people who believe that a detox is a wonderful thing to do and reported great benefit. I also firmly believe that beer swilling, high octane laughter and engaging entertainment is wonderfully therapeutic in the right measure.

What I want to share with you finally for this chapter, though, is a way to detox your mind and body using your thoughts, with a view to enhancing recovery when you are doing a lot of running. Imagine if you could cleanse your body and your mind by just using your thoughts. Regardless of whether you believe in purity of the body or pleasures of the flesh (sounds very sordid!), you

349

can use your mind to cleanse it all. Let me show you how in some simple steps:

Step One:

Induce hypnosis using your method of choice. Once you have induced hypnosis, move on to Step Two.

Step Two:

Using your imagination, in the area just above your head, imagine that floating up there is an energy of light, pure light, floating just above your head. Let the light be the size, colour, shape and dimensions that suit you the most or that you find most appealing or healthy.

You know that your body often knows how to do a great deal more than you consciously know. If you fell over and cut your knee, you would trust it to heal itself without you actually knowing what exactly your body is doing to heal, wouldn't you? Now imagine that the light has that wisdom, an energy, that 'know-how' to it. Imagine that it has the ability to heal, to help to access the wisdom of your mind and body to cleanse, to create a very balanced and healthy condition in your body. A condition of enhanced recovery.

Shortly, you are going to allow this light to slowly move down through the top of your head and to permeate and penetrate each and every cell in your body. That cleansing, healing light, guided by your thoughts, is going to travel slowly through, purifying, updating, healing and letting go of what it no longer needs.

When that light begins to move through your body, it then removes and collects anything unwanted and releases substances or toxins that your body is better off without. Imagine that the light neutralises it.

The light is going to move through and restore a condition of optimum health in every cell, leaving behind a condition that is for optimum health in the cells, the blood, the organs; removing and releasing anything that you are better off without.

Step Three:

Now give that light some movement — guide the light with your intention and focus, let that light begin to slowly move down through your body.

Tune in to the light and feel the energy of it slowly touching the top of your head, moving into every aspect of it. Some people say they feel a vibration or a warmth; just tune in to it and experience whatever you experience. Let it move down slowly through your head; anything unwanted at all is collected by the light and held onto.

Really use your imagination at this stage, notice that as that light slowly moves down through different areas, you can imagine that more and more particles collect within the light, let it continue moving slowly down through your body. You can allow your mind to know what the particles represent and what you are freeing yourself of.

Step Four:

As well as concentrating on the light itself, really notice the condition that it leaves behind. Make a difference between the colour of where the light has been, contrasted with where it is going. Maybe you prefer to notice the sensation or the sound of the area that is cleansed, choose how to recognise the difference for yourself. How do you notice that it has been cleansed and healed?

Make sure that the light moves down around and into the muscles you use most when running, including your heart and lungs as well as your arms and legs.

Allow that light to create the most optimum condition of health in every cell in your body, notice how much it collects, how much you can let go of.

Step Five:

Once the light has reached the tips of your toes, let it float away from your body. Just imagine it floating further and further away until it gets so far away that it becomes just so tiny and then you notice that it disintegrates into little sparkles and twinkles that float far, far away into the universe and beyond. Just let go and imagine them gone.

Step Six:

Trust your body, turn this over to your body and allow it to have that wisdom to heal. Accept your body and allow it to heal, to be healthy and strong.

Tell yourself that during the night tonight as you sleep your body will become healthier, stronger in every cell, down to every atom, healthier and stronger, and that this process continues to rejuvenate you throughout the next day.

Step Seven:

Exit hypnosis by counting from 1 through to 5.

Start to make all or any of these techniques an integral part of your training and get your recovery advanced and your performance enhanced.

Chapter Eighteen:
The Energised Runner

"May the road rise up to meet you. May the wind be always at your back."

Irish Proverb

I want to round things off by giving you three processes designed to help you have more energy. Be healthy and appropriate with this stuff. What I mean is, make sure that you trust you are healthy and listen to what your body tells you. If you are ill or injured, then don't go using your hypnosis skills to boost your energy levels to your own detriment.

The Energy Orchestra:

I have written often about people needing to make a concerted effort with their running and training, an effort to be disciplined, motivated and diligent. A number of years ago, following a blog entry on this theme of making an effort, I got a response from a lady who told me that effort should not be needed and that people needed inspiration. I think she wanted lightning bolts coming from the sky, which I did not think was all that practical.

Often, when I suggest to my clients that I have some continuing work for them to do outside of the face-to-face sessions together, they sigh with a sense of despair. They want the hypnotherapist to zap them without them having to do any work requiring effort.

Often, when my students are happily staring at me teaching them in class, when I tell them to get into pairs to do a practical exercise, they make a sound not too dissimilar to a teenager being asked to go to bed before midnight by his parents. A sort of cross between a groan and a whine.

Why is it that people do not necessarily like stepping into action? Even if it will undoubtedly result in their own betterment?

Runners sometimes can get into bad habits and suffer from the same lethargy at times. It seems that as soon as you hand over the effort to them, the very energy keeping them breathing and living seems to drain out of them right before your eyes. It is crazy: worse and more noticeable than when someone claims to have seen a ghost.

Apparently, according to a non-evidence based article I read in a tabloid newspaper, Paul McKenna is the most unread bestselling author in the UK. That is, many, many millions of people invest in his books, but never actually read them: it takes some effort to read. And then even more effort to actually understand the concepts in the book, and a colossal amount more effort to then apply the strategies and techniques to yourself and your own life, doesn't it? I know many people will think the same about all the effort required to engage with the processes in this book.

> *"Uurgh… Can't you just wave a magic wand over me and make things change without all that fuss?"*

Oh come on!

Firstly for this chapter then, I want to show you how to get more energised for change, more energised for running and more energised for training with a fabulous self-hypnosis technique. Follow these simple steps.

Step One:

Induce hypnosis using your method of choice. Once you have done this, move on to Step Two.

Step Two:

Now imagine yourself seated in a large, magnificent theatre. Make it of your own design entirely. The seats are coloured in your favourite colour, or a most conducive colour; note the surroundings, get a sense for this place that you create in your own mind.

You can hear that the orchestra is playing your favourite music. Just enjoy it for a few moments.

Also, there are many people in the theatre. As you look around, you notice that everyone is happy and contented and enjoying themselves. So soak up the atmosphere and let that deepen your state of receptivity and relaxation.

Step Three:

You notice that the people there are all smiling naturally and enjoying the music as much as you are.

As the orchestra continues to play, your attention focuses on the orchestra leader, for as he conducts the orchestra, he uses both hands, holding a baton in one hand. This baton controls the pace and tempo of the music and it fascinates you. Get absorbed in what he does for a few moments.

As the baton gradually slows down the music, you feel yourself becoming even more deeply relaxed. And when the music stops, there is complete cessation of movement and complete silence and complete relaxation. Every nerve and every muscle in your body is relaxed and you feel very connected.

Now, as you let yourself drift awhile, you become even more relaxed. Your attention now focuses on the orchestra leader who has turned around to face the audience. See him take a bow. As you gaze at the orchestra leader, you see that he is moving in your direction. As he nears you, you recognize him as a representation of your mind. That's it — he represents your mind!

Step Four:

You go ahead and greet each other; he holds a mirror in front of himself. You gaze into the mirror and see yourself.

And as you are looking at your own reflection, your mind (this man or woman) is telling you that you love and approve of yourself. You feel this so strongly, that you repeat it to yourself, over and over again. You feel so good that you want to tell everybody in the room just how good you feel.

Now here comes the fun. Without any hesitation, you stand up and tell everyone in a loud and clear voice that you love and approve of yourself. It fills you with energy just to exclaim it! You look around and as you sit back down, they begin clapping their hands. They liked what they heard you say.

Your mind smiles at you and asks you to look back into the mirror and to make a wish for something that you would really like to happen. Ideally, to be more appropriately energised.

Then go ahead and imagine that what you had wished for (increased enthusiasm and energy) is really happening in the mirror. Suddenly the mirror becomes a giant movie screen and you and all of the people in the room are viewing your wish coming true. At the end of the scene, everyone applauds you. You are touched so deeply that you want to stand up and say something.

You announce again to the audience:

1. I am more and more energised — thank you all!

2. Each moment of my life is becoming more captivating, even if I do not realise why or how. This energises me more — thank you all again!

3. I give thanks now for my life of running, health, happiness, and self-expression (you can add whatever you want to add here) — thank you all!

You might want to take a bow?

As the people clap and cheer with approval, you sit down and your mind turns around and returns to the podium. He raises his arms to signal the orchestra to prepare to resume playing. As you watch his baton swaying back and forth in rhythm to the music, the tempo begins to quicken and liven up. You feel so refreshed and recharged… So full of 'life'.

Take lots of time over this, really soak up more and more the energy of the orchestra playing and energising you. Just bask in it!

Step Five:

Once you have done this for long enough, count yourself out of hypnosis from 1 through to 5.

Take an action that is proof to you that you have more energy and enthusiasm for your running. Go and do something that you may not have done yesterday, for example.

Oceans of Energy:

The storms that we encountered in 2009 here in the UK were apparently nothing to do with global warming. A rising warm front of pressure from Canada, along with some icy currents in our waters, combined menacingly to create the worst storms for a long while here in the UK.

Luckily, my home, which is actually a very old house, managed to survive the ravages of the storms intact. Yay.

I started laughing at the news coverage. The TV channels found the windiest places in the country, or the most damaged, then decided to report the weather from there, or they'd have the reporter standing beside the single most huge puddle causing problems in that town, or positioned besides houses that have water up to their windows and a dinghy was required to get in and out!

We want to be safe, of course, but not terrified out of our wits!

Now I am all for utilisation. That is, I like the fact that we are starting to use wind energy and have wind farms out at sea and other places now, and it got me thinking, in what way can I utilise these storms for my own work and the benefit of my readers?

Anyway, when the storm onset earlier that week, Katie and I gazed up and out at it from within our conservatory. I love watching the elements, especially when we are snuggled up inside. My barber told me that he went to a sea front café when it was all happening and sat there and watched the waves roaring up and crashing and said it was a beautiful spectacle.

On the local news magazine on TV here, "South Today", they had a little section where viewers had sent in stunning pictures of the stormy sea and of other wonderful views and I felt a triumph for those of us truly appreciating what was going on rather than allowing it to onset doom and gloom.

The sea, ocean, winds and nature at certain times of year have an incredible energy. It is that incredible vigour, zest, energy and power that I want us to harness and share in the next self-hypnosis process. Simply follow these simple steps.

Step One:

Induce hypnosis using your method of choice. When you have hypnotised yourself, move on to Step Two.

Step Two:

Imagine you are walking near the sea, maybe along the sea front in some favourite place. It is right after a fierce storm. The surf is coming in to the shore on the back of those huge, magnificent waves. Then crash upon the beach. Look at the colours in the sea and the white curls of the waves. The sky is filled with sunlight that is bright and illuminating against the dark clouds. As you walk on the sand you can feel, sense or imagine the energy in the air.

Find a spot that is comfortable for you and sit down on the sand, facing the sea. Watch as the thundering waves come in to shore. Feel their power. Get a sense of the amazing power of nature. The waves coming in and out as you sit relaxed on the sand. As you watch the waves, breathe at the same rate as the waves coming in and then receding and get a lovely rhythmic sensation in your body reflecting the sea.

Once you have engaged and really developed a sense of being in this place, move on to the next step.

Step Three:

Once you have developed this rhythm, as you are watching the waves, you start to feel the air around you. It is so supercharged with energy. It has a magical energy, unique and filled with sensations that you notice in your own way. Take a deep breath and feel how this supercharged air goes into your body. Feel the air energising your body as you breathe it in. Feel your body respond. It tingles with all this energy. Feel the energy going to every part of your body right now, in this time, in this place.

Take all the time you need at this stage and feel the energy filling your body. When you have really noticed some tangible sensation, then move on to the next step.

Step Four:

Now take another deep breath and feel the supercharged air go into your mind. Feel it shift your mind, giving you energy, creativity, power. In fact allow it to give you anything you could do with more of right now. Feel the energy going to every part of your body right now, in this time, in this place. Again, take all the time you need to feel the energy in your mind before you move on to the next step.

Step Five:

Now take another deep breath and feel the supercharged air go into your spirit, your soul. You all know, I am not overtly spiritual, but I get a certain sense and awe when confronted with this form of nature. It is that which I refer to here. Feel the shift in your spirit, giving you energy you need to manifest your purpose and who you are. Feel the energy going to every part of your spirit right now, in this time, in this place. Again, bathe in this and spend some time feeling the energy in your spirit. It makes me smile just thinking about how good that feels to do.

Start to think of how good it is when you run with that sensation within you. Then move on to the next step.

Step Six:

Imagine and sense that you feel the most tremendous energy come over every part of you. Energising your body, mind and spirit. Exhale and feel any old stagnation of your body, mind, and spirit just disappear and dissipate. Let it go.

Look out over the sea and feel the energy of the sea enter into your body and your mind. Continue to breathe as long as you need to. Inhaling as much energy as you need for now and is right for you. When you are done, you feel you have all the energy you need. Ask yourself to ensure that this feeling stays with you for as long as you need.

Step Seven:

When you are ready and energised, begin to get a sense of your body again, take a deep breath of life and just let it radiate through you. Count yourself up and out of hypnosis from 1 through to 5.

Take some action today to use the elements around you and get them working for you. I find those storms inspiring, energising and very reflective. It is very exciting having them around. Whatever the weather is like in whatever part of the world you are in, make sure you use it to enhance yourself and your energy levels so that you are driven and feeling great about your running.

Atoms of Energy:

This is the final energising self-hypnosis process for you to use.

When the seasons change here in England, I find myself amazed to be up and walking around in the dark. Yes indeed, 6am becomes a dark time in winter when it has been so light throughout the summer. I have to start wearing warmer clothing to work and to sleep in and of course, to run in. I do not run in my summer vests when we arrive at winter here on the south coast of England. The water taps I use to fill up my water bottles when running in the summer no longer work along the sea front, so I have to train wearing my big backpack which carries two litres of water instead of a single bottle when running. All indicators that the summer is over and that winter is here.

I have said it before and I'll say it again, I love the changing seasons here in the UK. They are less severe here on the south coast, but I love watching the scenery change colour and I get

364

excited by the darker evenings just as much as I do when they get lighter in late spring. I love the changes in my own garden. I start planning for next year, moving shrubs around, choosing what vegetables I'll grow next year and finishing the harvest from this year's crops and goodies.

It all keeps me driven and motivated and moving.

With the change of season, also comes the new academic year for me and my school, I start with a new group of students on my hypnotherapy practitioner diploma and then have the second 9-day tuition block for my intensive hypnotherapy diploma, both in October, meaning that I have a very busy time of it in Autumn each year. Add to that my continued marathon training, my ongoing research studies, new audio product launches, my busy client schedule, and maintaining my marriage to my amazing and supportive wife. I would not have it any other way, though it can leave a man feeling pooped.

This next self-hypnosis process is aimed to help you stay healthily energised; using atoms. Follow these simple steps and atomically energise yourself.

Step One:

Hypnotise yourself using your method of choice.

Then imagine yourself in a special place, a favourite place, somewhere you have been to before or somewhere you create in your mind. Spend some time seeing the sights, colours and hearing the sounds, feeling the sensations of peace, tranquillity and safety here in this place. Tell yourself that being in this place in your mind takes you deeper into hypnosis. Once you have really established that in your mind move on to Step Two.

Step Two:

Engage your imagination in whatever way is the best for you, interpreting these things however you prefer. Find yourself in a tunnel that you cannot see the end of. Create the tunnel in your own mind with the colours, sounds, textures, dimensions and contours of your own choosing.

Imagine walking down the tunnel and as you walk further inwards and downwards, you can make suggestions to yourself that you are reaching deeper inside of your mind too.

As a side note, some people are not comfortable with tunnels. If so, you can have lots of big windows and access to light and air and design it in a way that ensures you feel safe, comfortable and at ease. Keep walking deeper into the tunnel and when you are ready to take the next step, move on.

Step Three:

As you walk further into the tunnel, start to imagine and notice a flickering of lights towards in the distance. You choose what colour the lights are, and start to notice that the lights are flickering and flashing and are very bright. They shine and feel good to observe and allow yourself to steadily get closer to the lights.

As you draw closer, you notice that the lights that are flashing before you actively are actually atoms of energy. There are hundreds of thousands of atoms flashing on and off, moving through the tunnel, foiled with energy and light.

As you draw nearer to them, start to extend your arms, stretch out and point your body and palms toward the atoms and notice them start to be attracted to you. Notice the atoms starting to fly towards you in a comfortable, vibrant and enjoyable way and sense how your body embraces the atoms as they land upon you and are absorbed by you. When you have started to notice this happening, move on to the next step.

Step Four:

Take as much time as you need now to enjoy absorbing all that wonderful energy, vibrancy and zest for life. Feel yourself being uplifted by the atoms filling you with vigour and energy and life force. Imagine the colours spreading through your body and get a sense of how it feels to have that flowing through you right now.

Absorb all that you feel you need, bask in the energy for a while, let it fill your senses and start to think of all the things that you can do now as a result of having this increased healthy energy. Imagine the energy getting more powerful and coursing through every cell of your body, and whenever you notice your thoughts becoming more positive and progressive as a result, move on to the next step.

Step Five:

Whenever you feel really filled up with positive energy, think about the actions you can take to make this an amazing day ahead, think about how you can make the most of the time you have and notice the energy within every part of you.

See the end of the tunnel and start to walk towards it as you glimmer and glisten with the vibrancy and inspiration of feeling so uplifted and ready to go.

As you get to the end of the tunnel and step outward, wiggle your finger and toes, open your eyes and go about your day keeping that energy with you.

This is a fabulous process to give yourself a pep and get yourself focused and feeling alive. Even if the days do get seasonally shorter, you can get energized and uplifted and feeling fabulous and productive with your time.

It gets said a great deal in personal development circles, but go and make sure you make the most of your day with this lovely way of enhancing your ability to do so. Use all of the processes in this chapter to make sure you have the energy to run, the energy to run with strength and the energy to make your running a more and more enjoyable experience.

Some final words and thoughts:

I think you'll already be aware that in order to derive the most benefit from this book you don't simply pick it up, read it through, and then put it on a shelf while you apply the skills and learning elements. To derive the most amount of gain and benefit as a runner, this book requires you to dip back in, it requires you to apply the skills on a regular basis and to practice, practice, practice.

By telling you now to start employing all the cognitive strategies I have outlined: use the mental imagery techniques I have described, engage your internal dialogue more progressively, set goals effectively, be motivated, optimistic, energised, focused and everything else… You could be forgiven for feeling a bit overwhelmed. There is a lot here in this book.

Therefore, I recommend that you set your running goal, and organise your physical training schedule. As you do that, also consider putting together a mental training schedule. Plot, plan and organise a theme or a technique that you focus upon each week, for example. Pick a lesson or a chapter that becomes central to that month and pull out the techniques you believe you'll benefit from the most and engage in them that week; even choose what you'll do each day and what mental strategy you'll employ within each training run.

If you get organised and focused, you'll have a system that you can simply follow and enjoy as you move forward.

I can help you stay on track a fair bit too; here are some ways to allow my work and I to keep you focused and exposed to more resources and sources of motivation:

Visit my blogs — they are filled with numerous other ways to heal, recover, advance thoughts and give you a number of other ways of doing the types of processes outlined in this book.

My hypnosis for running blog is here: **hypnosisforrunning.com**

My hypnosis blog is here: **adam-eason.com/blog**

These are regularly being added to, but there is an enormous amount of information there already for you to explore and advance your knowledge, skills and keep you inspired and driven.

You can follow me on Twitter here: **twitter.com/AdamEason**

You can engage with me on Facebook here: **facebook.com/hypnotistadam**

I hope you connect with me in some further way. It is the connection with other runners which helps sustain my running. It is the sense of community I get from you runners that keeps me on track.

If you would like me to be a speaker at your event, or if you'd like to bring me in to run a workshop, seminar or training, then get in touch with me via the contact page of my website — **adam-eason.com/contact/** — or email me directly at **ae@adam-eason.com**. I always do my best to reply within one working day.

Before I sign off, I'd like to share something with you. Running does not come naturally to me and I actually find it tough to keep up with it, to keep getting those miles ticked off and getting those marathons completed in times that satisfy me. The stuff in this book is all stuff I use all the time to help me continue to do it. Most of the time I love it, yet on occasions I do not. I hope you discover for yourself that by employing your mind, you can go on to find so much utter joy from much of your running. My wish for you is that you realise that you can go on to achieve so much with your running and that when you engage your mind well, running becomes exponentially more than just running.

As you run, your mind and body run together; that makes me feel so delightfully alive. That makes my life better in many ways.

GO RUN!

"Struggling and suffering are the essence of a life worth living. If you're not pushing yourself beyond the comfort zone, if you're not demanding more from yourself — expanding and learning as you go — you're choosing a numb existence. You're denying yourself an extraordinary trip."

Dean Karnazes (2006) Ultramarathon Man: Confessions of an All-Night Runner. Tarcher Publishing.

Bibliography

Chapter One:

Bannister, R. G. (1956)
Muscular effort.
British Medical Bulletin, 12: 222–225.

Bannister, R. G. (1981)
The Four-minute Mile.
New York: Dodd, Mead & Co.

Bingham, J. (2002)
No Need for Speed: A Beginner's Guide to the Joy of Running.
Rodale Books.

Morgan, W. P., Pollock, M. L. (1977)
Psychological characterization of the elite distance runner,
Annals New York Academy of Science; 301: 382–403

Morgan, W. P., Costill, D. L. (1972)
Psychological characteristics of the marathon runner.
Journal of Sports Medicine and Physical Fitness; 12: 42–46

Morgan, W. P. (2001)
Psychological factors associated with distance running and the
marathon.
In D. Tunstall Pedoe (Ed.), Marathon Medicine 2000 (pp. 293–310)

O'Connor, P.J. (1992)
Psychological aspects of endurance performance.
In Shephard, R.J., Astrand, P.O, (eds) Endurance in Sport.

Unestahl, L. E. (1982)
Use of Hypnosis in Sport Psychology.
Society of Clinical and Experimental Hypnosis Workshop text.

Chapter Two:

Albrecht, J. L., & Adelman, M. B. (1984)
Social support and life stress: New directions for communication research.
Human Communications Research, 2, 3–22.

Allen, J. (1903)
As A Man Thinketh.
In public domain.

Burton, D., Naylor, S., & Holliday, B. (2001)
Goal Setting in Sport.
In R. Singer, H. Hausenblas, & C. Jenelle (Eds), Handbook of Sport Psychology (pp. 497–528)

Burton, D. Weinberg, R. S., Yukelson, D., & Weigland, D. (1998).
The goal effectiveness paradox in sport: Examining the goal practices of collegiate athletes.
The Sport Psychologist, 12, 404–418.

Duda, J. L. (1992)
Motivation in sport settings: A goal perspective approach. In G. C. Roberts (ed), Motivation in Sport and Exercise (pp. 57–92)

Dweck, C. S. (1986)
Motivational processes affecting learning.
American Psychologist, 41, 1040–1048.

Gould, D. (1988)
Goal setting for peak performance. In J. Williams (Ed.),
Applied Sport Psychology: Personal Growth to Peak Performance (pp.
1820196).

Hardy, C. V., Richman, J. M., & Rosenfeld, L. B. (1991)
The role of social support in the life stress/injury relationship.
The Sport Psychologist, 5, 128–139.

Kingston, K., & Hardy, L. (1997)
Effects of different types of goals on processes that support
performance.
The Sport Psychologist, 11, 277–293.

Locke, E. A., (1968)
Toward a theory of task motivation incentives
Organizational Behavior and Human Performance, 3, 157–189.

Locke, E. A., & Latham, G. P. (1985)
The application of goal setting to sports.
Journal of Sport Psychology, 7, 205–222.

Locke, E. A., & Latham, G. P. (1990)
A Theory of Goal Setting and Task Performance.

Orlick, T., & Partington, J. (1998)
Mental links to excellence.
The Sport Psychologist, 2, 105–130.

Tubbs, M. E. (1991)
Goal setting: A meta-analytical examination of the empirical
evidence.
Journal of applied Psychology, 71, 474–483.

Weinberg, R. S., & Weigand, D. (1993)
Goal setting in sport and exercise. A reaction to Locke
Journal of Sport and Exercise Psychology, 15, 88–95.

Weinberg, R. S., Burton, D., Yukelson, D., & Weigand, D. (2000)
Perceived goal setting practices of Olympic athletes: An
exploratory investigation.
The Sport Psychologist, 14, 280–296.

Chapter Three:

Callen, K. E., (1983)
Auto-hypnosis in long distance runners.
American Journal of Clinical Hypnosis, 26 (1), 30–36.

Fromm, E., Brown, D. P., Hurt, S. W., Oberlander, J. Z., Boxer, A.
M. and Pfeifer, G. (1981)
The phenomena and characteristics of self-hypnosis.
International Journal of Clinical and Experimental Hypnosis, 29:
189–246.

Green, J. P., Barabasz, A., Barrett, D., & Montgomery, G. H.
(2005)
Forging ahead: The 2003 APA Division 30 definition of
hypnosis.
International Journal of Clinical and Experimental Hypnosis, 53,
259–264.

Johnson, L. S., Dawson, S. L., Clark, J. L. and Sirkorsky, C. (1983)
Self-hypnosis versus hetero-hypnosis: order effects and sex
differences in behavioral and experiential impact. International
Journal of Clinical and Experimental Hypnosis, 31: 139–154.

Kahn, S. P., Fromm, E., Lombard, L. S. and Sossi, M. (1989)
The relation of self-reports of hypnotic depth in self-hypnosis to hypnotizability and imagery production. International Journal of Clinical and Experimental Hypnosis, 37: 290–304.

Olness, K. (1981)
Imagery (self-hypnosis) as adjunct therapy in childhood cancer: clinical experience with 25 patients.
American Journal of Pediatric Hermatology/Oncology, 3: 313–321.

Orne, M. T. and McConkey, K. M. (1981)
Hypnosis and self-hypnosis.
In L. Kristal (ed.), The ABC of Psychology, pp. 115–118. Multimedia Publications, London.

Shor, R. E. and Easton, R. D. (1973)
A preliminary report on research comparing self-and hetero-hypnosis.
American Journal of Clinical Hypnosis, 16: 37–44.

Yapko, M (2003)
Trancework,
Brunner Boutledge, pp 301.

Chapter Five:

Beck, A. T. (1970)
Cognitive therapy.
Behavior Modification, 1, 184–200.

Dobson, K. S., & Block, L. (1988)
Historical and philosophical base of the cognitive-behavioral therapies.
In Dobson (Ed) Handbook of Cognitive Behavioral Therapies (pp. 3–34).

Ellis, A. (1982)
Self-direction in sport and life.
Rational Living, 17, 27–33.

Gauron, E. F. (1984)
Mental Training for Peak Performance.

Greenspan, M. J., & Feltz, D. L. (1989)
Psychological interventions with athletes in competitive situations: A review.
The Sport Psychologist, 3, 219–236.

Orbach, I., Singer, R., & Price, S. (1999)
Mental links to excellence.
The Sport Psychologist, 2, 105–130.

Williams, J. M., & Krane, V. I. (2001)
Psychological characteristics of peak performance.
In Williams (Ed) Applied Sport Psychology: Personal Growth to Peak Performance.

Zinsser, N., Bunker, L. K., & Williams, J. M. (2001)
Cognitive techniques for improving performance and building confidence.
In Williams (Ed) Applied Sport Psychology: Personal Growth to Peak Performance.

Chapter Seven:

Cook, C. E. and Van Vogt, A. E. (1956)
The Hypnotism Handbook.

Kabat-Zinn, J. (1991)
Full Catastrophe Living.
Piatkus Books. Pp. 75–93.

Morgan, W. P. and Pollock, M. L. (1977)
Psychological characterization of the elite distance runner.
Annals of the New York Academy of Science, 301: 382–403.

Morgan, W. P., O'Connor, P. J., Ellickson, K. A. and Bradley, P. W. (1988)
Personality structure, mood states and performance in elite male distance runners.
International Journal of Sports Psychology, 19: 247–263

Morgan, W. P., O'Connor, P. J., Sprling, B. P. and Pate, R. R. (1987)
Psychological characterization of the elite female distance runner.
International Journal of Sports Medicine, 8: 124–131

Perls, F., Hefferline, R., & Goodman (1951)
Gestalt Therapy: Excitement and Growth in the Human Personality.

Rohe, F. (1975)
The Zen of Running.
Random House.

Chapter Eight:

Bell, K. F., (1983)
Championship Thinking: The Athlete's Guide to Winning Performance in all Sports.
Englewood Cliffs, NJ: Prentice-Hall.

Buffone, G. W., Sachs, M. L., & Dowd, E. T. (1984)
Cognitive behavioral strategies for promoting adherence to exercise.
Running as Therapy: An Integrated Approach (pp. 198–214)

Cousins, N (1990)
Head First : The Biology of Hope and the Healing Power of the Human Spirit.
Penguin Books.

Dagrou, E., Gauvin, L., & Halliwell, W. (1991)
The mental preparation of athletes: current practices and research perspectives.
International Journal of Sport Psychology, 22, 15–34.

Dagrou, E., Gauvin, L., & Halliwell, W. (1992)
Effects of positive, negative, and neutral language on motor performance.
Canadian Journal of Sport Sciences, 17, 145–147.

Darwin, C (1871)
The Descent of Man.

Dreyer, D. (2008)
Chi Running.
Pocket Books.

Gauron, E. F. (1984)
Mental Training for Peak Performance.
Lansing, NY: Sport Science Associates.

Gauvin, L. (1990)
An experiential perspective on the motivational features of exercise and lifestyle.
Canadian Journal of Sports Sciences, 15, 51–58.

Gould, D., Guinan, D., Greenleaf, C., Medbery, R., & Pederson, K. (1999)
Factors affecting Olympic performance of athletes and coaches from more and less successful teams.
The Sport Psychologist, 13, 371–394.

Highlen, P. S., & Bennett, B. B. (1983)
Elite divers and wrestlers: A comparison between open- and closed-skill athletes.
Journal of Sport Psychology, 5, 390–409.

Kirschenbaum, D. S., O'Connor, E. A., & Owens, D. (1999)
Positive illusions in golf: Empirical and conceptual analyses.
Journal of Applied Sport Psychology, 11, 1–27.

Kirschenbaum, D. S., Ordman, A. M., Tomarken, A. J., & Holtzbauer, R. (1982)
Effects of differential self-monitoring and level of mastery on sports performance: Brain power bowling.
Cognitive Therapy and Research, 6, 335–342.

Kirschenbaum, D. S., Owens, D., & O'Connor, E. A. (1998)
Smart golf: Preliminary evaluation of a simple, yet comprehensive, approach to improving and scoring the mental game.
The Sport Psychologist, 12, 271–282.

Meichenbaum, D. (1977)
Cognitive-behaviour Modification.
New York: Plenum Press.

Meyers, A. W., & Shleser, R. A. (1980)
A cognitive-behavioral intervention for improving basketball performance.
Journal of Sports Psychology, 3, 69–73.

Orlick, T., & Partington, J. (1988)
Mental links to excellence.
The Sport Psychologist, 2, 105–130.

Schill, T., Monroe, S., Evans, R., & Ramanaiah, N. (1978)
The effects of self-verbalizations on performance: A test of the rational-emotive position.
Psychotherapy: Theory, Research, and Practice, 15, 2–7.

Van Raalte, J. L., Brewer, B. W., Rivera, P. M., & Petitpas, A. J. (1994)
*The relationship between observable self-talk and competitive junior tennis players' match performance.*Journal of Sport & Exercise Psychology, 16, 400–415.

Witt, J. K. and Proffitt, D. R. (2005)
See the Ball, Hit the Ball: Apparent Ball Size Is Correlated With Batting Average.
Psychological Science, 16: 937–938

Zinsser, N., Bunker, L. K., & Williams, J. M. (2001)
Cognitive techniques for improving performance and building confidence.
In J. M. Williams (ed.), Applied Sport Psychology: Personal Growth to Peak Performance (pp. 284–311).

Chapter Nine:

Edmonston (1991)
Hypnosis and relaxation: Modern verification of an old equation and Theories of Hypnosis,
In S.J. Lynn and J.W. Rhue (eds.) Theories of Hypnosis: Current Models and Perspectives, pp.127–240

Banyai, (1991)
Theories of Hypnosis: Current Models and Perspectives,
In S.J. Lynn and J.W. Rhue

Robertson, D (2012)
Cognitive Behavioural Hypnotherapy.
Karnac Books.

Wolpe, J. (1958)
Psychotherapy by Reciprocal Inhibition.
Stanford University Press, pp. 53–62.

Chapter Eleven:

Coué, E. (1922)
Self-mastery Through Conscious Autosuggestion.
New York: American Library

Felt, D. L., & Landers, D. M. (1983)
The effects of mental practice on motor skill, learning and performance: A meta analysis.
Journal of Sport Psychology, 5, 25–57.

Hardy, L., & Callow, N. (1999)
Efficacy of external and internal visual imagery perspectives for the enhancement of performance on tasks in which form is important.
Journal of Sport and Exercise Psychology, 32, 95–112.

Harris, D. V., & Harris, B. L. (1984)
The Athlete's Guide to Sport Psychology: Mental Training for Physical People.

Jacobsen, E. (1932)
Electrophysiology of mental activities.
American Journal of Psychology, 44, 677–694.

Mahoney, M. J., & Avener, M. (1977)
Psychology of the elite athlete: An exploratory study
Cognitive Therapy and Research, 3, 361–366.

Martin, K. A., Moritz, S. E., & Hall, C. R. (1999)
Imagery use in sport: A literature review and applied model.
The Sport Psychologist, 13, 245–268.

McDougall, C. (2009)
Born to Run: A Hidden Tribe, Superathletes, and the Greatest Race the World Has Never Seen.
Knopf Publishing.

Murphy, S., & Jowdy, D. (1992)
Imagery and mental rehearsal.
In T. Horn (Ed.), Advances in Sport Psychology (pp. 221–250).

Orlick, T. (1986)
Psyching for Sport: Mental Training for Athletes.

Paivio, A. (1985)
Cognitive and motivational functions of imagery in human performance.
Canadian Journal of Applied Sport Sciences, 10, 22–28.

Sackett, R. S. (1934)
The influences of symbolic rehearsal upon the retention of a maze habit.
Journal of General Psychology.

Suinn, R. (1972)
Removing emotional obstacles to learning and performance by visuomotor behavioral rehearsal.
Behavior Therapy, 3, 308–310.

Vealey, R., & Greenleaf, C. (1998)
Seeing is believing: Understanding and using imagery in sport.
In J. M. Williams (Ed) Applied Sport Psychology: Personal Growth to Peak Performance.

White, A., & Hardy, L. (1995)
An in-depth analysis of the uses of imagery by high-level slalom canoeists and artistic gymnasts.
The Sport Psychologist, 12, 387–403.

Weinberg, R. S., Seabourne, T. G., & Jackson, A. (1981)
Effects of visuo-motor behavior rehearsal, relaxation, and imagery on karate performance.
Journal of Sport Psychology, 3, 228–238.

Weinberg, R. S.,
The relationship between mental preparation strategies and motor performance: A review and critique.
Quest, 33, 195–213.

Chapter Thirteen:

Ellis, A., & Dryden, W. (2007)
The Practice of Rational Emotive Behavior Therapy (2nd edition).
Springer publishing company.

Kaptchuk, T. J., Friedlander, E. et al (2010)
Placebos Without Deception: A Randomized Controlled Trial in

Irritable Bowel Syndrome.
PLoS One, 5.

Kirsch, I., (2009)
The Emperors New Drugs: Exploding the Anti-Depressant Myth.
Bodley Head.

Seligman, M., (1990)
Learned Optimism; How to Change your Mind and your Life.
Vintage Books.

Chapter Fourteen:

Barber, T. X. (1966)
The effects of hypnosis and suggestions on strength and endurance: a critical review of research studies.
British Journal of Social and Clinical Psychology, 5: 42–50.

Chauloff, F. (1997)
The serotonin hypnothesis.
In: Morgan, W. P. ed. Physical Activity and Mental Health. Washington: Taylor and Francis: 179–198.

Dishman, R. K. (1997)
The norepinephrine hypnothesis.
In: Morgan, W. P. ed. Physical Activity and Mental Health. Washington: Taylor and Francis: 199–212.

Havens, R. A., & Walters, C. (1989)
Hypnotherapy Scripts: A Neo-Ericksonian Approach to Persuasive Healing,
pp.141. Brunner/Mazell Publishers.

Hull, C. L. (1933)
Hypnosis and Suggestibility.
Appleton-Century-Crofts, New York.

Mandell, A. J, (1979)
The Second Second Wind.
Psychiat Annals; 9, 57–69.

Morgan, W. P. (1972)
Hypnosis and muscular performance.
Ergogenic Aids and Muscular Performance, pp. 193–233. Academic Press, New York.

Morgan, W. P. (2001)
Psychological factors associated with distance running and the marathon.
In D. Tunstall Pedoe (ed.) Marathon Medicine 2000, pp. 293–310. Royal Society of Medicine, London.

Morgan, W. P. (2002)
Hypnosis in sport and exercise psychology.
In J. L. Van Raalte and B. W. Brewer (ed.) Exploring Sport and Exercise Psychology, pp. 151–181. American Psychological Association, Washington DC.

Morgan, W. P., Horstman, D. H., Cymerman, A. and Stokes, J. (1983)
Facilitation of physical performance by means of a cognitive strategy.
Cognitive Therapy and Research, 7: 251–264.

Morgan, W. P. and Pollock, M. L. (1977)
Psychological characterization of the elite distance runner
Annals of the New York Academy of Science, 301: 382–403.

Morgan, W. P., O'Connor, P. J., Ellickson, K. A. and Bradley, P. W. (1988)
Personality structure, mood states and performance in elite male distance runners.
International Journal of Sports Psychology, 19: 247–263

Morgan, W. P., O'Connor, P. J., Sprling, B. P. and Pate, R. R. (1987)
Psychological characterization of the elite female distance runner.
International Journal of Sports Medicine, 8: 124–131

Williamson, J. W., McColl, R., Mathews, D., Mitchell, J. H., Raven, P. B. and Morgan, W. P. (2001)
Hypnotic Manipulation of effort sense during dynamic exercise: Cardiovasular responses and brain activation.
Journal of Applied Physiology, 90: 1392–1399.

Williamson, J. W., Mitchell, J. H. and Raven, P. B. (2005)
Cardiorespiratory control: hypnosis and perceived exertion.
International Journal of Sport and Exercise Psychology, 4: 518–526.

Chapter Fifteen:

Gallwey, W. T. (1998)
The Inner Game of Golf (Revised edition).
Random House.

Nideffer, R. M. (1992)
Psyched to Win.
Human Kinetics.

Chapter Sixteen:

Weinberg, R. S., and Gould, D. (1999)
Foundations of Sport and Exercise Psychology
(2nd Edition). Human Kinetics.

Yerkes, R. M., and Dodson, J. D. (1908)
The relationship of strength of stimulus to rapidity of habit formation.
Journal of Comparative Neurology and Psychology, 18, 459–482.

References:

Fitzgerald, M. (2007)
Brain Training for Runners: A Revolutionary New Training System to Improve Endurance, Speed, Health, and Results
New American Library.

Galloway, J. (2010)
Marathon: You Can Do it!
Shelter Publications Inc.

Higdon, H. (2011)
Marathon: The Ultimate Training Guide (4th edition).
Rodale.

Mittleman, S. (2001)
Slow Burn.
Harper Collins.

Murakami, H. (2009)
What I Talk About When I Talk About Running.
Vintage.

Pfitzinger, P. and Douglas, S. (2009)
Advanced Marathoning.
Human Kinetics.

Tucker, R., and Dugan, J. (2009)
The Runner's Body.
Rodale Press.

1 - Getting Motivated to Run — 104
2 - Fall in Love with Running — 109.
3 - Let go of excuses not to train — 112.
4 - Mindful Exposure to Running — 144
5 - Thought Spotting — 149
6 - Mindful Meditation when Running — 157
7 - Ending Catastrophisation — 183
8 - Cognition to Lift Mood — 186
   Modifying Internal Dialogue
9 - Tone Your Inner Critic — 193
10 - Hypnotic Desensitisation. — 207
11 - Using Cognitions to Enhance Imagery — 225
12 - Unleash the Animal Within — 237
13 - How you Attribute success and failure — 246
14 Building internal encouragement. — 251
15 Guide your own performance enhancing drugs — 263

390

7205402R00216

Printed in Great Britain
by Amazon.co.uk, Ltd.,
Marston Gate.